Gays and Grays

Gays and Grays

The Story of the Inclusion of the Gay Community at Most Holy Redeemer Catholic Parish in San Francisco

Donal Godfrey

To Michael Schmidt,
in thanksgiving for your
work as AIDS support
group coordinator,
Donal Godfrey,
07.

LEXINGTON BOOKS

A division of
ROWMAN & LITTLEFIELD PUBLISHERS, INC.
Lanham • Boulder • New York • Toronto • Plymouth, UK

LEXINGTON BOOKS

A division of Rowman & Littlefield Publishers, Inc.
A wholly owned subsidiary of The Rowman & Littlefield Publishing Group, Inc.
4501 Forbes Boulevard, Suite 200
Lanham, MD 20706

Estover Road
Plymouth PL6 7PY
United Kingdom

British Library Cataloguing in Publication Information Available

Library of Congress Cataloging-in-Publication Data

Godfrey, Donal, 1959–
 Gays and grays : the story of the inclusion of the gay community at Most Holy
Redeemer Catholic Parish in San Francisco / Donal Godfrey.
  p. cm.
 Includes bibliographical refernces and index.
 ISBN-13: 978-0-7391-1937-2 (cloth : alk. paper)
 ISBN-10: 0-7391-1937-0 (cloth : alk. paper)
 1. Most Holy Redeemer Parish (SAn Francisco, Calif.)—History. 2. Church work with
gays—Catholic Church. I. Title.
 BX4603.S495G63 2007
 282'.79461–dc22   207018425

Printed in the United States of America

⊗™ The paper used in this publication meets the minimum requirements of American
National Standard for Information Sciences—Permanence of Paper for Printed Library
Materials, ANSI/NISO Z39.48–1992.

For my parents Mary and the late Robin Godfrey, and the parishioners at Most Holy Redeemer parish, living and dead, past and present

You will find the good people of our parish, old, young, married, gay, lesbian, straight, transgender, affluent, homeless, blue-collar, converts, cradle Catholics, radical, traditional, questioning and fervent. What you're least likely to find here is complacency or indifference. We seem to be a church with no accidental parishioners: everyone singing in our pews or making sandwiches for the poor in our hall is committed to a vision of a better world and a better Church to serve it.

Fr. Steve Meriwether, pastor

Contents

Acknowledgements

I want to thank my family and all who helped me with this book, most particularly the people of Most Holy Redeemer parish in San Francisco.

This book emerged from my dissertation: "Gay and Gray. The History and Significance of the Inclusion of the Gay Community at Most Holy Redeemer Parish, San Francisco," written in partial fulfilment for the degree of Doctor of Ministry at the Church Divinity School of the Pacific in Berkeley, California. My committee members were very supportive and I am very grateful to them. They were: the Rev. Dr. Louis Weil, Dr. William McKinney, and Fr. Zachary Shore.

Three others gave special support. They are Patrick Mulcahey, Dr. Patti Jung, and Robert Garrett. Patrick Mulcahey is a friend, three-time Emmy winning writer, and parishioner at Most Holy Redeemer. Patti Jung is Professor at the Department of Theology at Loyola University Chicago. Robert Garrett is a doctoral student of the same department.

I am also grateful to my fellow Jesuits; especially the communities of the University of San Francisco and Loyola University Chicago, as well as the Irish Province of the Society of Jesus. Among those Jesuits who have helped include Mario Prietto, Gerry O'Hanlon, John Dardis, Richie Salmi, David Stagaman, Dan Hartnett, John Savard, Robert Buenconsejo, Tom Leyden, James Harvey, Mark Bosco, Fergus O'Donoghue, Billy Hewitt, Pat Davis, John Coleman, Tony Pabayo, Brian Grogan, Patrick Hume, Kevin Ballard, Bob Doran, David Robinson, Jim Corkery, George Murphy, J.A. Loftus, Rob Marsh, Bob Curran, Jack Treacy, the late Phil Harnett, David Birchall, Senan Timoney, Paddy Carberry, John Dunne, Tom Lucas, and James Bretzke. Through the generosity of the Irish Jesuit provincial, Fr. John Dardis, S.J., all proceeds from this edition will support two charities at Most Holy Redeemer parish: the Wednesday night suppers begun by Patrick Mulcahey, and the MHR AIDS Support Group. However, neither my fellow Jesuits, nor the Society of Jesus, are responsible, nor necessarily share my views.

Thanks to all those who generously shared with me in my interviews. Many are named in the text. Thanks also to the following: Fr. Tony McGuire, Fr. Stephen Meriwether, Bernard Appassamy, Fr. Thomas Hickey, Jani White, Michael Maher, Michael Duffy, Don Crean, Michael Harank, Jeremy Langford, Ross Miller, Franco Mormando, Alda Morgan, Rachel Hart, Chris and Bren Murphy, Claire Noonan, Brendan Fay, Carita Kempner, Brian Foey, Jane Maynard, Arthur Holder, Richard Rodriguez, Eliza Escott, Andrea Ellington-Peyerl, Fr. Ned Phelan, Sr. Adele Appleby, Andy Heinz, Michael Mullins, Fr. Brendan O'Rourke, the late Peter Pierce, Michael King, Catherine Wolf, Bernard Schlager, Eileen Weston, David Moutou, Catherine Cunningham, Rozalyn Gallo, Pete Toms, John Golding, Danny Field, David Simmons, Sr. Cleta Herold, Arith Hayes, Jamie Cherrie, Jim Gunther, Jeffrey Burns, Kathleen Carey, Rev. James Mitulski, Mary Geracimos, Fr. William Young, Ramona Michaels, Rob Hopcke, Laurence Rolle, Bishop Randolph Calvo, Carmen Silva, John Oddo, Thomas Fry, Fr. Jim Schnexneider, Fr. Edmundo Zarate-Snarez, Fr. Bob Whiteside, Andrew Whelan, Rev. Mark Wilson, Bill Vicini, George Woyames, Linda Saytes, Archbishop John Quinn, the late Alfredo Armendariz, Joseph Stellpflug, Sylvia Sands, Antonio Quioque, Richard Rogowski, Michael Gorman, Gloria Swanson, Albert Marez, Edgardo Moncada, Daniel Dominguez, Deacon Chuck McNeill, Jerry Locsin, Jim Laufenberg, the late Kean Brewer, Krandall Kraus, Paul Bojas, Stephen Hutcheon, Br. Terry Cant, C.F.C., Fr. Joseph Healy, James Grant, Fr. James Alison, Brian Foey, Bernard Henry, Sr. Jane Ferdon O.P., Colin Crossey, Jeff Brand, Fr. Mike Greenwell, Richard Arugundi, Rev. Victor Arceneaux, Nick Andrade, David Barclay, Brendan McKeown, Norma Evans, Margo Webster, Jaci Neesam, Robert Pementell, Fr Tom Hayes, Sharon Thornton, Michael Mendiola, Bob Blouin, Richard Hardy, Linda Clardy, Stephen Reilly, Willie Little, Dan Hocoy, Sara Suman, Jerry Betz, Sr., Rory Desmond, Bill Mochon, Mary Talbert, John Yengish, Richard Levy, Robert Pementell, Dan Golden, Liah Burns, Francis Masson, Russell Moy, Jose Rosel Jr., Charles Fermeglia, William Benemann, and Daniel Toleran.

Where permission was granted, the audiotapes and hard copies of interviews given as part of the research for this book are available in the Bancroft Library at the University of California, Berkeley (Sexual Orientation and Social Conflict Collection).

Finally I want to express my gratitude to my publishers, Lexington Books, and in particular T.J. MacDuff Stewart and Patrick Dillan.

This book examines the remarkable story of Most Holy Redeemer, San Francisco, and the way two very different communities, the "gays and grays" created a new kind of parish. The story has a much wider significance for the church and world, one that continues to evolve. For the purposes of this book, however, it begins and ends with the centennial celebrations of the parish.

Ad Majorem Dei Gloriam.
Donal Godfrey, S.J.

Chapter One

The First Eighty Years

The good people of Most Holy Redeemer are used to bishops and gay politicians, just not to seeing them in the same place.

On this bright Sunday morning we celebrate the centennial of the parish's dedication. The Most Reverend John C. Wester, personable Auxiliary Bishop of San Francisco, is presiding at mass (for Archbishop Levada, who is in Rome). Supervisor Mark Leno is here too, with a city proclamation declaring today, January 13th, "Most Holy Redeemer Day." A former rabbinical student, and openly gay, Leno represents the liberal neighborhoods of District 8, none more liberal than the Castro, home to the city's largest concentration of gay restaurants, bars, discos, bookstores, sex clubs, gift shops, cafés, etc., and likewise home to MHR. Looking unfazed by all the unaccustomed pomp, MHR's much-loved pastor, Father Zachary Shore, stands by to accept the framed proclamation, which cites one hundred years of service to the neighborhood, singling out for special praise the work of the AIDS Support Group. The proclamation represents a rarity in San Francisco, Leno deadpans: its passage by the Board of Supervisors was unanimous. The joke is well received. Another pair of contrasts the congregation is used to: laughing and crying in public.

Emboldened by the warm reception—or maybe it's what he planned to say all along—Leno goes on to commend the parish and Father Shore for making a difficult stand at the time of the Knight Initiative. The relaxed rustle of a crowd in Sunday clothes comes to a stop: the sound of many people sitting very still. Two years, but the memory is fresh. After repeatedly trying to push a ban on same-sex marriage through the legislature, in 1999 state Senator William J. "Pete" Knight succeeded in placing a one-sentence ballot initiative before the voters: "Only marriage between a man and woman is valid or recognized in

1

California." The Knight Initiative was viewed here as mean-spirited; taking arms against a menace that didn't exist. It passed handily in March of 2000, as was expected, but not before generating many hundreds of thousands of sentences of debate, and attracting many hundreds of thousands of dollars in support: California's twelve dioceses, through the California Catholic Conference, contributed more than $310,000. Some MHR parishioners, on hearing about this surprise destination of their Sunday envelopes, left and never came back. Some demanded the parish respond—but how? When Father Shore read from the pulpit his anguished letter to the Archbishop protesting the gift of money to such a cause, he was met with the most thunderous ovation in memory, and the most emotional. It was a landmark in his tenure as pastor, soon receiving national attention.[1] Most in the congregation remember the equally thunderous laughter when, after the tears and the clapping finally stopped, Father concluded by saying: "I hope you'll all come visit me in Siberia."

The applause for Leno today is not of that order, but is very warm; even the bishop joins in. The congregation approves of them both. Wester may have squirmed a bit to hear the California bishops singled out for such strong criticism, but this morning's enthusiasm for his presence and his homily has been too sincere for any slight to be suspected. Besides, the locus of this sort of tension has been the health and the heart of Most Holy Redeemer for the past twenty years. I am confident Bishop Wester doesn't need this explained; but as I concelebrate the mass with him, I can't help but think how unimaginable this day would have been to Archbishop Riordan a century ago.[2]

Archbishop Patrick Riordan formally dedicated the new church on January 12, 1902; it had been consecrated the previous year. Jewish elected officials were not unheard of at the time, though certainly they weren't invited to mass and applauded for criticizing the Church. By no exercise of the imagination, however, could Riordan or his flock have conceived of what we now call the gay community—or, for that matter, of an "out" gay man or woman, someone whose homosexuality was a matter of record and widely accepted. The building Archbishop Riordan blessed has weathered the century's cataclysms, the earthquakes of 1906 and 1989, the Great Depression, both World Wars, the AIDS epidemic; has been renovated in recent years and reconsecrated by the Archbishop, the Most Reverend William J. Levada. Riordan would still recognize the tower of Most Holy Redeemer, but perhaps not what goes on inside. Its form is less radically altered than its function.

Riordan himself was born of Irish parents in New Brunswick, Canada, and in visiting Most Holy Redeemer was very much visiting his own people: the parish was at the time made up largely of Irish immigrants and their children.[3] An encyclical Leo XIII issued in November of 1900 may have suggested the name of the new church, his centennial letter to the faithful: "Tametsi Futura

Prospicientibus (On Jesus Christ the Redeemer)."[4] While San Francisco at the turn of the century was a thriving, growing city, Most Holy Redeemer was the newest parish in a still-remote Archdiocese,

> . . . an outpost of the American Church, far removed from the rivaling centers at Rochester, New York, and St. Paul. "We are . . . so cut off from the great life of the nation," Riordan explained to his satisfaction, "by two ranges of Mountains, the Rockies and the Sierras, and a vast desert intervening, that we seem to belong to a Foreign country."[5]

The first pastor for the 370 families living in the newly popular hinterland of Eureka Valley was the Reverend Joseph P. McQuaide. For a time he was a pastor without a church, offering mass at a temporary location on Hartford Street,[6] just a few blocks away from where the Douglas-fir-and-redwood frame of the present edifice was being erected. McQuaide supervised the construction, and no doubt the attraction of a new church played a role in helping the district, then on the outskirts of San Francisco, project the appeal of a respectable blue-collar neighborhood. Father McQuaide also founded the "Total Abstinence Tourist Club," with a view, one supposes, to combating the (then as now) famous affinity of the Irish for drink. He might be discouraged to find the Castro today is a tourist destination known for its bars. In truth, their relative abundance is probably not much changed from when the neighborhood was an Irish-Catholic stronghold, nor is the fact they are almost exclusively patronized by men.

Indeed the alterations wrought by a hundred years are striking, but care must be taken not to overstate them. Most Holy Redeemer still offers comfort to the exile and refuge to those fleeing oppression and intolerance where they were born. The Catholics in our pews now are no less loyal or faith-filled than they were then. True, they dissent to a degree that might have shocked their grandparents, but that is not novel either. Many American parishes allow heterosexual men and women the exercise of their own consciences on contraception, divorce, capital punishment, other issues, and do not consider them "bad Catholics" for it. MHR extends a like forbearance to Catholics of other orientations. It does not publicly oppose any Church teaching; certainly to do so would court great risks, but perhaps it is also unnecessary. For the parishioners provide a prophetic witness that it is possible to be gay and Catholic at the same time. This witness goes in two directions, to the rest of the church and the rest of the gay community. Most Holy Redeemer challenges the institutional church not by clamoring for change but by allowing gay, lesbian, bisexual, and transgender people of faith to be themselves and be Catholic, without shame or subterfuge. Quietly living their lives in the truth of who they are is thus both the meekest simplicity and a radically subversive act.

San Francisco has a long history of being home to the disreputable and the dispossessed. The earliest inhabitants were American Indians. The Spanish first sailed into San Francisco Bay in 1769, and not till seven years later did they establish a small *presidio* (fort) and a mission, dedicated to Saint Francis of Assisi, *San Francisco de Asis*. The church on the site known today as Mission Dolores dates back to 1791. The original mission church of 1776 was a small wooden structure located at what is now the corner of Camp and Guerrero Streets, between 16th and 17th. Most Holy Redeemer is only a short walk from the mission and originally was comprised in it.[7]

Mexico broke from Spain in 1821, and in 1846, San Francisco was captured from Mexico by the United States. The discovery of gold soon after and the subsequent Gold Rush years created new outlaws, new problems, and a population of thirty to fifty men (estimates vary) for every woman. In 1848, the first Protestant clergyman coming to San Francisco from Hawaii was warned his undertaking was wild, foolish, and futile, owing to the city's reputation for iniquity. In 1874, a New York newspaper reportedly wrote: "There are no people who so practically ignore and hold in contempt the legal marital relations as do Californians."[8] Oscar Wilde visited in 1882, and later put into a character's mouth (Lord Henry in *The Picture of Dorian Gray*) the celebrated remark, stripped of its irony when you hear locals repeat nowadays: "It is an odd thing, but everyone who disappears is said to be seen at San Francisco. It must be a delightful city, and possess all the attractions of the next world."[9]

The attractions of a better life in this world were what drew the earliest parishioners of Most Holy Redeemer:

> They came to Eureka Valley from all over in the 1880s, Irish, German, and Scandinavian, homesteading on the sunny slopes of Twin Peaks. Farms and dairies that had once belonged to Mexican land barons like José Castro were now a short streetcar ride from downtown San Francisco. It was every workingman's dream: to buy a cheap piece of land and build a stately Victorian, big enough for several generations of the family. Scattered houses soon yielded to whole city blocks. A bustling commercial strip sprang up at 18th and Castro, where the stream used to run. By the 1920s, Eureka Valley was a tight little neighborhood, promoting itself as the sunny heart of San Francisco.[10]

Succeeding Father McQuaide, it fell to Father Patrick McGuire to see the parish through the catastrophic earthquake and fire of April 1906. Thanks to luck, Providence, and one assumes, the high standards of McQuaide and his builders, any damage the young church sustained was not substantial enough to record. In 1917, the Reverend Charles E. O'Neile was appointed to replace McGuire. Father O'Neile oversaw the construction of Most Holy Redeemer School, across the street from the church, and of the convent, which for the next sixty-two years would house the sisters who taught in it. The physical plan of the parish buildings as we see them today was only completed in 1940, with the construction of the "new" rectory under Monsignor William Sullivan, who became pastor in 1932. All Mary Geracimos can recall of Msgr. Sullivan is that his sermons were long and dull—at least, that was her considered judgment at the age of four. Too she remembers the church bells rang all day long on the day of his death.[11]

Monsignor Henry J. Lyne was Sullivan's successor, serving as pastor for the crucial twenty years from 1948 to 1968. By the 1950s, the life of the parish was virtually indistinguishable from the life of the neighborhood. It was a predominantly Irish Catholic community, with the concomitant sense of mission, identity, and pride:

> It would indeed be difficult to define the limits of the spiritual service of the Irish race . . . and that, perhaps, is why the Holy Father said they are "everywhere, like the grace of God." "Everywhere," they are found the champions of morals, the apostles of liberty, and the emancipators of peoples and races.[12]

San Francisco was very much a Catholic city in those days, and except in the godless precincts of downtown, when asked where you lived you might well have answered with the name of your parish.

> The city maps have always called the area Eureka Valley, but to the people who lived there, it was just Most Holy Redeemer Parish. The Catholic Church dominated every facet of the neighborhood's life, from the schooling of children to the family picnics and weekly bingo games.[13]

And yes, there were children: big working-class Catholic families filling the playgrounds and the school on Diamond Street with children.[14]

Even then, there were other neighborhoods, not considered quite so wholesome, where homosexual men and sometimes women met. Embarcadero, North Beach, and later, Polk Street were more hospitable to single working people, more amply supplied with apartments and boarding-houses than single-family homes, and it was possible for gay men to socialize, carefully, in a scattering of bars and bathhouses. But Eureka Valley was a world apart from all that, having more in common with small-town America than it did with San Francisco's own waterfront. Parishioner Mary Ragusin O'Shea remembers:

> Everybody I knew went to Holy Redeemer. And Holy Redeemer would have picnics and everybody would go to them. I mean, going on the train for the picnics, what could be better than that? And with all of the people who . . . your parents, and the people you went to school with. . . . It wasn't just who lived in your house was your family. It was all the people around you who were family.[15]

Elsewhere San Francisco was changing; but the community life in Eureka Valley seemed a stronghold of stability, centered it was in the parish of Most Holy Redeemer:

> Though San Francisco may always have been home to a large gay population, Castro Street is one of the least likely locations for a gay ghetto phenomenon. Located in the geographical dead-center[16] of the city off Market Street, the city's main drag, the Castro area was built up during the 1880's as the city burgeoned with ethnic immigrants. The area was first populated by working people—stevedores, butchers, teamsters, and carpenters. Large Catholic families stuck their roots in the rows of ornate Queen Anne houses, which were nothing more than the tract housing of the era.
>
> John Murnin, now in his sixties, grew up there, the son of Belfast immigrants who fled the potato famine for America's West. Murnin recalls an area rich with ethnic names like O'Shea, O'Riley, Roselli, and McCarthy. He can point to the antique, record, flower, and gift shops and tell of times when the buildings housed stores selling candy, buttermilk, and kiddy-matinee tickets—all this just footsteps away from what is now called the cruisiest corner in the world.[17]

By the 1950's the forces driving the eventual change had begun to build. After World War II, many homosexual men and women from the armed forces, who'd been stationed in San Francisco or called it home port, chose to stay here. Living as a gay man or lesbian was unthinkable in the hometowns they'd left behind, but it was just possible in San Francisco, if you were cautious. For a few post-war years the city's gay life could even be described as "freewheeling"—which soon tested the city's legendary tolerance.[18] In 1955, the San Francisco chief of police had had enough; estimates vary, but there were perhaps 50,000 homosexual men and women in the city by then. The chief wanted a crackdown by the head of his sex-crimes squad, who formulated the problem this way:

> Homosexuals have flocked to this city from all parts of the United States—they are everywhere. They fill the bars in the city's cheap Tenderloin district. They throng together in the city's parks. Instead of being known as Golden Gate City, San Francisco is being tabbed Queer City, a haven for homosexuals. My orders from Chief Michael Gaffey were get rid of this offensive mess. It wasn't an easy job.[19]

Gays as yet had little defense against stepped-up police action, but a few struggling organizations had sprung up to campaign for change in their legal and social situation. One such group, the Daughters of Bilitis, was founded and headquartered in San Francisco.

And in the 1950s, factors emerged that in time enabled The Castro to become something new: the world's first gay neighborhood. Increased car ownership and more and better roads allowed the white middle class to work in the city's center but live further and further away, in the Sunset District, Marin County, the suburbs. People left Eureka Valley too, moving up and out (as they saw it) to a better way of life, leaving behind city life, with all its attendant problems, and a neighborhood that now seemed past its prime. Single-family dwellings became cheap rental flats. Businesses were closing. The exodus fueled itself—the more people you knew who left, the more you wanted to as well—bringing on a downturn in the neighborhood economy.

By the 1960s, the demographic shift taking place in Eureka Valley was accelerated by fear of what the neighborhood envisioned spreading over the hill from the Haight-Ashbury district—birthplace of the hippie. Throughout the world, the Haight became synonymous with "flower children" and the counter-cultural movement: "If you're going to San Francisco/Be sure to wear a flower in your hair. . . ." The news cameras didn't stick around long enough to notice that what began as a peaceful, fun-loving experiment in human living changed before long into something more troubled:

> The subculture that would soon colonize the Castro first took shape in the Haight-Ashbury heyday of flower power and acid trips. By 1970, after years of the counterculture ferment, the Haight had become a burned-out, devastated war zone and many residents began looking for other places to live.
>
> Eureka Valley, which already had signs of gay visibility, quickly became a magnet for counter-cultural lesbians and gays.[20]

"My ex-husband was a cop," says Mary O'Shea, a parishioner. "He worked Mission Station. He was totally afraid that our neighborhood was going down the tubes. So he says, 'Our house is for sale!' I say, 'What?!' 'We're selling the house, I don't want the kids raised here any more. All that stuff in the Haight, it's coming over the hill at us.' "[21]

Rumors of a gay bar's being established in the neighborhood struck dread in the hearts of the Irish-Catholic stalwarts of Most Holy Redeemer parish:

> The word went out. A former police officer, not a good Castro boy, but—the housewife flicked her wrist, raised her eyebrows, and, after a meaningful pause—a funny one, bought the Gem bar. And he's probably going to make it over for *his* crowd. Real estate agents were already writing obituaries for the Haight-Ashbury neighborhood over the hill. The hippies came in and wham, there went the neighborhood. Now the gays were going to do that too, right here in Most Holy Redeemer Parish.
>
> Baird never saw anything like the panic that followed the establishment of the first gay bar on Castro Street in the late 1960's.[22] The stolid Irish families sold their Victorians at dirt-cheap prices, fearing greater loss if they waited. By 1973, the numbers of gays moving into the neighborhood amounted to an invasion.

That's what the old timers called the new men of Castro Street—invaders. Now it was 1973 and Baird figured at least half of the people moving in were gay, while more and more of the old-timers sold out.[23]

In 1973, Dignity, the gay Catholic caucus, first met in San Francisco—at St. Peter's in the Mission, not at Most Holy Redeemer. St. Peter's at the time was a much more progressive and open parish. "From what I understand of the history of the Archdiocese in the 60's and 70's, MHR was a little fortress in the middle of a dynamically changing neighborhood," says David Simmons.[24] The story of St. Peter's parish parallels Most Holy Redeemer's: a predominantly Irish parish forced to adapt to changing demographics when the Mission district became a primarily Latino community in the late 1950s. Transformation at St. Peter's, as at MHR, took much pain and struggle. Latin Americans, however, have been part of the Catholic Church for a very long time; with openly gay men and women, a new kind of conversation had to begin. It has been the genius of both parishes to incorporate diverse groups, to learn their language and minister to them in it, while remaining within the larger church structure:

> St. Peter's became the premier Hispanic parish because of its commitment, at times grudging, to make a place for the newly arrived Hispanics within the parish. . . . At the heart of ministry to the Hispanic community at St. Peter's was not a fancy theory, or "strategy," but a basic acceptance of the people where they were, as they were. Hispanic ministry was successful ultimately because the newer Latino groups came to feel welcome at St. Peter's, to feel they were a vital and valued part of the parish.[25]

Monsignor Henry J. Lyne, Most Holy Redeemer's pastor from 1948 to 1968, was and remains a beloved figure in the parish's history, but Lyne simply did not know how to adjust to these drastic changes in the community's life. He too was Irish, and proud of it, and like many of the Irish a good storyteller; he was also very conservative. He was possessed of a sense of humor, of foresight and energy: he remodeled the school, the church, built an outdoor shrine to the Blessed Virgin, a playground for the schoolchildren, and had an Austin organ installed in the choir loft. He is remembered today by the Mercy Housing independent-living facility for seniors next door to the church, named after him. For all his charm and vivacity, however, nothing in Lyne's tradition-loving nature or seminary training could have prepared him for what was happening all around him in Eureka Valley.

Lyne loved gardening and planted the rose garden next to the rectory. Mary Geracimos remembers walking by one day while he was tending his plants; it was 1959, and she was wearing a JFK for President button. "You're voting for Kennedy?" Lyne inquired in his Irish brogue, dismayed. "Don't vote for the man because he's a Catholic! You're not voting for him because he is Irish, are you?" To which Mary responded: "No, I'm voting for him because he's so good-looking!" Lyne rolled his eyes and laughed, exclaiming: "Jesus, Mary, and Joseph!"[26] In the 1960s when the San Francisco Archdiocese was actively promoting the Fair Housing Act, the Social Justice Office sent a speaker, a priest, to Most Holy Redeemer. At the end of his presentation, Monsignor Lyne declared to the assembly, "You can disregard everything this man has said!"[27] Owing both to the force of Lyne's personality and to his shortcomings, an historical disjunction developed: Most Holy Redeemer had all the hallmarks of a successful, active parish, in the traditional sense—a full schedule of services, up-to-date facilities, dedicated women religious teaching in the school—and yet it was waning. Father Bill Young, still in residence at MHR, remembers the parish in 1968: "You just looked at the receipts. I went out on a Sunday Mass, hardly anyone there. The organist was an old lady who had arthritis; she could hardly get the right notes. It was really a dying parish. The doorbell hardly rang at all."[28] The changing profile of the community, and the new population that was changing it, were ignored or regarded with distaste.

Sharon Johnson, for ten years an aide to gay politico Harry Britt and later State Senator John Burton's chief of staff in San Francisco, grew up in the neighborhood and in Most Holy Redeemer parish.

> I remember those times well. I was astonished at the behavior of the parishioners at that time. It was the first time I realized how bigoted they were—you know how you idolize people when you grow up. I went to MHR School. Being Catholic you were special and those outside were not. In my household, anyone of color was frowned upon. My family was anti-gay, and very frightened and prejudiced. It was seen as anti-Jesus, anti-Bible to be gay. They changed, of course.
>
> I remember hearing about a town hall meeting at MHR. I was a child at the time, but I heard the father of my best friend had said that the church should not welcome anyone who was gay, as they were not welcomed in the Bible. He was very outspoken.[29]

Lyne was pastor when Most Holy Redeemer School was disgraced by an event terrible in its violence and far-reaching in its effects.

> On April 30, 1961, the *Chronicle* reported that William Hall, a 27-year-old Ross schoolteacher, had been robbed, thrown on the tracks at 19th and Church streets, and killed when a streetcar ran over him. By May 5, three [students] at Most Holy Redeemer . . . had confessed to the crime.

They had gone to a dance, the newspaper reported and fell into talking about "queers." Said one, "We hate them. You can't go anywhere anymore—downtown, to a show, or just when you're walking home."

When they came upon Hall waiting for the streetcar, they beat him and kicked him until he fell off the platform into the path of the J_Church. "He was able to raise his arm in feeble protest as the J car rumbled towards him," said *The Chronicle*, "but that wasn't enough." After Hall was run over, the boys stole his wallet.

"One of the boys stood up and argued that it wasn't murder," said homicide chief Ralph McDonald after the confession. "He seemed to think that it was all right to beat up homosexuals. I asked how they could tell whether a man is a homosexual, and they said all they had to do was talk with him, that they could tell."

The three were convicted and sent to a juvenile correction facility. . . . They were paroled on June 30, 1976.[30]

To Sharon Johnson, the incident changed the way gays and the long-established community in the Castro felt about each other, and about themselves:

> I also remember that incident when the MHR students rolled the gay man onto the track and he died. I was horrified by it. I felt people in Eureka Valley accepted all people and then was devastated to realize they did not. Members of the gay community were so hurt they called you breeder on the street sometimes.[31]

(Much later, in 1975, a Catholic priest, Father Reed, sitting on the San Francisco Board of Education, was told about the incident. He made an impassioned plea to the Board in favor of employment protections for the district's gay teachers; previously the Board had rejected the proposal by a 7-0 vote. Community activist Hank Wilson was there. "You could hear a pin drop when Father Reed spoke," he says. "It was very moving." This time the motion passed unanimously.)[32]

Sad and ironic that almost forty years later, when a similar tragedy occurred—the killing of gay college student Matthew Shepard in Wyoming—of all the Catholic parishes in San Francisco, it was Most Holy Redeemer that held a service in his memory:

> Thomas Van Etten, who helped plan an interdenominational service in San Francisco with his longtime partner, Robert Van Etten, said he was heartened when about 500 people showed up. "I think people are looking for healing and for a way to make a difference . . . instead of screaming and shouting," said Van Etten, a member of Most Holy Redeemer Catholic Church, where the service was held.[33]

By the end of Lyne's pastorate, parishioners were concerned that the church doors might close for good.[34] Most Holy Redeemer was in decline. The church Father Young remembers in 1968, with the near-empty pews and the arthritic organist, is in sharp contrast to the one Mary Geracimos recalls when Lyne arrived in 1948:

> The twelve-fifteen mass was always full. We went to the nine o'clock mass in class; the whole school was there, the nuns, the parents at the back. We had the first two sections. We had to wear a hat, not a scarf. You'd get a tap on the shoulders if you lapsed [i.e., nodded off].[35]

In 1968, Father John O'Connell became pastor, having already served two years as parish administrator under Msgr. Lyne. O'Connell was a former military man, as traditional as Lyne but less involved with the community socially. Some are persuaded he was homophobic. Between 1968 and 1976, while O'Connell was pastor, the area comprised within the bounds of Most Holy Redeemer parish became the most famous gay neighborhood in the world[36]—yet there was no outreach to the new gay neighbors. As the late, much loved, Evelyn Squeri recalls, "You know, people never talked about things like that in the parish. And when they first came to the area they seemed outlandish. That really scared people off." When children from Most Holy Redeemer School were caught going into the new gay bars of the neighborhood shouting, "Fags! Fags! Fags!" it was enough of an embarrassment that O'-Connell intervened to end the harassment, at the Archbishop's request.[37]

The vitality of the parish seemed lost. No new idea was the right idea. A youth Mass started in 1973 faltered and disappeared. Sunday bulletins from the time make no reference to anything going on in the wider neighborhood or the city. The impression they give is of a beleaguered community. Notes appear regularly disparaging other Christian churches. If this was the attitude to fellow Christians by the parish leadership, what hope was there for a fresh approach to the gay community?

> Did it ever strike you that a dying Catholic—be he good, bad, or indifferent—will never call for a Protestant minister? That no Catholic, so long as he leads a virtuous life, falls away from his faith or denies his religion. That ordinarily only the best among Protestants become Catholic? That only the indifferent, not to say the worse Catholics become Protestant? That the Protestant ministers who have become Catholic were among the most learned and the most virtuous of their calling?[38]

Good relations with churches of other traditions were plainly not a priority; but unlike Most Holy Redeemer parish, many of them were taking seriously the need to reach out to the gay community. Indeed, while some of the more progressive churches played a key role in the history of the gay movement in San Francisco, the Roman Catholic Church was conspicuous by its absence—especially conspicuous in the Castro.

The 1960s saw the creation of the San Francisco Council on Religion and the Homosexual, formed to initiate a dialogue between the burgeoning homosexual community and the more progressive Protestant churches. In 1965, the Council held the now famous New Year's Day Mardi Gras Ball, a costume event (giving those attending the option of masking their faces). Organizers secured assurances from the police that attendees would not be harassed, but even so, police officers arrived and demanded entrance, simply forcing their way inside when met with protests at the door. Ministers and clergy looked on in shock as partygoers were loaded roughly into paddy wagons and taken off to cells. The next day, CRH ministers held a press conference at Glide Memorial Church to express their outrage—a turning point in San Francisco's attitude towards its gay residents. All charges were dropped, and the police department took the unprecedented step of appointing an official liaison to the gay community.

In 1976, Archbishop Joseph P. McGucken appointed Father Donald Pyne as pastor of Most Holy Redeemer. Pyne was no more prepared to contend with the Castro's gay community than his predecessors were. He didn't want to be a pastor, especially of such a problematic parish. Deacon Laurence Rolle says that he never talked about the gay issue; he wanted to lead a quiet life and then retire.[39] Mary Geracimos, still the parish bookkeeper today, had left San Francisco for a few years, and on her return was struck by how changed MHR was:

> Numbers were declining, instead of it being packed as I remembered it. There were few people in the pews.
>
> I did the bookkeeping for the parish. The Irish were leaving, the school had closed, there were not enough students, and the parishioners were very upset about this. I think it was Fr Pyne—he had reassured them he would not close it, and then he did. There was a lot of angry feeling. The parish started declining. $400 to $600 was a good collection at this time.
>
> There was a housekeeper, Margaret, who lived in. No one was calling at the door; the phone never rang. The area was thriving, the church wasn't.
>
> Fr. Pyne was not friendly to the gay community. He once told me that the gays were like the hippies, coming in from the Haight, partying, and then they would leave. I said to him that hippies don't buy houses, real estate, and settle, but the gays do. He just shook his head like I was wrong. Fr. Pyne was a nice man, but he was very quiet, a loner I guess.
>
> If you were gay then, you didn't talk about it. You just didn't say anything. No one ever asked.[40]

Frances FitzGerald gives a vivid, detailed description of the Castro in *Cities on a Hill: A Journey Through Contemporary American Cultures.* FitzGerald argues that until 1965, San Francisco was much as it had been since the turn of the century:

A manufacturing city, a port, and a collection of ethnic villages—Irish, Italian, and German as well as Asian, Hispanic, and black. But in the sixties much of the shipping and manufacturing moved out—to be replaced, eventually, by financial and service industries. With the flight of manufacturing, the European ethnic communities scattered into the suburbs and beyond. Their members had conceivably "melted" into the white middle class. . . .[41]

It was this very flight to the suburbs that attracted the city's gay newcomers to the Castro: housing was cheap, and there were the stirrings of something exciting, liberating:

The Castro was the first gay neighborhood in the country, and as such it was something quite new under the sun. But the Castro was also a movement; it was part of the national movement for gay liberation, but Castro activists thought of it as the cutting edge. Gay liberation was a civil rights struggle, but it was much more than that. Now that the feminist movement had passed its radical phase, gay activists saw themselves as the avant-garde of the sexual revolution and the revolutionary change in sex and gender roles. Specifically, their goal was to overturn one of the oldest and strongest taboos in the culture, but beyond that, it was to challenge all the conventions surrounding the "traditional" nuclear family. The Castro—or what they called their "liberated zone"—was a kind of laboratory for experimentation with alternative ways to live. It was also a carnival where social conventions were turned upside down, just for the pleasure of seeing what they looked like the wrong way up. At the Castro Street Fair, on Halloween or on any other of the gay holidays, men would turn up as Betty Grable lookalikes, as Hell's Angels toughs, as nuns on roller skates, and as men in Brooks Brother's shirts and tasseled loafers. This was play, it was at the same time a meditation on the arbitrary nature of gender roles and costumes; it was also real life for men who had found themselves in the excluded middle of the terms male/female.[42]

FitzGerald argues that the sheer concentration of gay people in San Francisco possibly had no parallel in history. The Castro was a neighborhood, unlike Polk Street and South of Market, which were also areas where gays socialized. By the early seventies the Castro was the center of gay life in the city. By 1978, estimates of the gay population of San Francisco ranged from 75,000 to 150,000. One hundred thousand is a number commonly given— meaning that one out of every five adults in the city was gay. FitzGerald gives us a snapshot of the Castro at this time:

In fact the neighborhood was like other neighborhoods except that on Saturdays and Sundays you could walk for blocks and see only young men dressed as it were for a hiking expedition. Also the bookstore was a gay bookstore, the health club a gay health club; and behind the shingles hung out on the street there was a gay real-estate brokerage, a gay lawyer's office, and the office of a gay psychiatrist. The bars were, with one exception, gay bars, and one of them, the Twin Peaks Bar near Market Street, was, so Armistead [Maupin] told me, the first gay bar in the country to have picture windows on the street.[43]

In FitzGerald's judgment, 1978 marked a high point in the development of the Castro. "Given the homogeneity of its inhabitants, it had quickly and spontaneously evolved a new kind of politics, a new style of dress and behavior, new forms of couple relationships, and new sexual mores. It had an ideology rather different from that of gay groups on the East Coast, and it had, as the sociologists put it, institutional completeness. It was something new under the sun."[44] By 1978 the corner of 18th and Castro Streets had been dubbed "the crossroads of the gay world," or "the gayest crossroads in the world." The neighborhood had become an international gay mecca.

Into this gay crossroads Father Cuchulain Moriarty was thrust, appointed pastor in 1979 and remaining at MHR until his death in 1982. Moriarty was a new sort of priest for Most Holy Redeemer. He came to the parish from the archdiocesan Social Justice office, favored work boots and jeans, was socially engaged and aware. Unhappily, he never seemed very engaged with the parish, or aware of the turbulent social climate in his own neighborhood.

A parish questionnaire from February 1979 is illuminating. *Results of the Most Holy Redeemer Parish Questionnaire* present a snapshot of the parish at the time, reflecting wildly differing attitudes and perceptions about the crisis the parish found itself in and what should be done about it. Some parishioners are fearful, want to retreat; some have an impulse to embrace the new reality in the neighborhood, sensing the parish must change, loosen its grip on the past, or die. A representative sampling of the responses compiled:

[#30] Have felt up to now that the parish lacks vitality. It seems so lonely and alien in this hedonistic neighborhood. There must be some way to be a light in the darkness.

[#34] Greater hospitality, understanding, and outreach to the gay community.

[#36] I remember growing up and seeing this church full of people. I come now and it is not even half full. Something is definitely lacking.

[#37] Where are the children of the parish?

[#38] Abolish the sign of peace. I have never cared for it. Find it disruptive. Often the students break into conversation. I feel people are insincere.

They just shake hands because if they didn't, everyone would notice. Of all the churches I go to, I prefer this one: it's very non-controversial here. More traditional in the singing and readings.

[#43] HOPE SCHOOL REMAINS OPEN.

Why discuss the Gospel in your sermons, we always here [*sic*] about that in school, all your sermons bore me.

[#52] I feel MHR should lend its facilities to Dignity, an organization of gay Catholics—or at least provide some ministry to gay Catholics.

[#56] I'm disappointed that so few children attend our school and that there is a lack of interest in the altar boy program.

[#57] THE DOWNFALL OF THIS PARISH IS NO ONE PERSON'S FAULT. BUT THE ARCHDIOCESE WAS NEVER (OR SO IT SEEMED) AROUND DURING OUR MOST CRITICAL TIME. MAYBE WE'LL RESURRECT OURSELVES AS A PARISH, I ALWAYS HOPE AND PRAY SO.

[#58] HOW CAN YOU HAVE SOCIAL EVENTS IN A PARISH WHERE PEOPLE AREN'T EVEN SOCIAL TO EACH OTHER? WE SHOULD MAKE IT KNOWN THAT ALL THE NEIGHBORS ARE WELCOME TO MASS. THE GAYS SHOULD BE WELCOME IN THE CHURCH, GO TO A COMMUNITY MEETING AND EXPRESS THE DESIRE FOR COMMUNITY AND MHR TO WORK TOGETHER RATHER THAN TOLERATE EACH OTHER. THEY ARE HERE—WHY NOT LET THEM IN—OUT OF LOVE.

[#62] WHEN I MOVED INTO THIS PARISH 8 YEARS AGO, I DID NOT FIND MHR A WELCOMING, CHRISTIAN PLACE. WE LIVE IN A DIFFICULT NEIGHBORHOOD IN A DIFFICULT CITY. I BELIEVE THAT THE CHURCH CAN BE A PLACE WHERE THERE IS ACCEPTANCE FOR ALL, A FORUM WHERE WE CAN ALL LEARN TO LIVE WITH OUR DIFFERENCES. I AM SO HAPPY THAT MHR IS TRYING TO CHANGE, CHANGE IS DIFFICULT AND I PRAY THAT WE WILL SUCCEED.

[#64] MY FAITH IS FINE UNTIL I HAVE TO DEFEND IT, I WOULD LIKE TO BE ABLE TO VERBALLY DEFEND MY FAITH—GAYS ARE

NOT A GROUP THAT ALL CHRISTIANS CAN ACCEPT AS BROTH-
ERS AND SISTERS. INDIVIDUALLY YES, BUT NOT AS A GROUP.[45]

Most Holy Redeemer School was closed in 1979, the year Moriarty arrived.
There were parishioners who blamed Moriarty for not "saving" it, but in truth
it was a *fait accompli* before he set foot in the rectory. Changed demographics and declining enrollment had doomed it years before. On September 18,
1977, Father Pyne had written to the Superintendent of Schools and the Archdiocesan Board of Education for consultation regarding the school's closure.[46] There was no reason but sentiment to keep it open.[47]

Since the 1961 killing of William Hall, the school had been plagued inter-
mittently by tensions between the parish and the gay community. Teaching
duties were in the hands of a handful of lay teachers and the Sisters of Charity of the Blessed Virgin Mary of Dubuque, Iowa—better known as the
BVMs (which some students unjustly construed as "Black Veiled Mon-
sters").[48] The sisters lived in the convent next door to the school and con-
tended as best they could with the hostility of their charges toward the neighborhood gays. Marie O'Connor, formerly a BVM and the last principal of
Most Holy Redeemer School, attended meetings at the Eureka Valley Recreation Center and found herself receptive, even sympathetic, to the new gay
community's concerns. Not so the parents of her students. More and more
mothers and fathers were arriving to escort their children home, newly fearful for their safety, or guarding against what they deemed unwholesome
moral influences that might be encountered on the street. Gay-bashings became common at night in Collingwood Park, next to the school—often per-
petrated by her own sixth- through eighth-graders, O'Connor was to learn. In
1973 or '74, two polite men[49] came to call on her with an eye-opening list of
the gay community's grievances against MHR students—beatings, name-
calling, throwing things into gay bars and businesses: unrelenting harassment.
Her visitors did not know the names of the children involved, only that they
came from the school's upper grades. Mortified and distressed, O'Connor
went from classroom to classroom informing the children that such behavior
was not acceptable from Catholic school students. Her faculty was in accord.
But it was a message the children failed to hear elsewhere in the parish, which
seemed not to take the problem seriously.[50]

To Marie O'Connor, the final decline of the school was dramatic. In rapid
succession, twenty-one of the neighborhood bars became gay bars. Families
were leaving in droves, deserting the parish for nearby St. Philip's, just over
the hill in Noe Valley, or moving out of the neighborhood entirely. Father
Pyne seemed unable or unwilling to act to reverse the trend, and the archdiocese seemed distant and indifferent. The sisters were left to their own devices

to manage the failing school. Talk of parish closures was in the air.[51] O'Connor concluded the parish was so adrift that its closing would soon be inevitable and its passing not much lamented.

Such was the situation Moriarty inherited as pastor in 1979. That he was a fine man there can be no question. His reputation for activism was celebrated far and wide. Bianca Jagger was a guest at the rectory in 1982, as was Rigoberta Menchu Tum, the Indian catechist and Christian leader who later received the Nobel Peace Prize. Upon Moriarty's death, Dianne Feinstein, then mayor of San Francisco, eulogized him for "his tireless advocacy, care and service to our city's poor. By his life-long struggle for social justice, he has set a beautiful and impeccable example for us all."[52] Father Moriarty kept his illness very private, and his passing was sudden. But when it was announced to the congregation at MHR, there was little reaction.[53]

Why? Moriarty was passionately concerned about the plight of Central American refugees, rather than about the plight of the parish or about the sexual refugees who populated the Castro all around him. The parish became a center for the work that engaged him personally. At one time six or seven Central American refugees, mostly Salvadoran, lived in the Rectory, and twenty or thirty in the convent, unoccupied since the closure of the school. The parish paid the refugees' expenses—without the parishioners' knowledge, at the time. Even so, they resented the energy he poured into causes not their own. The Central Americans were never seen in church, which perhaps the language barrier can account for. Still, the perception was that the church facilities had been hijacked and the parish left to fend for itself. As Rev. Kevin Ballard, S. J., who grew up in the parish, remembers MHR in the early eighties:

> Moriarty was never a part of the neighborhood. He used the buildings for his own interest; that was refugees. He was dying of cancer at the time and not interested. . . . [A]s a Jesuit student, I would go to the nine-thirty mass. I was depressed. There were maybe forty people in the church, almost all elderly, and a few gay men. One of them was Jim Stultz. He wore blue jeans and plaid, a somewhat toned-down version of the "clone look" for church! He was not hiding anything, and he was a lector. This was the picture just before Tony McGuire arrived as pastor.[54]

Moriarty seemed ambivalent about the gays who had brought the Castro—his parish—such worldwide fame, or infamy. Perhaps it was inattention, indifference. According to Mary Geracimos, he never tried to stop gay people from coming to church, but neither did he reach out to them.[55] Father Young, who lived in the rectory with Moriarty, says he disliked gay people: "Now, that is an opinion, obviously, but I am basing it on the way he reacted to them and the way he talked about them."[56] Tom Fry, however, who co-founded the San Francisco chapter of the gay Catholic group, Dignity, thinks Moriarty was sympathetic to gays but simply had no time to develop a relationship with the community, ill as he was with cancer and preoccupied by his work with refugees.[57] The experience of Laurence Rolle, deacon to the parish at the time, was mixed:

> Moriarty was interested in the Spanish speaking community, but let everything else [just] happen. I organized having gay people in the rectory after the ten a.m. mass. Moriarty seemed pleased about this, but Bill Young told me recently that he resented losing his dining room with "these people." This was the first outreach to the gay community in the parish. Moriarty would go to a gay restaurant with me occasionally.
>
> [Services were] very traditional, with slow hymns, hymns sung four times slower than they should be. Moriarty wanted decent music, but Gertrude the organist, well, basically I fired her. She got confused all the time. Eventually we hired a gay man, John Oddo, as music director. I got the lectors going for the first time, lay lectors and Eucharistic ministers. And we had spaces after the readings too. Those who were gay came quietly and left quietly and didn't let anyone know. No one knew whom you were, why you were here, you just went to Mass like everyone else. You went to the coffee breaks, but they still weren't out to all the parish. The coffee mornings were informal, no agenda, no resolutions. Some of it was gay talk, but mostly it was just chat.[58]

Moriarty didn't oppose the innovations, but didn't support them so much as allow them. Perhaps it's too easy to forget at a distance of more than twenty years how new toleration of gay people was, how limited and tentative. Certainly Moriarty was progressive compared to many of the old-timers in the Castro:

> Some of the Irish Catholic neighbors and shopkeepers, people like the crusty old couple who ran Andy's Donuts, seemed resistant, even hostile, to the endless number of gay young men, and put up signs about how customers should dress and behave if they wanted to be served.[59]

Tension always accompanies demographic change. It was rife at nearby St. Peter's when the mostly Irish neighborhood of the Mission became mostly Latino.[60] But unlike MHR, St. Peter's was led by a series of progressive priests who were determined the parish should include rather than resist the transformed community in which it found itself. Its support of Dignity was of a piece with this intention. Meanwhile, in the new Castro, gay capital of the world, Most Holy Redeemer's principal role was to serve as an occasional lightning rod for the gay community's anger towards the Church.

When voters in Dade County, Florida, at the behest of Anita Bryant and others, repealed a gay rights ordinance in June 1977, MHR took the brunt of local gay outrage. A letter favoring the repeal, read two days before the vote in Miami's Catholic churches, may or may not have been decisive on election night—but it was a provocation San Francisco' gay community could not ignore.

> At the Gay Center on Grove Street, amid the glum remains of what was to have been a victory potluck dinner, the idea was born to gather at the crossroads of Castro and Market, and march in candlelit protest on the Church of the Most Holy Redeemer, the parish church and traditional cultural anchor of the old Castro neighborhood—and a center of resentment among conservative Catholic families engulfed by the gay migration.
>
> The word went out through the city's bars and clubs, and by ten-thirty, the intersection of Market and Castro was jammed with 1,500 people, almost all of them men in their twenties and thirties. Bearded, mustached, dressed in denim and flannel shirts or old military fatigues, they were holding up lighted candles, roaring with emotion as they began to move. Chanting *"Out of the bars—into the streets!"* they headed toward Most Holy Redeemer, drawing more and more marchers as they went. But the volume and energy were too great to be satisfied with a rally at a neighborhood church, and the crowd surged on—up Market Street, shouting "Two, four, six, eight, Gay is just as good as Straight!" . . . By the time the crowd pooled into Union Square for a midnight rally, it numbered more than five thousand. Holding candles, they listened as a few speakers shouted themselves hoarse over a ten-watt bullhorn, and then, with feeling, sang "We Shall Overcome."
>
> It was a defining night.[61]

The crowd was led that night by Harvey Milk,[62] without some mention of whom no history of the Castro in the seventies could be complete. Milk was elected to the San Francisco Board of Supervisors in 1977, the first openly gay man to be elected to public office on the West Coast.[63] Operating out of his camera shop, "Castro Camera," Milk was also the first gay businessman to make conciliatory overtures to the Castro's long-time residents and merchants. (For years "Castro Camera" was advertised weekly in the Most Holy Redeemer bulletin.)

> He soon became an ex-officio liaison between the established Castro businessmen and the new gay merchants who were moving into the once boarded-up storefronts. What surprised many of the merchants was that Milk never tried to drum up business with his visits, he just stopped by to chat.[64]

Still, despite Milk's best efforts, the merchants resisted the newcomers:

> The first skirmish came when two gay men tried to open up an antique store. The established burghers associated with the Eureka Valley Merchants Association (EVMA) were taken aback; an antique store just doors down from The

Family Store where the kids go to buy their Most Holy Redeemer uniforms? The antique store won the fight, but the fracas soured relations between the old and the new merchants. The EVMA would have nothing to do with the gay invaders.[65]

The upshot was the formation by Milk of a new association for the gay merchants: the Castro Village Association. In 1974, the CVA organized the first Castro Street Fair, which remains a major annual celebration in the life of the neighborhood; indeed MHR has a booth at the Fair each year. Once its staying power became obvious, even non-gay merchants began to join.

Milk and Mayor George Moscone were fatally shot in City Hall on November 27, 1978. Infamously, their assassin, Dan White, fellow Supervisor and pious Catholic, was found guilty only of voluntary manslaughter and served just five years in prison. The much-reported fact that White immediately fled to St. Mary's Cathedral after murdering the two men did nothing to help the image of the Catholic Church in the gay community.

Despite Father Moriarty's (possibly) benign neglect of the gay community, it was after all during his time as pastor that MHR's first outreach to gays began, albeit informally, thanks to the self-effacing parish deacon, Laurence Rolle. Perhaps because Moriarty was ill or distracted, Rolle had more influence than one might expect of a deacon. A gay man himself, Rolle had a personal interest in making Most Holy Redeemer a place where gay people felt welcome. His coffee hour each Sunday in the rectory dining room attracted mostly gay men, more and more of whom started coming regularly to church and found their way onto various church committees. Rolle would make a point of mentioning gay issues in a positive light when it was his turn to give the Sunday homily—a definite departure from the pastoral approach of Moriarty and his predecessors.

In spite of itself, the parish was beginning to accommodate the new reality that for so long it had tried to ignore. Tensions remained strong, between new parishioners and old, between Deacon Rolle and Father Moriarty, between Rolle and another priest, Father Jim Hagan, who had joined the parish staff. Like Moriarty, Hagan felt called to work on social-justice issues in the world at large rather than in the parish: when he left, it was to take an assignment in Mexico more suited to his temperament, working with the very poor. The friction in the rectory led to Rolle's being ousted as deacon.

The few cautious changes the parish had managed to make were not sufficient to revive it. When Moriarty died in 1982, Most Holy Redeemer was facing the possibility of its own demise. A choice had to be made: the parish could continue to move in the direction of decay and irrelevance, or engage the gay community in a new kind of relationship, with the prospect of becoming something traditional and radical at the same time.

The next pastor would be MHR's savior, or its last.

NOTES

1. The Data Lounge, "Priest Protests Church Backing of Knight Initiative," October 28, 1999; available from http:/www.datalounge.com/datalounge/news/record .html?record=4802; accessed August 7, 2001.

2. On MHR's centennial, see also Joe Dignan, "Most Holy Redeemer turns 100," *Bay Area Reporter,* January 10, 2002: "We're probably 70–80% gay and lesbian," said parishioner David Differding. "We're putting up banners for the centennial that say 'An inclusive Catholic community.'" Bishop Wester became the Bishop of Salt Lake City, Utah in March 2007. Wester is replacing Bishop George Niederauer in Salt Lake City. Niederauer had left Salt Lake City to himself become Archbishop of San Francisco replacing Archbishop Levada in February 2006. Archbishop Levada had been appointed Prefect of the Congregation for the Doctrine of the Faith in Rome succeeding Cardinal Joseph Ratzinger, who was elected Pope Benedict XVI on the death of Pope John Paul II.

3. Jeffrey M. Burns, *San Francisco: A History of the Archdiocese of San Francisco* (Strasbourg: Editions du Signe, 1999–), vol. 2, *1885–1945: Glory, Ruin, and Resurrection,* 2.

4. David Simmons, taped interview by author, San Francisco, April 9, 2001.

5. James P. Gaffney, *A Citizen of No Mean City: Archbishop Patrick Riordan of San Francisco, 1841–1914* (Wilmington, NC: A Consortium Book, 1976), 212.

6. No one seems to know precisely where the emerging Catholic community worshiped. It might well have been in the home of long-term parishioners at 4036 19th Street (and Hartford), the Dolan-Callan family. The house was built in 1887, the same year Lily Langtry visited San Francisco. The Dolans came from Galway in 1852, the time of the Great Hunger. Vincent Callan, Jr., who lived his whole life in the house, died in 2002. (John Callan, taped interview by author, San Francisco, May 12, 2001.)

7. See also John Bernard McGloin, S.J., "The Catholic Origins of San Francisco," chapter 6 in *Some California Catholic Reminiscences for the United States Bicentennial,* ed. Francis Weber (published for the California Catholic Conference by the Knights of Columbus, 1976). The first record McGloin finds of mass being said in San Francisco is on March 28, 1776, by Franciscan Pedro Font, on his journey with Juan Bautista de Anza to locate sites for what would become the Presidio and Mission of San Francisco. St. Patrick's was the young city's second parish, established in the Gold Rush days. Pope Pius IX established the Archdiocese of San Francisco on July 29, 1853.

8. Apocryphal, often repeated. E.g. Databay Travel E-guide, "Maiden Lane" (South Boston, MA: Hunter Publishing, 1999), available from hlttp://www.data bay.com/eguide/Bay_Area/San_Francisco/Maiden_Lane/; Internet; accessed November 5, 2002. Rev. Wilfreid Glabach, pastor of the First Congregational Church of San Francisco, tells me that the pastor coming from Hawaii who received this warning about San Francisco being wild and futile ground for the gospel was his predecessor. I had the honor of preaching at this historic Protestant church, which was founded in 1849.

This reputation for San Francisco being "wild, foolish and futile" seems to have staying power. During the 2006 congressional elections Nancy Pelosi Congressional representative for San Francisco was attacked for holding "San Francisco values," and I think that we have some idea of what this means. Despite these attacks Pelosi went on to be elected the first woman speaker of the house. Pelosi is a practicing San Francisco Catholic. MHR parishioners have informed me that while she is a regular parishioner at St. Vincent DePaul parish she has been seen worshipping at MHR.

9. *Dorian Gray* (London: Simpkin, Marshall Hamilton, Kent & Co., 1913), 234.

10. Peter L. Stein, *The Castro—a Neighborhood, a Battleground, a Mecca*. (San Francisco: KQED Books and Tapes, 1997). Originally an episode of KQED's *Neighborhoods: The Hidden Cities of San Francisco*.

11. Mary Geracimos, interview by author, San Francisco, February 20, 2001.

12. Francis Weber, *Catholic Footprints in California* (Newhall: Hogarth Press, 1970), 188.

13. Randy Shilts, *The Mayor of Castro Street: The Life and Times of Harvey Milk* (New York: St. Martin's Press, 1982), 81–82. Randy Shilts was planning a book on the Roman Catholic Church and homosexuality when he died in 1994 from AIDS complications at his ten-acre ranch in Guerneville, Sonoma. Guerneville is a popular gay resort north of San Francisco. Shilts is buried close to friend and MHR parishioner Kean Brewer at Redwood Memorial Gardens in Guerneville. http://en.wikipedia.org/wiki/Randy_Shilts, January 13, 2007.

14. "Holy Redeemer . . . the Catholic parish, was just overflowing with kids." C. Rodney Silk interviewed in *The Castro*, KQED.

15. KQED, *The Castro*.

16. When I took one of her renowned walking tours of the Castro ("Cruisin' the Castro"), Trevor Hailey called the neighborhood "the heart of the city."

17. Randy Shilts, "Castro Street: Mecca or Ghetto?" (1977) in *Long Road to Freedom: The Advocate History of the Gay and Lesbian Movement* (New York: St Martin's Press, 1994), 156.

18. "Both the large numbers of gay men (and lesbians) transplanted to San Francisco and the established enclaves of homosexual San Francisco quickly found themselves under renewed siege by the law." Les Wright, 173.

19. KQED, *The Castro*.

20. Susan Stryker, "The Castro: Journey to the Center of the Queer Universe," *San Francisco Frontiers Magazine,* April 5, 2001, 27.

21. KQED, *The Castro*.

22. The first gay bar in the Castro actually opened in 1963 and was known as the Missouri Mule, located on Market Street. It closed in 1973.

23. Shilts in *Long Road to Freedom*, 82. The parish itself influenced the name of another early gay bar in the Castro: "Tom Sanford, who was known to many by the nickname 'Sally,' had a metal statue of a nun in his yard and wanted to call the bar 'The Iron Nun.' A pharmacist called Eugene Longinotti who worked at the Star Pharmacy and was part owner of the building, refused to allow the name. He was a fairminded but conservative man as well as a Catholic. He was willing to allow a gay bar in his building, but he knew the good priests at Most Holy Redeemer, the church around the corner, would not tolerate a bar called The Iron Nun! So the bar was named Toad Hall after the name of toad in the children's story, *Wind in the Willows,* written

by Kenneth Graham in 1908. Toad was a charming and respectable but wayward frog, a misfit, who didn't quite fit into the community of quiet hard working rural creatures, nor could he handle the fast paced, hectic role of a city dweller," www.backdoor.com/castro/street/thallpage.html.

24. April 9, 2001 interview by author.

25. Jeffrey Burns, "*Que Es Esto*? The Transformation of St. Peter's Parish, San Francisco, 1913–1990" in *American Congregations*, vol. 1, *Portraits of Twelve Religious Congregations,* ed. James P. Wind and James W. Lewis (Chicago: University of Chicago Press, 1994), 453–54.

26. February 20, 2001 interview by author.

27. Father Anthony McGuire, interview by author, tape recording, San Francisco, February 4, 2001.

28. Father William Young, interview by author, tape recording, San Francisco, February 20, 2001.

29. Sharon Johnson, telephone interview by author, November 25, 2002.

30. *San Francisco Chronicle,* April 30, 1961, 5. See also from the Internet, newsgroups: ba.motss, October 18, 1998, posted by Frank Martinez Lester, October 15, 1998.

31. November 25, 2002 interview.

32. Hank Wilson, telephone interview by Patrick Mulcahey, December 9, 2002.

33. Martha Irvine, Associated Press, "Vigils Held for Gay Student," *South Carolina Gay and Lesbian Pride Movement* website, http://www.scglpm.org/news/vigil3.shtml, accessed August 22, 2002.

34. Evelyn and John Squeri, interview by author, tape recording, San Francisco, January 22, 2001.

35. February 20, 2001 interview by author.

36. An interesting assessment of what created what we now call the Castro can be found in Peter Liuzzi's *With Listening Hearts: Understanding the Voices of Lesbian and Gay Catholics* (New Jersey: Paulist Press, 2001), 67. "Many homosexual people simply feel left out of mainstream life. That sense of alienation finds its fullest expression in what could be called the gay ghettos in most major cities. Los Angeles has its West Hollywood and San Francisco has its Castro. Such communities attract some people who are really on the fringe of society and who exhibit an in-your-face attitude and bizarre behavior and dress that are meant to draw negative attention and are so often exploited by the media. At their worst, such places are the gathering of persons around their brokenness. At their best, such places provide a temporary refuge for people who have nowhere else to go or who just need to be with other homosexual people for entertainment and a sense of community. I have been accustomed to seeing such a neighborhood as the marketplace where evangelization is waiting to happen. My attitude has led me to find goodness and light there as well. What is important to realize is that such places speak clearly to the fact that all human beings are called to relationship and community by their very nature. Exclude any group of people from traditional communities and they will establish their own communities as a means of survival."

37. Fr. Anthony McGuire interview by author, February 4, 2001.

38. Most Holy Redeemer bulletin, November 11, 1973.

39. Laurence Rolle, interview by author, tape recording, San Francisco, March 20, 2001.

40. February 20, 2001 interview by author.

41. Frances FitzGerald, *Cities on a Hill: A Journey Through Contemporary American Cultures* (New York: Simon and Schuster, 1981), 16.

42. FitzGerald, 12.

43. FitzGerald, 34.

44. FitzGerald, 48.

45. *Results of the Most Holy Redeemer Parish Questionnaire*, distributed February 1979.

46. Most Holy Redeemer bulletin, February 12, 1978.

47. A terse note in the parish bulletin of July 4, 1982 declares: "We have decided to lease the premises to the Live Oaks [*sic*] School, with classes from kindergarten through the sixth grade. The cafeteria will remain as our senior center." The building was later rented to the San Francisco Friends School, a Quaker school.

48. Two other women's religious congregations served the parish: Sisters of the Holy Family coordinated religious education for public-school students and Sunday school, and sisters from the Missionaries of Charity did parish visitations.

49. O'Connor thinks they were Tom Edwards and Harry Britt, major figures in the gay community at the time and subsequently, Britt does not recall the episode, but allows it might have been he. (Harry Britt, telephone interview by author, November 25, 2002.)

50. Marie O'Connor, telephone interviews with author, San Francisco, November 10–11, 2002.

51. Several parishes were finally closed in the 1980s, though some (Holy Cross, for instance) were re-opened later, to serve a demographically new congregation.

52. Letter published in Most Holy Redeemer bulletin, December 19, 1982.

53. Laurence Rolle, interview by author, San Francisco, November 12, 2002.

54. Kevin Ballard, interview by author, tape recording, San Francisco, October 22, 2001.

55. February 20, 2001, interview with author.

56. February 20, 2001, taped interview with author.

57. Tom Fry, interview with author, tape recording, San Francisco, August 21, 2001.

58. Laurence Rolle, interview with author, San Francisco, March 20, 2001, tape recording.

59. Dudley Clendinen and Adam Nagaourney, *Out for Good: The Struggle to Build a Gay Rights Movement in America* (New York: Simon and Schuster, 1999), 337.

60. Burns, *"Que Es Esto?"* 396–464. St. Peter's successfully negotiated the transition and also provided a home to San Francisco's Dignity chapter, whose first mass was at St. Peter's in January 1973. The group used the parish auditorium at three o'clock on Sunday afternoons. When news of the meetings became public, a clamor of protest arose, mainly from outside the parish. Burns records how Pastor Monsignor James Flynn defended the decision in a letter to Archbishop McGucken, saying "Our involvement at St. Peter's is limited to making available to the group our meeting

rooms" and warning that refusal to allow Dignity to hold mass would cause greater publicity and disruption. Dignity was allowed to continue to meet at St. Peter's. As Burns points out, while the Hispanic community has been stereotyped as fiercely anti-gay, at St. Peter's no conflict ever surfaced between Latinos and gays.

61. *Out for Good*, 336.
62. *The Mayor of Castro Street,* 159.
63. *The Mayor of Castro Street*, 170–85.
64. *The Mayor of Castro Street*, 87.
65. *The Mayor of Castro Street*, 89.

Chapter Two

Father Anthony McGuire, Pastor

After Father Moriarty's death, representatives from the archdiocese came for a "listening" session with parishioners, in order to assist the archbishop in selecting a new man. For Laurence Rolle, it was principally an exercise in side-stepping the proverbial elephant in the room:

> They came from the chancery, the personnel board, to ask questions, to see whom to send. We have to replace Fr. Moriarty, they said; "What kind of pastor do we need in this parish?" At some point it came to me: no one had said anything about the new demographics of the area. I said, "The parish is gradually becoming more gay. These are the demographics of the area. This needs to be thought about in making this decision." There was absolute stone-dead silence around the room. Everyone looked down; no one would look up. Dead silence, not just a pause, a shocked silence until someone mumbled something. How dare I say such a thing! And the meeting went on to another point.[1]

Fortunately, Archbishop John Quinn was well aware the question needed to be asked, and chose a man who turned out to be especially suited to the new sociological profile of the parish. Under Father Anthony McGuire—"Father Tony"—MHR was reborn.

I asked Archbishop Quinn how he decided on Fr. McGuire:

> I wanted someone I knew would be kind, but would also be true to the Church's teaching. And be a true witness to the Church, but in a way that is kind and with genuine pastoral concern for the people in the parish. I admired him very much. He was very right for the job. He was very kind, very intelligent, and he was pastorally zealous with his concern for the good of the people. He had all the best qualities.[2]

Anthony McGuire became the ninth pastor of Most Holy Redeemer parish in 1982. McGuire already had a full-time job as Secretary of Ethnic and Cultural Affairs at the Chancery of the Archdiocese. He'd only held the position for two years, and was taken aback when Quinn asked him to take on Most Holy Redeemer—not instead of but in addition to his current duties.

> I knew the parish by name. I did not know much about the parish but I knew it was complex. I was torn; I went over to the church. I just went inside in the church for an hour, and I was very moved by that stained glass window of the most holy Redeemer. It just said, let it happen. It was a very soothing kind of experience.
>
> For two years I was pastor at MHR and also kept my other job.[3]

That window of the risen Christ has become an emblem of the parish. Small replicas can be purchased as gifts. The image appears as a logo on the front of the parish bulletin. In it, McGuire saw something like a job description—a plan for the path Most Holy Redeemer was to take.

> Several months ago one of the parishioners pointed out to me the stained glass window over the altar—the figure of the Risen Lord, Our Most Holy Redeemer. He felt he was being pulled forward and drawn closer by the hands of the Risen Lord.
>
> They were welcoming him along with all the needy, all the sinners, all the weary, and oppressed of the world. The figure expresses the fact that Jesus, raised from the dead, is now like the Father's magnet, able to draw to Himself all the creatures of the world. . . .
>
> Because of this, the figure in this stained glass window was sent as an Easter card to all the parishioners, so that they could meditate on this figure in their homes and sense unity with other members of the parish as they did so. [It is] so expressive of compassion and the love which comes as a fruit of suffering; an unyielding, constant faithful love which translates out to touch all our hearts, especially when we are troubled.[4]

McGuire's approach was careful, deliberate: fact-finding was his first order of business. He was unsure what the parish needed most and took the novel step of asking:

> Within about three months I went to visit all the old-timers and the gay men who would come to the church, and then formed with them an advisory board, and someone from the chancery came, and I asked, "Where do we go?" The group was twelve people, mostly old-timers, and two gay men. . . . This was before the parish council was formed; it was just an advice group.
>
> Well, we had a great day. The two gay men were wise and faithful Catholics and they offered some very clear proposals to the group. To an individual, even

the strongest curmudgeon knew that something had to be done. They were concerned about their parish, that very few came any more, that it was moribund. Everybody said that.

The two gay men, Dale Meyer and Jim Stultz, suggested we start a gay and lesbian outreach. And that was approved 12 to nothing.

I was stunned. I did not know what to do when I arrived, but I was happy with this idea. There was no canon in Canon Law that had the requirements for a Gay and Lesbian Outreach Committee! I don't know if it had ever happened elsewhere. . . . Dale was on disability, a fine man and very bright, very easy to talk to. So he started collecting names, addresses, and phone numbers.

We had this event at Christmas, like a reading, over dinner in the rectory. We set up small tables, very festive. A gay man read from a book called *Embracing the Exile*,[5] about gay men's desire to be in the church and yet their struggle with their sexuality. A section was read and then we had a discussion about it. Marie Krystofiac, a widow from the parish, said I have the same trouble. This tension around sexuality came to be seen as part of life, not just a gay issue. I also mentioned tension with celibacy as a celibate priest.[6]

Dale Meyer moved into the Castro in 1983. When he started attending MHR, it was a dying parish. What did the parish have to lose by starting a lesbian/gay outreach?

Much to our surprise, we sent out some invitations and 65 people showed up for a potluck. Over about a year's time and many potluck dinners, the group grew to over 100 people. Every one of those people then became an agent for change within the church and the community. They drew other people in. Sunday mornings at ten o'clock mass these days, you can go and find the place nearly full. About 60% of the people are gay or lesbian.[7]

The Gay and Lesbian Outreach Committee—so unique,[8] so bracing, so critically what the parish needed when it needed it—eventually withered away, a victim of its own success, when the entire parish had taken on the work it was formed to begin.

Its formal existence commenced in June 1983 when the Parish Advisory Board, later called the Parish Council, was founded. At a full-day retreat, the Board formulated as one of its goals an "effective and inclusive" outreach to the gay community. At its next meeting on June 13, the Board set up four task forces to address the priorities it had set for the parish, and one of them was the Gay and Lesbian Outreach Committee.

In the report for their first year of operation, 1984, the Committee declares its role is to reach out to gay and lesbian Catholics who are alienated from the Church. "We wanted to show them that there was a place for them at Most Holy Redeemer and that they would be welcome here, just as most of us on the Committee who were gay had been made welcome. We wanted to spread the Good News and share the joy this Parish had allowed us to feel—some of us for the first time, perhaps."[9]

In 1983, Jim Stultz, the chair of the parish board, in an unpublished letter to the local gay paper, *The Bay Area Reporter* (the B.A.R.), described the development of the ministry:

> When I arrived in the neighborhood five years ago, there [were] no visible gay people attending Most Holy Redeemer. We started a meager outreach with our regular ad in the B.A.R. This started a movement of local Gay people into parish life, until the present time in which we see, as The Task Force's letter stresses, Gay people actively involved in most areas of parish ministry and service. The progress which we have witnessed over the years has sometimes been halting; we make mistakes; we naturally have big obstacles to overcome; but we now have an *active, organized* outreach of ministry to Gay Catholics. . . . Indeed, the fact that the Chair of the parish's first Parish Council is an outspoken Gay Catholic is evidence itself of the extent of the involvement of Gay people at MHR. We are actively seeking the participation of greater numbers of sexual minority people, both in worship and in parish service activities such as our "Friends of the Aging" group. (As an example of the "service" oriented participation of Gay people at MHR: in our project to provide transportation for needy Seniors, 80% of the volunteer drivers are Gay, and so is the project coordinator.)[10]

What MHR was doing was without precedent anywhere in the Roman Catholic Church. The parish was exploring new territory in ministry.

That conflict should accompany such an endeavor is to be expected; it's possible that time has made the conflicts seem milder than they were, in the minds of some of those I interviewed. Difficulties can be felt in the minutes of a meeting between McGuire and the chair and subcommittee heads of the Outreach Committee[11] (Dale Meyer, Richard Davis, Frank Oliva, and Ron Messineo). McGuire must have felt some anxiety about this genie he'd released from its bottle, but he was both prophetic and wise enough to know the parish had to change or die.

Some were angered by his firm stand against MHR doing what Dignity does—working for change in the Church's teaching. He felt powerless to defend the Outreach Committee if it placed itself squarely and publicly outside what the Church taught. Instead the Committee should pursue the goal of cooperation with the whole faith group in the parish. To that end, it was important to find ways of de-emphasizing "gay" and emphasizing unity—"we." Messineo too was concerned about trying to do too much too fast and alienating the parish. To Oliva, it only seemed "too fast," that a group oppressed or ignored by the Church for centuries, and by the parish for decades, should have a coffee hour and a committee. He estimated that perhaps 6,000 alienated Catholic gay and lesbian people lived within the parish boundaries: since the Outreach Committee had only 40 or so members, maybe it meant they weren't moving fast enough.

McGuire saw his point, but was sensitive to the needs of the parishioners. Meyer insisted the Outreach Committee had done nothing to embarrass or detract from the Parish—it had, in fact, involved itself in the whole spectrum of parish activities. As a member of Dignity, Meyer felt there was a place for political and theological change, but agreed that was not MHR's function. Dignity was moving on a broad front and MHR on a local one; Dignity's own charter calls for its members to become active in their own parishes.[12]

The Outreach Committee drew up an "Education, Organization, and Purpose" document on January 8, 1984, the same month as this important meeting. In retrospect this document seems too ambitious for such a small group of people, forty-five in number at the time. It succeeds however in expressing their optimism, their drive and desire for change. During the year the group held a meeting with Bishop Walsh, then Auxiliary Bishop, at which they spoke about the official policy of the archdiocese on ministry for homosexuals—the so-called "Blue Book," which was the Senate of Priests Report on Ministry to the Homosexual Community in the Archdiocese[13]—and also about the role of Dignity. There were also discussions between Dignity and the Outreach Committee; and with the archbishop's Board of Ministries, which was responsible for implementing policies regarding homosexuals in the Diocese. On September 22, 1984, four members of the Outreach Committee, along with Fathers McGuire and Brenneman and Sister Cleta Herold, hosted a social hour, dinner, and extended conversation with Archbishop Quinn in the parish rectory. This very significant event not only helped educate Archbishop Quinn, it was a sign of hope for parishioners that the institutional church in San Francisco was beginning to take gay Catholics seriously.[14] The Outreach Committee also set up a booth at the Castro Street Fair:

> Sunday at the Castro Street Fair was a day of contrasts for me. In the middle of a laid-back crowd and many money making booths was the booth sponsored by the Gay and Lesbian Outreach Committee—just down from the "Return to Atheism" booth. It was set up to benefit the restoration of the convent as a hospice. The cookies and cakes made by many of the parishioners, and the flowers which were donated by friendly florists of the parish, were given out with a heart that said "WE CARE," a beautiful symbol of the sentiments of so many of our parishioners who had cooperated to make that booth possible, and an important message to the carefree passersby on that day.[15]

In these matters McGuire showed his great gift for bringing people from very different backgrounds together and creating something new in the process. In an early parish bulletin, Fr. Tony describes his inclusive vision for the parish in his regular "Note from the Pastor":

> The view of San Francisco on a clear day from the top of Market Street is a stunning one. In the distance crowding into the foothills are Berkeley and Oakland with a bustle of ships in and out of the port. The back of the bay is set off against the tall white buildings climbing into the sky downtown and the shorter buildings sitting like St. Mary's Cathedral on a throne with the sunlight sparkling off its white marble and radiating light to the buildings around.
>
> Lately I have become more interested in the great variety of buildings in all colors of the rainbow, which cling to the hills leading up to Market Street. This is the complex of architectural styles and colors and shapes, which reflect the variety of persons and life styles, which make up Most Holy Redeemer Parish. It surely is a beautiful parish. To curve down Market Street and turn off one of the side streets, the driver can get lost on narrow streets, which end in beautiful cul-de-sacs and open out to breathtaking views. Small rugged hills still have avoided the developer's jackhammer but most of the open spaces have long since been replanted with houses and flats, and now with plague-like condominiums.
>
> As I look down from Market Street or wind through the crowded streets, I can't help but think of the works of Jesus in the Gospel today: "The harvest is rich, but the laborers are few;" therefore ask the harvest master to send workers to his harvest from house to house, like the disciples in the Gospel. Their salute would be the same as in the Gospel, "Peace to this house." Peace to the old lady worried about her Social Security, peace to the parents at odds with their teenagers, peace to the gay man who has drifted from the church, peace to the lonely man locked behind his iron gate, never visited and never visiting. This is the peace, which Jesus gives. "Not as the world gives do I give you peace."[16]

After so many years of resentment, disaffection, even hostility between parishioners and the gays who had refashioned the neighborhood, the parish proved an ideal place for reconciliation and friendship. It initiated a new way of relating for the two very different communities.[17]

Older women who had outlived their husbands were missing their own children, who in many cases had moved to other parts of the country. The new gay parishioners had mostly come to San Francisco from other parts of the country, were largely male, and were happy to find a new extended family at Most Holy Redeemer. Fr. Tony wanted his parish to stand for this sort of improbable yet natural coming-together: he often spoke of "the gays and the grays." "To my mind it is much better when people get out of their own groups. The gays can get silly together, and the older people get together just to talk about their pains. When they mix there is a lot more going on. I really think that a parish has the possibility of being a sign in the neighborhood of bringing people together, especially in fast-changing neighborhoods."[18] Pastor John Thornburg makes a similar point from a different tradition: "The greatest sense of trust between gay and straight people in the congregation will come from shared leadership of major responsibilities. Justice demands that *neither* gay nor straight members of the congregation be allowed to engage in segregation. People feel care when their talents are respected and employed. Likewise, they feel rejection and loss when their energy is ignored."[19]

McGuire and Thornburg express in concrete terms the central insight in an important book: *faith beyond resentment: fragments catholic and gay* by gay Catholic and regular visitor to MHR, James Alison.

> Once we start to learn to see people not as caricatures but as brothers, then maybe we can begin to read in quite a different way the texts, like those of the "woes to the Pharisees," which before served to keep the caricature alive. The texts themselves become a gift which both shows us what an idolatrous building of our home looks like, and how to move beyond it in charity. Rather than a confrontational Word creating a "we" and a "they", they become gratuitous words helping us to detect our own involvement in a world of "we's" and "they's" and enabling us to begin to imagine what it might look like to live together without such a barrier.
>
> This is, I think the real beginnings of access to Eucharist.[20]

In a passage from *Inclusion: Making Room for Grace*, Eric Law captures what was happening at Most Holy Redeemer:

> In every age, there are individuals and groups, usually minorities, who are discriminated against and constantly put into a disadvantaged position. In every age, the people of God must have the courage, as Joseph did, (in *Matthew 2: 19–23*) to adopt the excluded. In that adoption, we move with the excluded into exile. In that exile experience, we discover the presence of God, renewing our faith and our understanding of God's salvation history in our present context. When we embrace the exile, we relive and reinterpret the meaning of our own liberation from bondage. When we return, we gain new insights into our reason to exist. We reaffirm our living, dynamic covenant with God. We gain renewed energy for Christ's ministry of compassion and justice. When we emerge from the grace margin, we give birth to new creation. . . .[21]

By moving in the direction of inclusion the parish was being faithful to God. The parish began to see that their perception of God was limited and thus learned more about God. As Law points out, it is we, not God, who exclude the things we consider bad, to be feared. And we make God think the way we do. We want God to have the same categories of good and bad. The community at MHR began to move from asking, "What do we want?" to "What does

God want?" And in the process MHR became a community of grace. McGuire knew just how far he could stretch the community and when to hold it back. If he had gone too fast, the community might have shut down; not going fast enough might have alienated gay parishioners. By keeping this delicate balance, Most Holy Redeemer could provide a sense of stability, continuity, in a changed neighborhood, even (or especially) to those who had changed it.

McGuire used his marvelous sense of humor to touch his flock's imaginations and to lubricate tense situations. His humor was even on display at his final Mass of Thanksgiving in the parish. In his homily he deadpanned that when he first arrived in the parish, he just thought "Hail Holy Queen" was a good entrance hymn! This line was captured on tape in a television news story about McGuire's leaving the Castro. Of course, the entire assembly broke into laughter. At MHR, McGuire often let humor enliven the liturgy.

> It was liturgy as a place of fun and joy. The first time I was part of the liturgy as deacon, Tony gave the job of the sprinkling to me. Tony said, "Get your mother, good!" In the liturgy, I learnt from him that you could be normal and happy. I have carried this with me. It was really valuable. The liturgy did not have to be too intense or heady. The Spirit moved us to laughter as well as to tears. The Liturgy Committee did not become a place of wars. We had arguments, yes, but we knew we were here to help people celebrate and respond to real needs such as grieving. There was a sense of purpose, which included happiness.
> Once we were in ordinary time, with green vestments, and one woman said, "Oh, we don't have ordinary time at Most Holy Redeemer!"[22]

McGuire surrounded himself with people who had the right qualities for the parish and brought out the best in them. He invited Fr. Randy Calvo to live in the Rectory and assist in the parish, even though he too worked full time in the Chancery as a canon lawyer.[23] Calvo had recently returned to San Francisco after completing his doctorate in Rome. He managed to combine a compassionate heart with intellectual rigor. McGuire also hired Sr. Cleta Herold as Associate Pastor. Having a woman in such a role did cause a stir among the old guard in the parish. Herold placed a note in the bulletin to explain that her new position was perfectly orthodox and approved by the diocese: "When Mrs. Q. met Mr. R. recently at the neighborhood supermarket, she promptly questioned R about what was going on at Most Holy Redeemer Parish. 'Look at this, will you R,' as she pulled out the Sunday bulletin from her purse. 'It says: Sister Cleta Herold, P.B.V.M.—Associate Pastor' what does this mean? I just don't understand. Is this part of the whole women's lib movement, or something new that Most Holy Redeemer is initiating?" Herold went on to become a vital part of the parish, especially in her compassionate ministry with countless people, mostly men, living and dying with AIDS. She also ran the Rite of Christian Initiation for Adults, which helped many negotiate their way to, or back to, the Roman Catholic community. Herold—just Cleta or Sister Cleta to the parishioners—is a Presentation sister who had experience with the gay community through her work with the deaf in San Francisco. Later she was appointed to the Archdiocesan Board of Ministries to Homosexual People (now defunct). Herold found McGuire caring and compassionate, the kind of person who when he believes in something, will stake his life on it. Such defiant commitment, she believes, is the reason McGuire is not a bishop today.[24] Herold continues to be held in great respect in the parish and has had an enormous impact in the life of the parish over many years.

The changes transforming the parish came to the notice of the *San Francisco Examiner:*

> Most Holy Redeemer Church, the Roman Catholic beacon in the Castro, was a parish on the skids. Established at the turn of the century to serve the neighborhood's burgeoning Irish Catholic population, the church had become a refuge for old-time parishioners weathering the gay invasion of the Castro.
>
> "The parish wasn't taking into account the gay population," said the Rev. Anthony McGuire, who was named pastor of the church in 1983. "The older people would come to Mass. They would die off, and nobody would replace them."
>
> Inside the Diamond Street church today, old time parishioners are sharing their pews with a growing number of openly gay worshipers.
>
> Ron Black, a lapsed Irish Catholic and gay immigrant to the Castro, first visited the church on Easter 1984. He is now an active member.
>
> "It never occurred to me to go to the church around the corner," Black said. "But there was a unity between everyone there. There was a real spiritual presence. It was mostly older people and younger gay men who—because of AIDS—were facing the same fears of disease and death."[25]

Black mentions another transforming issue for the parish: AIDS. McGuire's and MHR's response to the epidemic will be dealt with separately in the next chapter.

Another sign that change was beginning to stir in the parish was a public letter distributed by parishioners "Jimmy and Derrick" on July 9, 1989:
The Challenge We Put Forth

> You have changed many outlooks at Most Holy Redeemer. Now is the time to reach out and enlighten the minds of your fellow Catholics in the Archdiocese. There are dozens of parishes where people have yet to see a loving Gay couple hold hands. Just as African-Americans in the 60's (and into the 80's) showed

courage every time they dared to enter a White Establishment, so, too, we must be brave in venturing forth into unknown territory.

Go to a different parish each week and act as you do at Most Holy Redeemer. Remember the Early Christians and the risks they surely took to spread the Word.

And so, we must go to each and every parish in this BEAUTIFUL CITY before election in NOVEMBER and SPREAD the WORD:

Be Witnesses to the TRUTH —

GAY LOVE IS GOOD.

Dear Gay Sisters and Brothers,

We are Greatly Angered and Deeply Disturbed by the support the Catholic Church has given to the Domestic Partner repeal ballot measure.

We have talked with two Gay couples of the Most Holy Redeemer Community who feel at this time that their presence at Mass (i.e. holding hands, showing affection at the Kiss of Peace) is the best course of action against a hierarchy that does not understand the goodness and beauty of Gay Love. It is The People who are The Church—Not a misguided upper Echelon, they say.

Perhaps MHR parishioners did not sign the repeal petition. But [as our 83-year-old grandmother] at Saint Cecilia's testifies there were lines of people waiting to sign the petition. And Saint Cecilia's was not the only parish where uninformed unenlightened Christians are being cajoled into supporting a ballot measure that will X away an ordinance that simply gives us the right to visit our sick lovers and be present at their funerals and recognizes our relationships as something Good!

The Most Holy Redeemer Community *is* enlightened thanks to your presence. Hopefully because of that presence they will not vote in favor of the repeal measure come November.

Harry Britt's office is very confident that the repeal measure will be soundly defeated. The taste of victory is sweet, but the fact that so many Christians are unenlightened about Our Goodness leaves a bitter lingering [*sic*] because our Catholic Community will continue to perpetuate homophobia and continue to threaten Our Civil Rights.[26]

Not everyone liked the changes McGuire brought about with his fresh approach. When he arrived, he had never seen the Castro at Halloween. The Halloween party in the Castro is notorious internationally for being flamboyant, wild, and exotic. When a former Catholic asked McGuire if his AA group might use the hall for a Halloween party, McGuire thought it sounded like a very appropriate request. When he said yes, he had no idea everyone would turn up either in drag or wearing practically nothing! The next day the woman who, in his words, was "the second most uptight parishioner," called and was furious. She berated him over the impropriety of such goings-on on church property. "It was like Sodom and Gomorrah!" she thundered. To which McGuire answered meekly, with his mischievous humor, "Well, maybe Sodom."

McGuire also had tensions with parishioners who opposed using the parish hall for homeless youth:

> Danny Barutta was a gay parishioner who worked for Catholic Charities and had this project for homeless youth. Many were coming to San Francisco, mainly on Polk Street, many young gays hustling and homeless, and Catholic Charities was looking for a place for them to stay overnight. We had the hall under the Church and all it was used for at the time was bingo on Sundays. So the possibility was to use that space.
>
> Now the guy in charge of the bingo at the time was difficult. He lived right next door to the church, a house the church owned, where the Msgr. Lyne Community is now. He lived in it rent-free, but he was in charge of the bingo. Our parish bingo was kind of the last straight bar in the Castro! They were a good group of old cronies and they worked hard for the parish, but there was this mean-spiritedness that he had, but the others did not share. Unwelcoming to the new, he and some others did not like me, as I was allowing all this change. I invited them to the Rectory for dinner, but still there was a tension. Not with all, but with this guy especially. So anyhow, somehow he got in a fight with the rest of them, and they said they wanted him out of here.
>
> We had a parish meeting, about the use of the bingo hall at night during the week as a shelter for homeless youth, and the only people who showed up were against the project, about fifteen people, led by this man in charge of the bingo. The Advisory Board and I sat at a head table.
>
> We had Danny Barutta give testimony.[27] A priest from Liverpool happened to be there, and he gave this speech; he had the same kind of program, and he gave a magnificent testimony, "All you are doing is throwing a life preserver to children who are drowning, children who are drowning." Others were saying, "Ah, they will rape our women." When you get a group of Catholics together who detest something, it is the worst.
>
> Then the parish council voted for it something like 10 to 2 in favor of the project. They, the gang that came were furious, the result was that that group was no longer in control; their voice was no longer the only voice, so it was great. It was the worst night, but it was really the turning point, a group that had held sway, they no longer had that sway.
>
> And actually the bingo people became very helpful in the whole process; it did cost them a lot. Everything had to be set up, but they would bring extra food for the kids, and it was a very good project for everybody. So it became like, this is a parish that is interested in the larger community, so that was a nice reputation to have.[28]

The Diamond Street Shelter for homeless youth that evolved out of this meeting was later the subject of an editorial in *The San Francisco Chronicle:*

> The Diamond Street Shelter for homeless youths, located at Most Holy Redeemer Church and operated by Catholic Social Service, is marking its first

anniversary. In the past year, the shelter gave refuge to more than 450 young-
sters from throughout the United States and abroad. Family reunification, coun-
seling, health care and job opportunities are some of the services provided. The
Most Holy Redeemer parishioners and the Eureka Valley/Castro neighborhoods
aid this unique operation. All segments of the San Francisco community can be
grateful for the presence and success of this service to young people.[29]

Some disgruntled parishioners did go up the hill to worship at St. Philip's.
McGuire very much wanted to keep people in church and bring the different
factions together, but with all his gifts, even he could not keep everyone
happy. Kevin Ballard was there on one occasion when someone confronted
McGuire, demanding to know how he could accept all those people living
"alternative lifestyles."

> It's true, [McGuire] said, people in our parish do need to be called away from
> gossip and from promiscuity and much else; but isn't it easier for people to make
> hard moral choices in a community that loves and accepts them. He just avoided
> the moral stuff. People were challenged to leave behind dangerous lives, and
> they were drawn in as people who would minister to others. Later the questions
> were asked. It was not saying everything was okay—but first come and relax.
> What can you do? Get involved. Later people can be challenged if it is needed,
> or maybe it will just happen naturally.[30]

St. Philip's provided a more traditional and less threatening environment for
MHR parishioners who were unhappy with the change. I remember a conversation I had with a long-time parishioner, the late Peg O'Malley, who had
come to San Francisco from Ireland as a child. She told me she had argued
with her husband over it: she wanted to continue to go to Most Holy Redeemer, while her husband indignantly stated he would never set foot there
again—because "those gays were being welcomed." They ended up worshipping in separate churches. Peg had the last word, though: she held her husband's funeral at Most Holy Redeemer.

Many of the old-timers who stayed found they began to like the new parish.
When Christmas came around one of the gay men put together a beautiful
crèche. In the previous, moribund parish, no crèche had been used in years. The
older people just loved the manger scene. It was handsomer than it had been in
the past, they declared. Even the altar was decorated in a way they had never
seen before—but liked. Many of them, too, were coming back to church. The
seniors were just happy to see people in the pews again. They thought, "It's
thriving, it's full, just like the old days," rather than, "It's full of gay people."

McGuire had to contend not only with hostility toward gays but also with
hostility toward Catholicism in the gay community. Even at his installation
Mass there were protesters outside the church, picketing. They condemned

visiting Archbishop Quinn, shouting to all who entered, "Quinn is a homophobe!" "Quinn is a homophobe!" McGuire showed his style at the end of this mass, saying: "Well, even though there are pickets outside, and we don't really agree with them, why don't we invite them to the gathering downstairs and show them some Christian hospitality?" Improbably enough, the angry gay men picketing outside accepted. Some of them even ended up dancing with the female parishioners.

In his early days as pastor, McGuire also had to deal with protests from the Sisters of Perpetual Indulgence. The "Sisters" first appeared in San Francisco on Easter Sunday 1979 as a group of four gay men in nun's habits. "Through 'drag activism'—cross-dressing—they combine street theater with political awareness of gay and lesbian issues."[31] Not surprisingly, the Sisters have a history of conflict and tension with the Catholic Church. Their feud with the Archdiocese of San Francisco culminated when they obtained a permit from the city to close down the streets of the Castro on Easter Sunday of 1999 against the wishes of William Levada, the Roman Catholic Archbishop, who protested it was offensive to Catholics. For McGuire too, contending with the Sisters was a thorny proposition:

> What happened was that one day before Christmas a notice on a telephone poll said the Sisters of Perpetual Indulgence are coming to Most Holy Redeemer for Christmas Midnight Mass. I was outraged, because they were very provocative. My first reaction was to find out who they were, I got an address, and I just went and rang the doorbell. I said, what is this, you are very provocative, and he said no we will not provoke, we will be coming in festive garments. I was still outraged. I said we will have our lawyer speak to you.
>
> Within a half hour I had a call from *The Advocate* in New York. "Is it true you are suing them?" "Well maybe not, let me think about it." I did not know what to do.
>
> So I called the Liturgy Committee together and the parish council and asked, what are we going to do. This is something we all have to face. This is *our* problem. The mix in the meeting was gay and gray. So we found out the limits. One, they cannot interrupt the service. Two, if they stand up and cause some kind of commotion, we can have people physically remove them. We began delineating what are our rights and what are their rights. Everybody was on board, especially the ushers. They would take action, not me.
>
> The Sisters came dressed as Marie Antoinette. Festive garb is the way people dress in the Castro on big occasions. So they came in and sat around the front row, and during the homily one of them was giving me these eyes, it was very distracting; but other than that they went away saying it was a nice service.
>
> There was a sister there who had been on retreat and she came that night to the Mass and wrote a letter complimenting me on the beautiful liturgy. She said [of the "Sisters"] she thought they were the three kings who were in the procession.

I mentioned to the parish the next week: poor Sister, I said, she has been in the convent so long she can't tell three kings from three queens![32]

Randy Calvo remembers the tension in the church at that midnight mass. At the beginning of the service someone started screaming—but he turned out to be "one of our own crazies: Charles, a former Cistercian, who hung around the parish. Well, there was a great deal of relief once we identified it as one of our own crazies!"[33]

The "Sister" who answered the doorbell when McGuire rang was Gil Block, or "Sister Sadie." Block remembered the encounter too and later wrote about it, from a very different point of view—one that illustrates the depth of bitterness and alienation some in the Castro felt toward the Catholic Church:

> It wasn't until the papal visit that we decided to do another Christmas mass in the Castro at the Most Holy Redeemer Church where Tony Baloney was the cappo di tutti fruiti. Actually, he was known as Father Anthony McGuire. Many may have liked him but I found him ridiculously crude.
>
> Now why would we bother going to holiday church services in the first place. Well, standing up to oppression is enough reason but doing so in the Castro after having the Vatican call us morally evil was sufficient to justify a riot. We simply called for others to join with us in "Making Mary."
>
> With our posters plastered around town, it didn't take long for the good father to pay an unannounced visit to yours truly. Filled with the nectar of human kindness, Minister McFire knocked on my door the day before Christmas. I had been home with a little cold and warned him before entering.
>
> "What makes you think that cold didn't come upon you for a reason?," inquired the preacher creature. "The Lord works in mysterious ways."
>
> "Oh, really," said I, "does that mean that if I'm well enough to attend mass tomorrow that it will be preordained?" He was not amused.
>
> "You mock us," he continued. Like, no, really? I stifled a yawn as he proceeded to threaten me with law suits and even arrest if we dared to come into his church. This was a great opportunity to get into a rip-roaring argument, but that's not my style. I simply replied that we both had our jobs to do so let's get on with it. I also mentioned that he might think about becoming part of the solution rather than the problem by challenging his boss in Rome, unless, of course, he enjoyed being in cahoots. His blank expression spoke volumes.[34]

Block describes a local television interview about the protest at Most Holy Redeemer, and the actual midnight mass itself. It would seem that an unfair burden of his anger with the institutional church is projected onto McGuire, since I found no one else who shared his complaints about Fr. Tony:

> As we approached the church, it was clear that they were prepared. A paddy wagon was parked right across from the entrance and dozens of uniformed cops

were sprinkled around the main hall, which was packed to the rafters. I spotted many a familiar face, a number of which were from the major press.

With our commodious costumes capturing considerable capacity and constant comment (someone said I was alliterate . . . hah!) we stood out like blazing sore thumbs, just as planned. While first being seated, a white-haired grandma parishioner looked up at us, her face agape. Suddenly all was silent as we waited for our first encounter.

"Oh, it's the Three Wise Men," she cooed. "Merry Christmas." I couldn't have said it better myself (although Scarlot Harlot is a bit too zaftig and reveal-ing to pass for a man—but ya never know, does ya?). Moments later, the service began and we were perfect ladies (and gentlemen).

At service end, we were very Oy Vey Maria-ed as all were invited next door for milk and cookies. We slowly passed through the hallway exit, where stood Squire McGuire wishing each one in turn his holiday happies. As I came before him, I said through several layers of gold eyelashes and even more layers of lip gloss: "Tony, dost thou not recognize me? I come to thee as a thief in the night."

He was livid but smiled through his teeth. How dare I refer to Jesus-talk right from his bible. My eyes finally broke from his and I sauntered triumphantly out the door.

We reassembled on the street and made a bee-line for the paddy wagon where two tired cops were twiddling their thumbs. "Easy night with great overtime, huh, kids?" They smirked. We smirked. We left. They left. Buh-duh-bing. Buh-duh-bang.

P.S.: Soon thereafter, after years of 'service,' Phony Tony was transferred out of the Castro. Bye. Bye.[35]

Since that Christmas, MHR and the Sisters of Perpetual Indulgence have con-tinued to interact from time to time. Indeed the Sisters have often volunteered for (and attended in full habit) the annual Thanksgiving Dinner for the home-less that was held at the parish's Ellard Hall. This event was until recently hosted jointly with the Metropolitan Community Church, an almost exclu-sively gay Christian congregation that until recently met on Eureka Street, one block from MHR.[36] At this dinner they meet and work alongside real Catholic nuns who are parishioners at MHR, but unlike the "Sisters" don't wear habits. Nonetheless many of these Catholic nuns find this parody offensive, even though they are on occasion willing to work alongside. There is a picture of Fr. Zachary Shore, the pastor who succeeded McGuire, talking with Sister Hedra on the Sisters of Perpetual Indulgence website.[37] Interestingly, in a video fea-ture made about gay San Francisco, the Sisters chose to be interviewed in front of the statue of Mary at Most Holy Redeemer.[38] Their relationship with the Catholic Church is much more complex than the media picture allows. It would be more accurate to describe it as love/hate rather than a simple parody.

In this relationship, as in much else, Most Holy Redeemer stands apart from the rest of the Catholic Church, even in San Francisco. For instance, in

1982 the Sisters of Perpetual Indulgence provoked much outrage in the
Catholic media when they attended an interfaith prayer service in the Roman
Catholic cathedral of St. Mary's:

> The gay community newspaper, the *Bay Area Reporter,* reported that the [S]is-
> ters did not intend their presence to be an affront: "The Sisters state that they are
> emulating, not mocking the Roman Catholic nuns. Their comment is they honor
> the spiritual and feminist quality which is represented by the nuns." The good
> intentions of the sisters were doubted by most Catholics who found the names
> of sisters such as Sister Hysterectoria and Sister Boom Boom totally outrageous
> and demeaning to the Catholic sisterhood. *The Monitor* [the Catholic newspaper
> at that time] concluded, "The organization, their names, and their use of reli-
> gious habits is an affront to religious women and Catholics in general."[39]

Sister Boom Boom, also known as Jack Fertig and quoted in the above article, actually ended up becoming a Catholic at Most Holy Redeemer some
years later. I remember commenting on the occasion that it must have been
the first time in history anyone left the convent to become a Catholic! Fertig
is a long-time gay activist who became famous as the Sisters' spokesman
(spokesperson?). Although regarded with horror by some, it is clear the Sisters see something valuable in Catholicism—paradoxically, perhaps, in the
tradition of powerful women—and in the Catholic sense of ritual. Fertig
wrote about his experience of becoming Catholic at Most Holy Redeemer:

> When I went to a Catholic mass, asking if this really was my direction, the an-
> swer was clear. I had finally come home. As I went back again and again, and
> went through the RCIA I knew I was finally coming to a place that had been
> waiting for me.
>
> When I spoke with the Sister [Cleta Herold] about entering the RCIA,[40] I was
> clearly not about to compromise anything regarding my sexuality. I didn't go
> into a lot of details, but I showed up in my Levis and leather jacket and talked
> about my background as a Gay activist, clearly not about to change that. This
> parish, Most Holy Redeemer, is in the heart of the Castro, perhaps the Gayest
> place on earth. I talked about my background with witchcraft and the Sisters of
> Perpetual Indulgence, and my disagreements with certain points of the cate-
> chism. Sister never batted an eyelash, but asked if I could show up Sunday
> mornings at 8.
>
> Steven W. D is absolutely right about my "localized situation." I surely could
> not have done this in Nebraska. But the Church is not monolithic. It is too filled
> with the diversity of humanity to be monolithic. And the Church is not the Pope.
> The Church is all of us. The Church has done a lot of good and a lot of harm. I
> am very glad that I wasn't raised Catholic, that I was spared the strictures and
> complexes of a religious upbringing, that I could look and think, and choose as
> an adult rather than having dogmas shoved down an innocent and naïve throat.

... This Church of ours is a wonderful collection of humanity, all nations, sexes, ages, shapes, and colors; with Baroque effulgence, Franciscan asceticism, everything in between; and a spectrum of politics ranging from Opus Dei to Pax Christi. . . . Through God's creation of humanity in the divine image, through Christ's life on Earth, through the communion of Saints, we see in this special Church how our humanity is sacred. That sanctity of humanity may be observed in other churches, but ours does it in such a special way that I have always wanted to be part of that celebration. And I feel supremely blessed to have found a home in this wonderful family of God and Humanity, this fallibly human, yet gloriously divine Roman Catholic Church.[41]

McGuire was also challenged by gay Catholics within the Church, some members of the MHR community, some not. Perhaps the most difficult, divisive issue was the question of what to do about Dignity.

Dignity is an organization of gay, lesbian, bisexual, and transgender Catholics, formed for mutual support and as a voice for reform in the Church. It began in San Francisco with a simple mass in the parish hall of St. Peter's in January 1973, not long after the very first Dignity chapters were founded in San Diego and Los Angeles. Dignity's "Statement of Position and Purpose" declares its intention to work for the acceptance of gay men and lesbians as full and equal members of Christ. It organized to unite gay Catholics and be an instrument through which they could be heard by the Church and society.[42] In one homily, McGuire spoke openly of some of the issues:

In a calm way, let us review some truths, which may help us.

First, the Church's teaching on sexual morality is difficult for everybody. It is a hard saying. And it will not change in our lifetime. Many people live according to it and live admirable Christian lives. Others find aspects of it do not correspond to their experience. After study, prayer, consultation, in their consciences, they come to a different decision. We have to presume that such persons are doing the best possible before God. They are still part of the family that is the Church. . . .

Bishop Malone, head of the National Bishops Conference talked of the Church in this way: A family comes together, each member expresses the pain, the anxiety, the doubts they feel. These things are listened to with respect and sympathized with deeply, and in the heart. Then support is expressed for the persons as persons, and for the responsibilities they must bear.

This is our experience of Most Holy Redeemer. We are a family. This is our home. As Robert Frost says: "Home is a place where when you have to go there, they have to let you in."

We should also deal with authority in the same calm family way.[43]

In the early days, Dignity met every Sunday for Mass at three p.m. in St. Peter's hall. Tom Fry, a former priest of the diocese of San Francisco, helped organize

Dignity/San Francisco. In 1971 Fry had founded the Catholic Gay Ministry, which survived until 1974 and was funded by sixty priests and by the Franciscans. Dignity moved from St. Peter's to St. John of God, which they soon found too small for their growing numbers. Dignity then asked Most Holy Redeemer for the use of the church for liturgies. A parish in the Castro seemed the best and most natural location for a gay Catholic caucus.

McGuire brought the matter to the parish council, where the issue was debated heatedly and at length. The archdiocese had just formulated a policy pamphlet called *Ministry and Homosexuality in the Archdiocese of San Francisco* (1983). When the Dignity/San Francisco group asked to relocate to Most Holy Redeemer, they had not rejected this document; subsequently they did, which presented a quandary for McGuire. The archdiocesan document reiterated that Catholics involved in ministry could not speak officially against the teaching of the Church in any church forum, though it exhorted them to a patient and pastoral approach. Dale Meyer at Most Holy Redeemer strongly urged that Dignity be allowed to come to Most Holy Redeemer, even in the light of their rejection of the archdiocesan policy. Meyer argued it would be a critical gesture the parish could make in inclusiveness of the gay community. McGuire, on vacation in Ireland at the time, was torn:

> I would wake up and say, Why not, they want to be close to the church. Then how am I being consistent with the teachings of the church?
>
> So when I got back, Dignity did a manifesto, rejecting the document from the Diocese on the pastoral care of homosexual persons. So I said at the council we cannot accept them. Dale said we have to nuance this. "No," I said. "We cannot accept them."
>
> It was really the first time I manipulated the council. It was more about the principle than about the consequences for the parish. What helped me clarify my position was the way I was running the parish; we would accept conscientious decisions on the part of people and their full life in the parish, but not promotion. Promotion was the line. One of the lectors got up and said, "Today is John and Jim's tenth anniversary, for them let us pray to the Lord." I asked him not to do that. I said, you pray in your heart. Not [in] a public prayer at this point. We are not promoting. I have no problem with a private prayer, but not in the public forum. I thought the bishop might come down on us.
>
> If we had allowed Dignity to come, they would have stolen the show, the whole thing would have moved in their direction, rather than the building up of an integrated community. That was my reading of it later.[44]

McGuire explained his decision in the parish bulletin:

> When I first arrived at the parish, Dignity, an organization of Catholic gay men and lesbian women, asked if they could use our parish facility for their Sunday

evening Mass, since their present facility was overcrowded. The parish advisory board met first with Fr. Gerry Coleman of St. Patrick's Seminary and myself and reviewed the Archdiocesan policy. The next day Dignity announced publicly that they would not accept that policy. So the next effort was to see in what way we could live with their public statement.

1. The organization Dignity should be treated with respect and fairness. Though everyone doesn't agree with all of their statements they deserve an honest hearing and should be treated in a brotherly way. When they asked to come to Most Holy Redeemer, that request should be taken seriously.
2. The unity of the parish community also has to be taken into consideration, and has a prior claim to the arrival of one group or another to the parish. Thus it became clear that if any group's coming was going to make it difficult for the different elements in the parish to come together, then that group should not come.
3. The third aspect was to ask the question, "What would Jesus do?" As I read the Scriptures, Jesus did not reject anybody, but called them and invited them to conversion. So, the initial effort was to accept and to try to work out ways in which they could be called to a deeper conversion to Christ.

The first response to the advisory board, after meeting with the board of Dignity was yes, you can come, but there is to be no public statement against the teaching of the Church either from the pulpit or in other forms that would be divisive to the Parish or Archdiocesan policy. Responsible dissent is acceptable, but inflammatory statements are not. This was not acceptable to Dignity. They came up with this rewording: ["]Dignity/San Francisco will on matters pertaining to the Roman Catholic Church and its teachings like all other Catholics, exercise the right of reasonable dissent, and will strive to express that dissent lovingly and through established, appropriate channels.["]

I was not comfortable with that. Likewise, I felt the timing was bad for Dignity's coming. I'm still new in the parish; the goals of the parish are not in place or in process. Everything is just beginning to move in the direction in which members of the parish are working closely together. To accept a big group without assurances that they would not keep pushing against the Church authority and thus causing division in the groups, which were forming, seemed unwise. Likewise the advisory board, in interviews with parishioners, were picking up much negative feedback on Dignity, mainly with the question "Why do they have a separate Mass?" On a grass roots level Dignity had to have a better communication.

So I made the following recommendations to the Board, which passed 3 for, 2 against, 1 abstaining. [The vote expresses the difficult nature of this decision.]

"I recommend that the response of Dignity is unacceptable, that more time is needed to work out our goals for the parish. There must be an education program before Dignity would come."[45]

In retrospect, McGuire's decision seems wise. McGuire would ultimately have been accountable to the diocese for Dignity's openly promoting change in the Church's teachings. Too, he had the foresight to realize that having Dignity at MHR might allow the parish to sidestep the delicate work of building up its own distinct identity, rather than simply existing in Dignity's shadow. Dignity found a Catholic church where they could and did meet, St. Boniface in the Tenderloin. McGuire admits: "Dale was really angry. He recognized that I had manipulated the council and strong-armed them. [His leaving subsequently] was a big loss, but eventually he came back on his terms. He got involved in other things but would come back for solemn occasions."[46] Meyer himself says: "We will go to our graves disagreeing about what that was all about. Tony is a rare fellow. He is strong, has a wonderful sense of humor, and can be as obstinate as hell."[47]

In the end, Dignity was forbidden to meet anywhere on Catholic Church property. Archbishop Quinn expelled them from St. Boniface. In a letter to the *New York Times* Quinn asserted the expulsion was not owing to any pressure from Rome,[48] though the climate created by Rome would certainly have pushed the diocese in this direction. If Dignity had met at Most Holy Redeemer and been expelled, the damage to the parish, the division it surely would have caused, might have been irremediable. Even Tom Fry, who helped found Dignity/San Francisco, agrees with this assessment now.

> I always fought for mutual respect rather than rivalry. I think [Dignity and MHR] are both very valuable, and yet they have different strengths and weaknesses. The great strength of Dignity is that it can be a prophetic voice of theological criticism. MHR got the message early on, in relation to Dignity, that the archdiocese did not want them to do this; they are not encouraged to speak out on the theology of the church. They also have the ability to do more coalition building with other church and synagogue groups and civil gay groups. And for the very few, hardly any have taken advantage of it, Dignity has the ability, unlike Most Holy Redeemer, to bless same-sex marriages.
>
> I think the negative thing about Dignity is that it is a bit ghettoized. It is almost all gay men, with hardly any straight people, and this is a disadvantage. Most Holy Redeemer has diversity, with seniors, and more women, and they are part of the structure. For many, just being part of the structure, they have more influence within the archdiocese.[49]

Dignity, pushed out of the Catholic Church, was welcomed at the Dolores Street Baptist Church, which, though at that time in the Southern Baptist tradition, was open and welcoming to gays. When their church burnt down, Dignity was again without a place to worship. The Metropolitan Community Church—MCC, or sometimes known as the "gay church"—just a block from

MHR, offered to make room for Dignity for the year. Rev. Jim Mitulski, then pastor of MCC, found it somewhat incongruous:

> The irony was, here we were, on top of each other in this cramped, somewhat ramshackle building, a block away from a Catholic Church that was sitting empty on Sunday afternoons, that would easily have accommodated them. And even when we had a fire at our church and were unable to use our sanctuary, no invitations came from Most Holy Redeemer, even until our space was habitable again. [Dignity] did ask if they could meet at MHR and were told, "No." So I think this highlights some of the difficulties they faced as a parish.[50]

The passionate conflict of opinions about Dignity inflamed other conflicts in the parish. Father Calvo, living and working in the rectory with McGuire, found a philosophical approach to the tension:

> My first-ever homily at MHR was on the feast of Sts Peter and Paul. I guess that became one of the frameworks of working at MHR. First to talk about the fact that there was conflict and tension. The operative image I had was that there would be tension in the church and the ministry: this image was found in [the Church's] history from the beginning. A major conflict. I phrased it in terms of necessary and inevitable tension between the need to conserve, which would be Peter, and the one who was on the frontier, who had to ask questions, and how to respond. These two approaches, there will be a tension. And Most Holy Redeemer was in a way a frontier, so there will be a tension with how we do this as a Church. There is no image or pattern — that was the basis of my first homily.
>
> Later I had other approaches to the parish from the Gospel. . . . [A] theology professor of mine was emphatic about new ideas in church: we are not to condemn or condone; we are to understand. We are there to try to understand and find out where people are. . . . We hold to what we believe and we try to understand where people are coming from. . . . There is space for middle ground. I faced this in going to dinner at the homes of gay couples. Was I condoning or whatever? I resolved it from this framework. It does imply an acceptance of people. Once you get down to people it is a whole different story.
>
> The other part was Luke 15 and Jesus with sinners and tax collectors. Well I can do this too! The connection Jesus made with people who are labeled sinners was to be with them and to be at table with them and be in their company. It was an image that was very powerful to me — that if we were to evangelize, you need to be at table with them and in their company. Rather than to stereotype and pigeonhole people, and therefore not be able to converse with them.
>
> So, the church teaches this about homosexuality, and I think we all know it — so what else do you want to talk about? What do you say after you say no! There has to be something else to discuss besides saying no.

One of the first encounters I had was with Jim Stultz, President of the Parish Council at the time. He came up to me and said I'd like to interview you before you get to the parish—well, I have opera these nights, when are you free? Jim was a very fascinating individual, and forthright. I remember one thing he talked about. He criticized someone who gave a homily at MHR bashing people for going to the gay baths, and all that. He said that was uncalled for. My point was, you can hardly expect me to teach what is contrary to the church, and he said, oh no, absolutely not. But is there not a lot more for us to talk about in the Gospel that is useful for our lives? I said yes. Broaden the whole thing, the focus in this parish does not have to be one thing.

That was an eye opener. An important thing for me to have someone say that.[51]

McGuire also had to face the challenge of the papal visit to San Francisco in 1986, part of the Holy Father's ten-day trip to the United States. The visit put a great strain on the relationship between the church and the gay community. It came shortly after the Vatican office of the Congregation for the Doctrine of the Faith had written a letter to the world's bishops called, "On the Pastoral Care of Homosexual Persons." This was better known in the gay community as "the Halloween Letter," because it was issued in October. Friction between gays and the Catholic Church had also worsened after the murder of Moscone and Milk by pious Catholic Dan White. The community saw the Halloween Letter as a hostile attack. Archbishop Quinn was upset about it too, in that the Congregation argued that although the particular inclination of the homosexual is not a sin, it is a more or less strong tendency ordered to an intrinsic moral evil, and thus the inclination itself must be seen as an "objective disorder." Quinn, on meeting Cardinal Ratzinger in the Vatican, urged him not to use such language in the document, telling him that the traditional teaching could be upheld with a more pastoral approach, one that didn't bandy fraught terms like "disorder" and "intrinsically evil."[52] Archbishop Quinn was even more distressed that the document declared gay people brought violence on themselves by being too open about their orientation:

I mean, that was an editorial comment, it was not a doctrinal teaching, and it had no place in such a document. How it got in there and who permitted it to be there—it was most irresponsible. In any case, what the gay community seized on was not that but the statement about "intrinsic evil." I mean, I think it was a very wrong thing to say in a public document of the church. And I said that to Cardinal Ratzinger myself. And so I made some reference to that, and I said that would not mark the activity of the church in this diocese. I tried to show concern and compassion, as far as we were able to do so.[53]

Quinn tried to address the outrage the document caused. The archdiocese opened discussions with the gay community.

Through the untiring efforts of George Wesolek, representing the Archdiocesan Social Justice department, negotiations were held between church, city, and gay leaders. The discussions defused the tensions and culminated in a joint statement against violence during the visits. As a result, the city was relatively free of major protests during the papal visit.[54]

Dignity was one of the groups involved in these conversations. Archbishop Quinn also had dinner with selected MHR parishioners at the rectory to discuss the issues raised by the visit.[55] Those present—Tom Kaun, Dale Meyer, Raymond Messineo, and Jim Stultz—later wrote a letter on parish stationary to the Archbishop thanking him for the visit. It included a copy of a letter they had sent to the pope, reflecting their concern that the visit have a genuinely pastoral character for the gay men and women, and particularly for those who live with AIDS. They were concerned gay Catholics, they told the Pope, who were troubled when "we desire help in our struggle to live out lives of holiness and we are confronted with unloving, un-Christlike sentiments such as those expressed by the October 1986 letter of Cardinal Ratzinger, presently Pope Benedict XVI, then Prefect of the Congregation for the Doctrine of the Faith: that document seems to contradict what our own bishops in 1976 said of the homosexual condition—that it is not sinful—and more importantly that gay people have rights as human beings and members of the Catholic Christian community in society and in the Church which must be respected."

We are most concerned because the language of the letter justifies "irrational and violent reactions" when gay and lesbian people seek ordinary human rights to which the letter says we do not have "any conceivable right." These statements are offensive to us, and have caused a terrible backlash in our city, which has us concerned—especially in the light of your visit in September of this year. We welcome you as a flock welcomes a shepherd, but there are many in our city who will find it difficult to welcome you and easy to condemn you, calling you un-Christian, a "foreign prince," a discriminator. We have a tradition of free and open dialogue in this city and all will have their say. We are doing what we can to counter violent demonstrations with our own prayerful appreciation of concern when you visit. . . .

Our own bishops, your brothers, have said that "homosexuals, like everyone else, should not suffer from prejudice against their basic human rights. They should have a right to respect, friendship, and justice. They should have an active role in the Christian community." The statement from the Vatican has caused a great deal of confusion which you can help remedy by uttering a simple statement, "I greet all of you, gays and lesbians, too, as my sisters and brothers in Christ Jesus.". . .

We would like to suggest that you consider speaking to the gay and lesbian communities of the cities you visit—in Miami, or New Orleans, or Los Angeles, or in all of these cities where our brothers and sisters bear the cross of Christ Jesus and try to live lives of quiet Christian joy. Just repeat your message of love, dignity, and of compassion to counter those, even in our own Church, who find us less than human, less than Christian.[56]

There were protests when Pope John Paul II visited San Francisco, but they were peaceful:

> . . . [T]he visit went remarkably well. During the planning stages it was suggested that the pope demonstrate his good will by visiting the Catholic AIDS hospice in Most Holy Redeemer Parish in the Castro. This could not be worked out, so it was arranged that on the first night of the papal visit, Pope John Paul II would meet with AIDS patients, their families, friends, and caretakers at Mission Dolores. The event packed an enormous emotional wallop. In a particularly touching moment, the Pope embraced a young four-year-old boy named Brendan O'Rourke who was suffering from AIDS. Pope John Paul then delivered a powerful sermon, which many interpreted as an olive branch to the gay community. The pope reminded the congregation of the "all embracing love of God . . . God loves you all, without distinction, without limit. . . . He loves those of you who are sick, those who are suffering from AIDS and from AIDS-related complex."[57]

There were tensions at Most Holy Redeemer over the pope's visit. A poll was taken in April, and of those who responded, 45 had negative feelings about the pope's visiting; 151 felt positively about it. One hundred sixty-nine parishioners signed up to go to the papal mass in Candlestick Park, and Joan Healy, who worked long hours with the MHR AIDS Support Group, was chosen to receive communion from the pope. The issue was handled sensitively by Fr. McGuire, who himself was very enthusiastic about the outcome.

> When the pope came, two parishioners with AIDS were in the group that would meet the pope. Then there was that boy with the photo. There was one guy who offered up all his sufferings for the safety of the pope.
> There were protests. I was working, doing the radio stuff in front of the Basilica. There was a gang protesting down on Guerrero Street. Maybe one hundred or so, but they were loud. We were trying to help people see the pope in a kindly light. We would write articles in the bulletin—some people felt I was going a little too far in that. "Who are you trying to defend?" they would say.
> In one of the bookstores, there was a book called *The Sex Life of the Pope*. You look inside and it had empty pages. I wrote a letter in protest to the owner of the bookstore. I went down by the bookstore and my letter was pinned to the window so everybody could read it. Well, I was so angry, I went in and huffed with the manager and he took it down. There was always some tension around.[58]

A gay priest with AIDS, Father Bob Arpin, who later became involved in the life of the parish and a regular presider when Zachary Shore was pastor, went to see the pope at Mission Dolores:

> Even though the media thought the pope was coming to see me, it took a while for the Archdiocese to catch on to the idea. In fact, my invitation to be one of the hundred people with AIDS who would be in Mission Dolores Basilica to meet the pope arrived just about a month before the event. We were instructed to gather by 2.00 P.M. at Most Holy Redeemer Church in the Castro, from which we would be bused to Mission Dolores. We were made to go through metal detectors, security screening, and ID checks. It was a long and difficult wait, especially for those of us with AIDS.
>
> When we got to the Basilica we were confronted by a large and angry crowd of protesters. Many were from the gay community and they were yelling: "Shame! Shame!" in justified anger at the homophobia of the Church. Among them was a familiar face, Leonard Matlovich, who had been thrown out of the Air Force for being gay and who was spending lots of his time and his energy now as an activist for gay and AIDS-related causes. The crowd inside was no less excited. In an attempt to keep us busy, the organizers had put together prayers and the recitation of the rosary. To his credit, Father O'Connor, the pastor of the Basilica, prayed not only for the Holy Father but for those who were outside, too. "Let us thank God," he said, "that we live in a land where everyone is free to say what they think."[59]

And the message of the pope inside the basilica was very inclusive, though he did not mention the gay community by name. I suspected Archbishop Quinn was partly responsible for the note His Holiness struck, but he told me no.

> In a particularly emotional moment, the pope embraced a young four-year-old boy named Brendan O'Rourke, who was suffering from AIDS. The congregation cheered and the pope cried. As Miles O'Brien Riley put it so beautifully, "The Vicar of Christ, picked up a little boy with AIDS—and hugged the whole world." Pope John Paul then delivered a powerful reminder of "the all-embracing love of God." "God loves you, without distinction, without limit. . . . He loves us all with an unconditional and everlasting love. . . . The greatest proof of God's love is shown in the fact that he loves us in our human condition, with our weaknesses and our needs. Nothing else can explain the mystery of the cross."[60]

McGuire constantly had to help the parish negotiate the delicate relationship between the parish and the wider Church. He agonized about this at times. In one homily he dealt head-on with the letter from the Congregation for the Doctrine of the Faith that had upset so many in the parish:

This past week has been somewhat unsettling for us Catholics. . . . U.S. News and
World Report had a cover of the Pope looking very grim with the title: "Pope
Cracks Down: Taking on American Catholics." The Congregation of the Doctrine
of Faith came out with a letter, which not only restated the teaching on homosexuality, but tightened it in a tone which was mean and belittling. The bishops
of the country gathered and seemed to leave their confreres swaying in the
breeze. The net result today is the same as the crisis in the early church: people
are disillusioned, angered, filled with anxiety, depressed. Some leave, others drop
out from responsibilities. The words of Jesus, passed down through the Church,
the tradition holds: "By your patient endurance you will save your lives."

McGuire then made bold to suggest that authority may be confronted, even
questioned, lovingly, and:

. . . if authority is [still] blowing the same horn, polite humor helps. Other times,
the words of authority must be taken to heart and reflected on very seriously.
This is not to belittle authority—but to defuse excess of authority.
"By your patient endurance you will save your lives."[61]

McGuire kept in touch with Archbishop Quinn and invited him regularly to
the parish. In fact Quinn came frequently and loved his visits to MHR.
McGuire did not always consult him, however—for instance, about an issue
involving the Eucharistic Ministers and Lectors:

Well, the question in my mind was, the people who make a conscientious decision to live together as a gay couple, and then they can come to communion, just
like people who make a similar decision on birth control, you don't harass them.
You respect their decision. The next step was, "Can a clearly gay couple take on
open ministries in the church?" Like if a gay couple apply for ordination, that
would clearly be an obex.[62] What about Eucharistic ministers? I thought maybe
I should consult [Quinn], but then we already had them!

I went to the seminary and Father Gerry Coleman gave me this information
of the Italian hierarchy on this issue, about heterosexual couples living together:
they decided the issue by asking, "Would it be scandalous if this was done?" I
decided in this parish it would be scandalous if we did not do it—to the other
people coming to the church. They would sense that they were not being welcomed as members of the church.

The bishop never brought it up. I don't know what his response would have
been. I must ask him now that he has retired.[63]

Archbishop Quinn, far from regretting having appointed McGuire, continued
to hold him in high regard—even if the parish had its own way of doing
things. The bishop was free enough to allow McGuire to guide him in learning to know the parish better. At his first visit, the archbishop found it diffi-

---

cult even to say the word "homosexual" aloud; but over the years, he became comfortable acknowledging publicly gay Catholics and the gifts they brought to the Church. That Quinn grew in sensitivity and understanding of the gay community was owing to his experience of, and love for, the parish of Most Holy Redeemer.[64]

There were then, however, and still are limits to how far the parish could go in embracing the gay community. A neighbor and friend of the parish, Rev. Jim Mitulski of the Metropolitan Community Church, has a perspective not everyone at Most Holy Redeemer could comfortably share:

> Most Holy Redeemer continues to walk a fine line between responding pastorally to its principally gay constituency while also being accountable to the Roman Catholic Church, which teaches that gay and lesbian people are intrinsically disordered. Father Zachary Shore succeeded Father McGuire, and has continued to ensure that Most Holy Redeemer serve the neighborhood in which it is located. This has been particularly challenging under the leadership of Archbishop William Levada, who has been sent by Rome to replace the more liberal Archbishop Quinn. Since Levada took over, the Archdiocese has repeatedly positioned itself against domestic partner registration, and filed a lawsuit in order to be exempt from the Human Rights ordinances requiring city contractors to provide domestic partner benefits. In 1999 the archdiocese vigorously protested the Sisters of Perpetual Indulgence being granted a street permit for their twentieth anniversary celebration because it coincided with Easter. Later that year the Archdiocese contributed heavily and visibly to the Proposition 22 campaign, the anti-gay and anti-gay-marriage ballot measure narrowly approved that fall by California voters. Despite all this Most Holy Redeemer continues to welcome gay and lesbian parishioners, and was home to many vital AIDS services throughout the AIDS years, most notably the Most Holy Redeemer AIDS Support Groups.[65]

McGuire once went with Archbishop Quinn on a private visit to Mitulski at MCC, the "gay church next-door," so to speak. McGuire told me about the visit:

> It appeared one time in the paper that the woman who was the minister with Jim Mitulski had been beaten up in the street. It had front-page coverage in the *San Francisco Chronicle*. The archbishop was very upset about all this, and wanted the people of the Metropolitan Community Church to know that . . . this was not condoned. So he called me up and I arranged a meeting with him and Jim Mitulski, and we went to his church and we waited and waited. Jim's mother was visiting from Chicago, a good Catholic woman, and she was just stunned to see the Archbishop of San Francisco visiting her son.
>
> Well, he came half an hour late, and he was terribly embarrassed, as it turned out the woman had made up this whole story and had inflicted the violence on herself, and it was a way to draw attention to violence on the gay community.

But it turned out to be very embarrassing for Jim and his church. The archbishop really went out of his way to be in solidarity with the community that was in trouble.[66]

Quinn too remembers the visit, and says it was a gesture he would make again, despite the event that prompted it having been fabricated. Mitulski also remembers the visit fondly:

> I had a staff member that I had just hired have a public nervous breakdown, and it was in the media.
>
> Fr. Tony and Bishop Quinn came over to MCC to just pay a visit and offer support privately, at a time that was extremely stressful for me personally. And then my mother, who was Catholic, from Michigan, would come to visit from time to time, and she always went to Mass at MHR. . . . She was there the day the bishop came over—in fact, she was the only one in the office. She was so proud because she could go back to her friends in Michigan and say, "Oh yes, I met the Archbishop of San Francisco."[67]

McGuire initiated a relationship between MHR and the Metropolitan Community Church that continues to this day. MCC was founded by the Rev. Troy Perry, a Pentecostal minister who'd moved to Los Angeles from Florida. In October of 1968, Perry held the first service in his living room: "We organized with the hopes of reaching those people who cannot or will not attend church because of the attitudes of other religions concerning homosexuality. Most gays believe very strongly in God, but most churches simply refuse to let them worship Him. . . . God made us all. He loves homosexuals as much as any of His children."[68]

Jim Mitulski has very fond memories of "Fr. Tony": "He was a great help to me personally when I came to MCC. He was a well-respected leader in the Castro and in the gay community—very well loved as well as respected."[69] Mitulski speaks of a certain revolving-door factor operating between their respective congregations. Some attended services at both churches. Mitulski estimates that half of MCC's members are ex-Catholics. Sometimes parishioners from Most Holy Redeemer went to MCC for same-sex weddings they could not hold at MHR. Most Holy Redeemer could welcome gay couples at Mass, even as Eucharistic ministers, but anything like a commitment ceremony for a gay couple was impossible. Nonetheless, sometimes parishioners would ask McGuire for such a service—people could always be referred to MCC from MHR, or vice versa. Joint prayer services were also held from time to time.[70]

Few would dispute that Father Tony McGuire was the right man at the right time for Most Holy Redeemer parish. As Kevin Ballard commented to me:

Sister Cleta and Tony were kind of Ma and Pa—not in a paternalistic way. It was just that at MHR people seemed able to drop whatever separated them and find what united them. People could drop their barriers when they found common passions and interests. In finding that they had the same ideas.

My own father became friends with a leather lesbian called Dawn. She came to church in her bike leathers sometimes. At parish events they would be the quiet ones. And so they sat in the corner—and suddenly my father spoke of her as a "friend"![71]

McGuire was the catalyst in creating the kind of community where such unusual friendships developed. It was part of his vision of the Gospel, and what he saw as the continuing work of Christ in the Castro. Towards the end of his time at MHR, McGuire along with the Pastoral Council put together a mission statement for the Parish. After several revisions and inviting comment from the parish, the statement was presented to the parish in May 1989. Fundamentally it is a communal theological reflection on the experience of the parish over the time McGuire was Pastor:

Most Holy Redeemer Parish is a Christian Community in the Roman Catholic tradition. The parish draws people from isolation to community, from searching to awakening, from indifference to concern, from selfishness to meaningful service, from fear in the midst of adversity to faith and hope in God.

The community of Most Holy Redeemer shares God's compassionate love with all people. The parish offers a spiritual home to all: senior citizens and youth; single people and families; those who are straight, gay and lesbian; the healthy and the sick, particularly those persons with HIV disease.

As a parish community, we celebrate God's loving presence in our lives. In worship and sacrament, especially the Eucharist, we are nurtured and challenged to respond to extend God's kingdom of justice, truth, love and peace by growing in the spirit of Jesus, the Most Holy Redeemer.

McGuire would agree with Jim Mitulski's assessment that the Castro is a sacred place. Indeed McGuire's greatest gift as pastor was to allow the holiness and activity of God, already present in the neighborhood, to come to life again and become manifest in the parish. And so MHR was renewed and reborn:

There are certain places that are recognized universally as sacred places. A combination of geography, culture, and history blend to produce an environment where mystery and awe are commonplace, and where the people who live or even visit them are forever changed. . . . The Castro is one such sacred place, a tiny neighborhood with tremendous importance that extends beyond its physical boundaries.[72]

Randy Calvo uses almost the same words:

> I always felt Most Holy Redeemer was very holy, a sacred place. The Spirit was palpable. And I believe AIDS had a lot to do with it, we were walking the line of life and death, and we had to figure out what it was all about.
>
> It was also a place that was missionary territory, so there was more sense of urgency involved, touching people's lives. It was Eucharistic; the Forty Hours devotion brought that out. And in the Easter homily, when I talked of all the dead, I talked about our response to the death of people, but how our response was "Let us brunch." Someone in *The Tablet* wrote an article about the parish and the brunches. And we go out and celebrate in the midst of all the tragedy, but it is tied to the Eucharistic, the Eucharistic is lived out in this community, the body of Christ.
>
> Something spiritual was found. It was a place that I don't think we can ever replicate. It is a completely unique experience in my life, it stands as a moment of what the church could be, a dream kind of coming true, never pure, that brought to mind an image of God and Christ and Spirit. That we don't control, that God is experienced in whatever way, and we more than often are surprised by the Spirit.
>
> The categories of our understanding don't always fit. We cannot box God in. And this parish taught me that.[73]

What Calvo refers to may have been both the parish's worst crisis and the single most influential factor in its maturation: the AIDS epidemic.

"Acquired Immune Deficiency Syndrome" was named in 1982—the same year Father Anthony McGuire was named pastor of Most Holy Redeemer. The two newcomers to the Castro were soon to be all too terribly, intimately acquainted.

NOTES

1. Laurence Rolle, interview by author, tape recording, San Francisco, March 26, 2001.

2. John Quinn, interview by author, tape recording, San Francisco, February 13, 2001.

3. Anthony McGuire, interview by author, tape recording, San Francisco, February 4, 2001.

4. Anthony McGuire, Most Holy Redeemer bulletin, April 22, 1984.

5. John Fortunato, *Embracing the Exile: Healing Journeys of Gay Christians* (San Francisco: Harper & Row, 1982).

6. February 4, 2001 interview with author. John Thornburg, pastor of Northaven United Methodist Church in Dallas, Texas, says: "Being a re-created congregation must be rooted in an initial act of radical hospitality. Because very few congregations

make it plain that gay men and lesbians are as welcome as anyone else, merely making an internal statement of the intention to be inclusive is not enough. It's one thing to have an open house. It's quite another to actually invite people to come in." "The Congregation as a Caring Community for Gay Men and Lesbians," in *Pastoral Care of Gays, Lesbians, and Their Families,* ed. David Switzer (Minneapolis: Fortress Press, 1999), 140.

7. Dale Meyer, then director of AIDS/ARC Programs, Catholic Social Services, quoted in *Proceedings of Interfaith Conference on AIDS and ARC* (held in San Francisco, March 21–22, 1987), ed. Weston Mulliken and Paul Stearns (1988): 130. Most estimates of MHR's gay parishioners are considerably higher now.

8. For a study of a Roman Catholic parish that in recent years has successfully integrated gay and straight people see *Congregation and Community* by Nancy Tatom Ammerman (New Brunswick: Ruthers University Press, 1997), 161–74. Ammerman has studied St. Matthew's Catholic Church in Long Beach, California, around which has grown up a gay business district. Since about 1986, the parish has integrated openly gay parishioners with the rest of the parish. A group, Communidad, is listed in the bulletin as a "Lesbian and Gay Outreach," somewhat the equivalent of the Gay and Lesbian Outreach Committee at Most Holy Redeemer in its day. The parish does not raise gay issues publicly, although the parish is supportive and many gay Catholics do feel at home. One major difference: it was the archdiocese, in particular Cardinal Mahoney, who in 1986 suggested beginning the ministry. However, Communidad did not begin to thrive until parish members embraced and took it over.

9. MHR Gay and Lesbian Outreach Committee, *Annual Report,* 1984. MHR Parish archives.

10. Jim Stultz, unpublished letter to *The Bay Area Reporter,* November 22, 1983.

11. The tensions are also expressed in the minutes of MHR Parish Council for November 7, 1983: "Some rather vigorous discussion followed centering on what some saw as a movement (the Gay and Lesbian Outreach) toward separating the Parish into factions, although assurances were given that this was not the intention of the Task Force. It was nonetheless agreed that the November 20 meeting would be held after the regular coffee hour and that greeters from the Gay/Lesbian Task Force would greet everyone, gay and straight, all the same. Fr. McGuire felt that the number of greeters were proper and that we could rely on the Task Force to act for the interests of the whole Parish."

12. From the Parish Council minutes of June 10, 1985: "A question was raised about the parish being divided in view of the seemingly large number of gay individuals on the volunteer committees. Fr. Tony responded that of the 18 people commissioned to do volunteer work on 6/2, 10 were gay, 8 were straight and these numbers represent a 'pretty good mix.' Thus the matter subsided."

Congregations that systematically avoid conflict also are very likely to avoid changing, Ammerman observes. "Adaptation can take many forms, but it is not an easy process. It requires determined effort at finding new resources, establishing new partnerships, and developing new leaders, new programs, and new ideas, and often involves fighting among people who love each other. Most congregations do not choose adaptation. They may be aware that the ecology in which they were born no longer

exists, but they continue doing what they know to do. . . . After a period of slow decline, these congregations are likely to disappear from the scene, perhaps making way
for utterly different congregations to sprout up in their stead. As with any other ecology, death is an inevitable part of the life cycle." *Congregation and Community*, 345.

13. There was however another, much more radical voice in the diocese: "Growing
concerns about violence against gay and lesbian men and women spurred the creation
of the Archdiocesan Task Force on Gay/Lesbian Issues in 1981 under the auspices of
the Archdiocesan Commission on Social Justice. In July 1982 the Task Force issued
a report approved by the Commission entitled *Homosexuality and Social Justice.* The
report created immediate controversy. The report gave voice to the lived experience
of many Catholic homosexuals. It ran into trouble by suggesting the Church was an
'oppressor' that validated violence against gays, and by calling for a new sexual ethic,
with a more positive theology of gay sexuality. Though published by the Archdiocesan Commission on Social Justice, the report was not an official statement of the
Archdiocese, and Archbishop Quinn quickly distanced himself from the Report."
Burns, *History of the Archdiocese of San Francisco,* vol. 3, *A Journey of Hope,
1945–2000,* 40.

14. One of the most colorful members of the committee was simply known to
everyone as "Pansy." I remember him working in A Different Light Bookstore. Pansy
Bradshaw helped write a definitive gay guide to San Francisco with Betty Pearl; although Pansy no longer revises this guide, it continues to be known as *Betty &
Pansy's Severe Queer Review of San Francisco: An irreverent, opinionated guide to
the bars, clubs, restaurants, cruising areas, performing arts, and other attractions of
the queer Mecca* (Cleis Press, San Francisco, sixth edition 1999). Most Holy Redeemer was reviewed positively in the early editions; more recently, the parish is simply listed along with other "queer-positive religious organizations and churches."

15. Anthony McGuire, Most Holy Redeemer bulletin, September 22, 1985.

16. Anthony McGuire, Most Holy Redeemer bulletin. July 3, 1983.

17. Naturally there is a tension between being inclusive and also being able to survive as an institution. Eric Law could be describing Most Holy Redeemer parish at
this time when he writes: "One of the central missions of the Christian community is
to welcome those who are excluded. This inclusive stand is at the heart of the complicated boundary function of the Christian community. In other words, the boundary
function of a faithful Christian community begins with inclusion. Yet, in order to survive, the church has to maintain its identity by defining its boundary and protecting
it. . . . Jesus pushed his followers and the church out of their safe zone into an area
that required constant reflection and reconnection with God as a living, compassionate being. Therefore, from it's beginning, the Christian boundary function is very
complicated, multilayered, time-consuming, and sometimes contradictory. It can create great uncertainty and confusion. It definitely requires risk taking. In order to understand and live this often unsettling Christian inclusive boundary function, we must
first understand grace. . . . In the grace of God, we can let go of our insecurity, let go
of our rigid rules, let go of our power, and invite Christ to help us discern the will of
our gracious God in the ministry of inclusion." *Inclusion: Making Room for Grace*
(St. Louis: Chalice Press, 2000), 26–27.

18. February 4, 2001, interview by author. See also: Cindy Bologna, "When Gays and Catholics Meet: Homosexuals, Church Can Get Together," *Bay Area Reporter,* December 14, 1985: "Quite often, the Catholic Church has been viewed as an enemy of gay and lesbian families. But for the past four years, in the heart of the Castro, a Catholic Church has been sponsoring a support group for people with AIDS and their families. . . . Our support group is for all people affected by the AIDS epidemic," said Franciscan Brother Regan Chapman, program director. "That means parents, lovers, siblings, grandparents. . . ."

19. John Thornburg, "The Congregation as a Caring Community for Gay Men and Lesbians," in *Pastoral Care of Gays, Lesbians, and Their Families,* ed., David Switzer (Minneapolis: Fortress Press, 1999), 145.

20. James Alison, *Faith Beyond Resentment: Fragments Catholic and Gay* (Darton, Longman and Todd Ltd: London, 2001), 122.

21. *Inclusion,* 109.

22. Fr. Kevin Ballard, 22 October 2001 interview with author.

23. I attended the ordination of Fr. Randy Calvo as Bishop of Reno on February 15, 2005 at the Hilton Hotel in Reno, Nevada.

24. Cleta Herold, interview by author, tape recording, San Francisco, January 15, 2001.

25. Don Lattin, "How AIDS Brought Gays and a Parish Together," *San Francisco Examiner,* July 28, 1986, sec. A, 1.

26. "Jimmy and Derrick," unpublished pamphlet found in parish archives, July 9, 1989.

27. Danny Barutta worked as Director of LYRIC, the Lavender Youth Recreation and Information Center. This center was founded in 1988 as a community center for lesbian, gay, bisexual, transgender, and questioning youth ages 23 and under. Until 1991 it was entirely staffed by volunteers. In 1993 it purchased property near MHR at 123–27 Collingwood Street. At the planning stage large numbers of parishioners testified in support of the application to open the center, against the opposition of other neighbors in the Castro. When Barutta was director, the parish regularly held fundraisers such as pancake breakfasts after Sunday mass to support LYRIC.

28. February 4, 2001 interview by author.

29. *San Francisco Chronicle,* January 16, 1985.

30. October 22, 2001 interview by author.

31. Angela Aleiss, "Mock Nuns Delight Some, Offend Others," Religious News Service, 2001. In 2006 the Sisters of Perpetual Indulgence, in a decision that aroused anger from some Catholics around the country, were given a lease to rent Ellard Hall at MHR for their "revival bingo." In October 2006 the parish ended the lease when the "Sisters" invited a drag artist "Peaches Christ" to participate in the Bingo. This decision generated intense and very different feelings from both the parish and the gay community. At a town hall meeting on the issue, Sr. Cleta Herold questioned why the Sisters of Perpetual Indulgence felt the need to parody catholic nuns in doing their good works. An example of the anger MHR has aroused on this and other issues is a website developed by Randy Engel, Director of the U.S. Coalition for Life, www.traditioninaction.org/HotTopics/ao2xAlert_MFR_Engel_ntml.

January 13, 2007, Engel attacks the use of the hall by the Sisters and continues: "Among the pro-homosexual speakers, lecturers and preachers to be invited to MHR are 'gay' Dominican Fr. James Alisson (misspelt), Richard Hardy, author of *Loving Men, Gay Partners* and a popular speaker on St John of the Cross, and Charlene Tschirard from the Center for Lesbian and Gay Studies." (Richard Hardy is a parishioner at MHR.)

32. February 4, 2001 interview by author. To confuse matters further, Robert Morse had written an article on December 22, 1989 in the *San Francisco Examiner,* which mistakenly implied that the sisters had been invited by the parish to come to a carol service! Several people called the rectory to complain.

33. Father Randolf Calvo, interview by author, tape recording; Redwood City, California, March 28, 2001.

34. Gil Block, *Confessions of a Jewish Nun: The True Adventures of Sister Sadie, Sadie, Sadie, the Rabbi Lady* (Fog City Press: San Francisco, 1999), 160–61.

35. Block, 164–165.

36. Most Holy Redeemer cooperates on many issues with MCC. In contrast, the Diocese of Denver gave up voting privileges in the Colorado Council of Churches after MCC was admitted. See "Catholics Curb Role in Interfaith Group After Organization Admits Gay Church," *San Francisco Chronicle,* 30 June 2000. In July 2006 cooperation between MHR and MCC reached a new level after the MCC church building on Eureka Street was declared structurally unsound. MCC now meets for worship at the LGBT Center on Market Street. However on Wednesday nights MCC uses MHR church for a Taize style prayer. Rev. Tessie Mandeville is quoted on the MCC website, http://www.mccsf.org, January 9, 2007: "Penny (Nixon) and I met with Father Stephen Meriwether yesterday morning and received a wonderful blessing. . . . Most Holy Redeemer will share their worship space at no cost to us!. . . As Penny (Nixon) said, "This partnership between MCC San Francisco and Most Holy Redeemer gives both communities the opportunity to go to another whole level of working together." Most Holy Redeemer has also agreed to host our Prevention Point Brown Bag program on Tuesdays."

37. Available from http://www.thesisters.org/gallery/thanksgiving00.htm; Internet September 7, 2001, page 3 of 5: "Father Shore and Sister Hedra discuss comfortable shoes."

38. Rosa Von Praunheim, *Queer Mecca,* 1998. In the interview outside MHR, one of the Sisters describes how they give all they raise to charity. One says that Catholic sisters understand them: "They wave and give us a blessing." Former parishioners Kevin Gogan and Dan McPherson are also interviewed in *Queer Mecca,* about what it is like to be a gay family as they raise their adopted child, Sarah.

39. Jeffrey M. Burns, "Beyond the Immigrant Church: Gays and Lesbians and the Catholic Church in San Francisco, 1977–1987," *U.S. Catholic Historian,* vol. 19, no. 1 (Winter 2001): 81.

40. The RCIA is the Rite of Christian Initiation of Adults.

41. Jack Fertig, "Why Be Interested in Catholicism?" at the Lesbian, Gay, Bisexual and Catholic Handbook: http://purl.org/NET/lgbh/, posted December 30, 1995.

42. Quoted by John McNeill, *Taking a Chance on God* (Boston: Beacon Press, 1988), 178–79.

43. Anthony McGuire, undated and unpublished homily provided to author.

44. February 4, 2001 interview by author.

45. Anthony McGuire, Most Holy Redeemer bulletin, September 18, 1983.

46. February 4, 2001 interview by author.

47. Quoted by Don Lattin: "The People's Priest Looks Back: the Life of Father McGuire mirrors 50 years of change." *San Francisco Chronicle,* May 30, 1990, B3.

48. John Quinn, letter to the *Times,* December 22, 1988. (I received the letter from Archbishop Quinn himself, and am unaware whether it was published or not.)

49. Thomas Fry, interview by author, tape recording; San Francisco, August 21, 2001.

50. James Mitulski, interview by author, tape recording; San Francisco, February 1, 2001. More recently Dignity hosts a Sunday 5:30 pm mass at the Seventh Avenue Presbyterian Church. Interestingly, for Christmas midnight mass, 2006, Dignity advertised that they were meeting in a Catholic church, St John of God on Irving Street. In the light of Mitulski's remarks it is somewhat ironic that MCC was given the use of MHR Church when their building was declared unsound.

51. March ,28 2001 interview by author.

52. John Quinn, interview by author, tape recording; San Francisco, 13 February 2001.

53. February 13, 2001 interview by author.

54. Burns, *Journey of Hope*, 41.

55. The 1984 minutes of the MHR Parish Council mention an earlier meeting of the Gay and Lesbian Committee with Archbishop Quinn. Dale Meyer spoke of this social meeting on October 22nd. Two focal points emerged: first, strengthening the relationship between the archdiocese and the gay and lesbian community (e.g. how MHR's gay and lesbian committee might work with the Board of Ministries); and second, defining a central ministry for MHR's gay and lesbian committee. In the latter regard, Meyer reported, the Committee has chosen to help people with AIDS, and to this end they set up a food drive in the parish. The minutes for March 12, 1984 mention a meeting between members of the Gay/Lesbian Outreach Committee, with representatives from St. Boniface, St. Dominic, and Mission Dolores parishes, and four members of the Archdiocesan Board of Ministries, established by the Archbishop. There was also a meeting of the Outreach Committee with the auxiliary bishop, Bishop Walsh. Walsh encouraged the committee's efforts, since he felt there was a critical need for parish-based outreach.

56. Unpublished letter to His Holiness, Pope John Paul II, signed by parishioners Tom Kaun, Dale Meyer, Raymond Hermann, Ronald Messineo, Dan Turner, and Jim Stultz, March 8, 1987.

57. Burns, "Beyond the Immigrant Church," 91–92.

58. February 4, 2001 interview by author.

59. Robert Arpin, *Wonderfully, Fearfully Made: Letters on Living with Hope, Teaching Understanding, and Ministering with Love, from a Gay Catholic Priest with AIDS* (Harper: San Francisco, 1993), 39–40. An interesting article in *The Los Angeles Times* (Peter King, "The Papal Visit: Game of Life; Church's Weekly Bingo Keeps AIDS Hospice Operating," September 18, 1987) described Most Holy Redeemer's bingo at the very time when other parishioners were meeting the pope at Mission Dolores. "The

Pope was only blocks away, concluding a poignant encounter at Mission Dolores with 62 people diagnosed with AIDS, and in the basement social hall of Most Holy Redeemer Catholic Church, about 150 of the faithful were convened. They had not come in conjunction with the papal visit but to partake in a weekly ritual. It is an activity that in many parishes across America seems to carry almost liturgical weight. They bowed their heads as one and contemplated white sheets of paper spread out before them on folding tables. . . . A little over a year ago, the archdiocese agreed to lease a convent across the street from Holy Redeemer . . . the parish itself pledged $45,000. To raise its portion, Holy Redeemer fell back on a staple of church fund-raising across America—bingo. For the last year, every Thursday at 6 p.m. a crowd of anywhere from 150–250 players has filled the basement hall and for three hours played serious bingo. . . . On this Thursday night, the crowd was a bit smaller, a result of anticipated traffic tie-ups and public protests stemming from the Mission Dolores event. More than a few of the players wore papal miters made up of folded newspapers. Other than that, it was bingo as usual. 'Initially we were going to cancel,' said Trey O'Regan, 28, the volunteer who runs the game. 'But when we announced it to the crowd, everybody protested. They said that they wanted bingo.' Most, but not all, of the players were gay men, keenly aware of the games' higher purpose. [I.e., funding the hospice across the street, in which their dying friends were cared for.] 'A lot of people have come and played and then disappeared for a couple of months,' O'Regan said. 'And then you find out they are dead. It's not morbid. It's just life and the reality of what is going on around here.' . . . 'I think the Pope should be made aware of this bingo game,' said Chas Dargis, a 34-year-old professional singer who was distributing cards among the players. 'Gays are pulling together in a Catholic church to help people with AIDS. It is disgraceful the bigotry that comes out of the Vatican.' There was an option other than bingo. Protests by gays upset with the Pope's stance on homosexuality were under way near Mission Dolores. Still, Dargis said, it was more important to be in the church. 'The Pope doesn't care about what I say or think,' he said, 'but this makes a difference.''

60. Burns, *Journey of Hope*, 41.

61. Undated and unpublished homily. ". . . McGuire, a self-described 'middle of the road progressive,' says the most difficult thing about being a priest today is dealing with the hard-line conservative doctrine coming from the Vatican—being a priest caught between the church of the people and the Church of Rome. 'The tone throughout the church today is one of imposition from above, rather than acceptance from below, doctrinal clarity rather than pastoral flexibility, and a kind of rigidity that requires a great deal of patience,' said McGuire. 'There's not enough room to breathe.'" (Lattin, *Chronicle,* 30 May 1990.)

62. *The Dictionary of Latin and Greek Theological Terms: Drawn principally from Protestant Scholastic Theology* by Richard A. Muller (Baker Book House Publishers: Grand Rapids, 1996), translates obex as a hindrance or an impediment: specifically, a spiritual obstacle in the way of sacramental grace.

63. 4 February 2001 interview by author.

64. "On May 5, 1980, he [Quinn] issued a 'Pastoral Letter on Homosexuality.' Quinn clearly restated the Church's opposition to homosexual activity, but noted homosexual 'orientation' was not condemned. In addition, the Church clearly con-

demned violence and discrimination against homosexual persons. 'While it is clear that the Scriptures condemn homosexual behavior, this does not imply any justification for the exploitation of the homosexual or injury to his or her dignity as a human person. Thus there is a clear difference between the acceptance of homosexual persons as worthy of respect and as having human rights, and approval of the homosexual lifestyle." He noted that like everyone else, homosexuals had to strive to overcome sin and 'become rooted in the person of Jesus Christ.' The Church had to be pastorally sensitive to this struggle and assist all people to holiness." Burns, *Journey of Hope*, 40.

65. Jim Mitulski, "The Castro Is a Sacred Place," in *Out in the Castro: Desire, Promise, Activism* (Leyland Publications: San Francisco, 2002), 221–22.

66. February 4, 2001 interview by author.

67. February 1, 2001 interview by author.

68. Troy Perry, quoted in *Long Road to Freedom*, 19.

69. February 1, 2001 interview with author.

70. The warm relationship between MCC and MHR, spoken of above, was never more on display than in the Thanksgiving dinners they later sponsored jointly. "In the physical realm Most Holy Redeemer and Metropolitan Community churches are only a block apart. Theologically they're on different planets. But that will not stop these two Castro area congregations—one righteously gay, the other Roman Catholic— from sitting down at noon today and breaking bread for a community-wide Thanksgiving dinner. 'This is the first big community event we've co-sponsored,' said Rev. Penny Nixon, lesbian co-pastor of Metropolitan Community Church, part of a nationwide denomination of gay and lesbian Protestant churches. . . . 'We're trying to do different things together,' said Rev. Zachary Shore, pastor of Most Holy Redeemer. . . . Shore said it is not surprising that the two Castro area churches have formed a holy union. According to Nixon, many of the MCC congregants were brought up Roman Catholic. And according to Shore, about 90% of his Catholic flock are gay or lesbian." (Don Lattin, "Giving Thanks Together," *San Francisco Chronicle*, November 26, 1998.)

71. Kevin Ballard, interview by author, tape recording, San Francisco, October 22, 2001.

72. Jim Mitulski, "The Castro Is a Sacred Place," 225, in *Out in the Castro: Desire, Promise, Action*. Ed., Winston Leyland. (San Francisco: Leyland Publications, 2002.)

73. March 28, 2001 interview by author.

Chapter Three

Bearing Witness in the Hour of AIDS

Tony McGuire

. . . [A]round 1985 we began to experience a number of people in the parish and the community at large dying of a strange disease. AIDS was unknown up until that time, and there was a great deal of fear about it. The specific method of transmission was not clear, although it was clear that it mostly affected gay men.

As a result, parishioners began gathering together to talk about what was happening. At that time we used to have these big gatherings in the parish's convent, which was still a vacant building. Around 50-60 people attended these meetings, all with a variety of ideas of what could be done to help those afflicted with this new disease.

I would attend these meetings and just listen, as I believed it was very important for members of the group to decide the course of action they would take. What developed little by little out of the discussions was that the group would try to set up some kind of support system. The support system would be volunteer driven, and involve real personal connections with the people who were sick, and the service would be provided to them in their homes.

We recognized that there were other kinds of services that were being put into place, both medical and social. Because of the fear of transmission of AIDS, many people were not willing to step forward to give that personal touch. This is where I thought the organizing group was very courageous. The people who began this group were very wise, reading all the material available about AIDS, and they became very well informed. It was then discovered that AIDS was not easy to contract, and especially not through casual contact.

Because of the fear that existed in society at large, many of the young men infected with this virus were very isolated. Their families rejected them, and they didn't have much connection in the community because many had just arrived in San Francisco. The support group really was a very significant instrument for bringing hope and a sense of a "caring community" to the people who were sick.

As the support group evolved, those who kept coming to these meetings formed a board of directors and hired Bill Reese as the Executive Director. The core leadership was parishioners, supplemented by others outside of the parish. That is the way it was from the beginning. It started clearly as the Most Holy Redeemer Support Group and not meant to serve only members of the parish, but meant to serve the community at large.

The MHR support group expanded as Project Open Hand began to use the MHR church as a drop off point for food and meal distribution.[1] The volunteers who distributed the Project Open Hand meals would see first-hand the type of assistance the clients needed, then inform Bill Reese. That is how the client services provided by the MHR support group evolved. . . .

There were a good number of older parishioners who were particularly helpful when the hospice opened. They visited patients, and volunteered in the office answering phones, etc. Bill Reese developed a weekend training program for volunteers, and at the end of their training the volunteers were invited to the MHR church to be recognized by the community.

In the beginning I believe the money came from the parish. The idea was that the support group should become an independent entity so that Bill Reese could get funding from foundations and fundraisers. Bill had a whole network of fundraisers. I don't really recall the exact financial aspects other than the start-up money came from the parish.

I eventually became a board member and followed up on the spiritual aspects of the group. I became the spiritual advisor for people wanting communion or an appointment, and as a result a spiritual community of friends developed.

I did have fears about what would happen once the initial state of founding spirit was over. I felt very good when I attended a fundraiser several weeks ago and saw that the second stage of volunteerism had "kicked in." There appears to be a solid organizational structure, and salaries and benefits are in place. . . .

One of the inspirations that I have always found in Most Holy Redeemer Church is the beautiful stained glass window above the altar. . . . I would always meditate on that figure. I think that it is the impetus, in the sense that God is among us, redeeming us, and we are part of making that redemption happen.

I'm also happy that the support group maintained the name [i.e., "Most Holy Redeemer AIDS Support Group"]. There is a symbolism that is deep and rich, and is reflected by the support group. By providing services for people who are in various stages of HIV disease, we assist them as they walk through those moments and feel the accompanying love of God.[2]

At the outset of the epidemic, the fear of catching AIDS terrified the city and the nation. Until 1985, no one knew how AIDS was spread, which caused not only panic but great isolation for those with the disease. Most Holy Redeemer parishioners were worried too. Many wondered if it was all right to shake hands at the sign of peace. Was it all right to drink from the cup? People, good loving people, would abandon a friend in his time of greatest need—because who was to say whether being with him, caring for him, might not put them in mortal danger too?

Thomas and Robert Van Etten

[Thomas:] In the early eighties, Walgreen's pharmacy was called Star Pharmacy,[3] and they had pictures on the windows of people with these spots on their bodies: "This is a gay cancer." It really freaked you out. You went home and looked at your body. [Robert:] No one knew how you got it. [Thomas:] But then John got sick, and—I am not able to admit this so easily, but we turned our back on him, and I really didn't want to go over there. He had thrush, and it was very visible on his tongue. He had periods of dementia. I didn't want to be around him, and I didn't know if being near him I would be sick. I might catch this from him. More and more of our friends were getting sick, and then we saw the estrangement that they were going through. And we had kind of done that to John. So we started delivering meals, it just grew, we just got more involved.[4]

Tony McGuire

The most important step in moments of doubt and darkness is to pray. I remember one day a gay man came in after church to complain, "Why don't you pray for people with AIDS?" Of course, why didn't we? So, we started making that a constant petition at Mass at the prayers of the faithful: "For persons with AIDS, let us pray to the Lord." A simple thing, yet a very powerful one. . . . In praying for them, our hearts open to them.

The next step in terms of prayer was that we began to add the names of all the sick to the prayer of the faithful. Because so many know someone who is sick with AIDS, sometimes the list is long. I wonder if this is the best thing. Some complain of the length. But one man who had AIDS gave a public testimony that when he was in hospital he heard that he was prayed for publicly in our church. He said that it gave him great strength and courage.

Another visitor, a Jesuit priest (James Hanvey) from England, wrote in the April 4, 1987 issue of *The Tablet*: "On Sundays I would try to say Mass in the church of the Most Holy Redeemer. It is in the Catholic parish church in the heart of the Castro—the gay section of San Francisco. The long litany of names in the prayers for the sick seemed to me to have an unusual power which came from the community—a *community* was suffering and in pain. It was also a community discovering a new liberation and strength."[5]

The parish council announced in a bulletin in December 1984 that the parish would begin a visiting program to AIDS patients the following year. This volunteer initiative is what evolved into the MHR AIDS Support Group, which continues its work to this day. There were serious tensions early on. The first full-time director, Bill Reese, found it hard to work at Most Holy Redeemer.

"Part of his problem came from the fact that he had worked previously for the government, and he was used to processes of evaluation," says McGuire. "I did not do that. I just told him he was doing great work, there was no formality to it, and he began to resent that. So eventually he left and brought me before the state board, and I had to go to a hearing. They ruled against me. I was devastated."[6] The Support Group managed to be Catholic and at the same time acceptable to people with AIDS who'd had bad experiences with the Catholic Church, especially in regard to their being gay.

Rudy Carcia

I grew up gay. I knew I was gay before I entered elementary school. By the time I was fifteen, being gay was just another part of me. It seemed very natural to me. God makes all sorts of people . . . I never had any dispute with God's choice.

I grew up Catholic. Even though I don't have much to do with Catholicism now, I can still pick and choose what I want from those beliefs. . . . I guess the biggest problem for me is the isolation. I used to have a lot of friends. And I've watched them all—ALL—die. I'm . . . the . . . only . . . one . . . left. It's just very hard.

And if they're not dead, they've moved back to Oshkosh, U.S.A. To die . . . I lost my lover, I lost my brother and I lost my mother all within a three-year period. And then I lost the only three people I had left in my life in the last six months. So I just shut everything down.

I have two new friends that really, really care for me. Pete Toms is one of them. He is a friend. He was brought to me because he's a volunteer coordinator with Most Holy Redeemer Support Group. He was just doing his job. I needed some emotional support and he was trying to connect me with a volunteer. But Pete, he and I just hit it off so well. . . .

He listens to my pain. He's concerned about my pain. And he's there; whenever I need him he's there. Almost at the drop of a hat. I like the man. He's very sensitive. Inside we're very much alike. You know, I have a good act. But I'm the same as Pete on the inside. And he's very sensitive to my spiritual devotion. Even though we differ. He's very . . . Catholic. That's okay. He cares for me.

It's very special. . . . He gives 101 percent. And I can't help but believe that there *is* a God.[7]

The Most Holy Redeemer Support Group's motto is "We Care," and over the years this group emanating from a small parish has provided a Herculean proportion of the care given locally to people with AIDS, their partners, families, and friends. Full training weekends have always been required for volunteers; I have gone through it myself. Support provided range from in-home care, which provides clients with a one-to-one companionship, to emotional support groups and bereavement groups. The model of ministry in the parish also empowered people with AIDS to minister to each other, not just to be the object of ministry.[8] And often enough, there were volunteers who became clients.

Tom West

In the winter of 1988 I began meeting every Tuesday afternoon in a back room of Most Holy Redeemer Rectory with a group of very inspiring and courageous men. My co-facilitator then was Radule Weininger, M.D. In her fifteen years as a psychotherapy group leader, she has never known a deeper or richer experience of group process. Joe Chinowth, my co-facilitator, and I agree with that assessment.

Over the years our group moved from the rectory into the church, we now meet in the side vestibule known affectionately as the St. Theresa room. Joe and I show up each week, but it is the group that does the work. It is a safe and reliable place for group members to show up and share who they are and what is happening to them. They share their pain and anger, their grief and loss, and their joy and hope. They consistently show up for each other in many concrete and subtle ways.

Three years ago I received a Christmas card from one of the guys in the group. Five months later I would help him prepare for his funeral service and take part in it. In his card he wrote:

"During the closing time at our little group I imagine the Holy Spirit like a mother hen brooding over us and helping us all make the transitions into our new life situations. Her presence is just one of the many blessings in my life because I joined up with our MHR group. I am feeling less isolated now and more committed to staying flexible during the process of being sick."[9]

Jean-Guy Lussier, in an unpublished thesis partly on Most Holy Redeemer, gives the example of one parishioner who found his way back to the church through an AIDS diagnosis and Most Holy Redeemer parish. Those infected at the parish in the early days of the epidemic are largely dead; this is true of parishioner Jerry, who at the time Lussier was writing, was a "long-term survivor" of AIDS. A "long-term survivor" in 1989 was someone still alive three years after diagnosis. Indeed, in 1989 only nine percent of those diagnosed with AIDS in San Francisco survived so long. Only three percent lived longer than five years. While he still had the strength, Jerry got involved in helping others, through the Support Group. Once a week he and his lover, Bill, would go to visit Andrew, whose lover had abandoned him when he was diagnosed with ARC (AIDS related complex).

Jean-Guy Lussier

Jerry was born and raised Catholic in the Midwest. Like many of his gay companions who came out of the closet and settled in San Francisco in the late 60s and/or early 70s, Jerry deserted Sunday Mass and parochial organizations. An estimated one quarter of the gay and lesbian community in San Francisco are believed to be born Catholic, an estimated 15,000 out of the 70,000 people who make up the gay and lesbian population in the City by the Bay. . . .

For a while, Jerry experienced only deep sadness and anger at the way the Church handled the presence of gays and lesbians within the Church and society. He could not find the so-called hallmark of the Catholic Church expressed in unconditional love for anyone, regardless of sexual orientation and lifestyle. That is why, in order to come out of the closet, Jerry has closeted God for a long time.

When Jerry was diagnosed with [AIDS] he felt a great emptiness. Illness forced him to journey at a different pace, and to initiate an inward quest to peace and reconciliation. He used his spiritual process as a way of becoming more human, to reach out his innermost nature which is called to greater holiness. He was challenged by all sorts of questions: Why do I exist? Where am I heading? What is the meaning of what is happening in my life? . . .

Although many gays have rejected traditional beliefs, almost all, when they are infected with the HIV virus turn to the spiritual, and initiate a spiritual quest which can take many avenues. Some to follow "new age" spiritualities where the sacraments become long hugs and slow sensuous massage, and its altars are votive candles burning wherever people with HIV congregate, and its great totem is a sprawling quilt imbued with sacred power, or a return to a more traditional religiosity.[10] As Rev. Bob Arpin, a San Francisco diocesan priest, since deceased from AIDS, pointed out vividly: "God has a wonderful sense of humor. . . . The ones who are rejected by society as having perverted love are the ones teaching the world to love again, and teaching the world the meaning of life." . . .[11]

For Catholic believers, AIDS became the occasion of a rapprochement or a closer relationship, a way to deepen one's faith with works of compassion and mercy at the parish level. For many it was the occasion to the rich heritage left by ancestors. MHR was established at the turn of the century to serve the new Irish Catholic community that had just settled the area. As Rev. McGuire puts it at Sunday Mass: "These early immigrants in one generation built a church, a school, and a rectory which serves us still today." The very first immigrants "gave themselves to this enterprise with great discipline and dedication, with a sense of urgency and detachment."

Jerry met with men and women for whom, as one interviewee pointed out, "it is important that people with AIDS/ARC are not 'excommunicated' in any sense—they are part of [the] community and need to be treated with the same love and respect [the local church] would direct toward any member of the parish, [the] neighbourhood, or the city."

Many faithful [at MHR] have understood that the parish is more than an ecclesiastical structure. It is rather "the family of God, a fellowship afire with a unifying spirit, a familial and welcoming home, the community of the faithful." Meanwhile, the reign of God is not merely sitting on our pews, and maintaining our cosy and pretty ideas about Church. It needs more boldness than that. The Reign of God calls on every baptized person, according to one's anointed charisms, to build up, in concrete manner, a fuller human and fraternal milieu, a milieu in harmony with God's dream for everyone of his/her children.

It will be the place where truth and life, holiness and grace, justice, love and peace will prevail for everyone. As McGuire pointed out: "This is a call to exercise our God-given creativity in finding new ways to disclose God and serve his people, new ways to facilitate the emergence of God in our midst." . . .

When the AIDS crisis began to strike among the ranks on a large scale, long-time parishioners came together with the gays and lesbians to help relieve the AIDS suffering.

Catholics and people of good will at MHR wanted to provide an environment in which a person can suffer with dignity, surrounded by love, die in peace, and be buried with all the hope and consolation, which our Liturgy offers.[12]

Donal Godfrey

[Most Holy Redeemer] parish has an AIDS Support group that has been a model for many other Catholic parishes around the world. Through this support group and in many other ways this parish models a truly Christian pastoral response to people with HIV. Like every human community it is sinful and flawed, but the labels of gay-straight, old-young, conservative-liberal, black-white, simply do not mean very much in a place like that. It is a truly prophetic Christian community.[13]

Richard Rodriguez

Cary and Rick's friends and family wish to thank the many people who provided both small and great kindness.

He was attended to and lovingly cared for by the staff at Coming Home Hospice.

And the saints of this city have names listed in the phone book, names I heard called through a microphone one cold Sunday morning in Advent as I sat in Most Holy Redeemer Church. It might have been any of the churches or community centers in the Castro district, but it happened at Most Holy Redeemer at a time in the history of the world when the Roman Catholic Church pronounced the homosexual a sinner.

A woman at the microphone called upon volunteers from the AIDS Support Group to come forward. Through the church, people stood up, young men and women, and middle-aged and old, straight, gay, and all of them shy at being called. Yet they came forward and assembled in the sanctuary, facing the congregation, grinning self-consciously at one another, their hands hidden behind them.

I am preoccupied with the fussing of a man sitting in the pew directly in front of me—in his seventies, frail, his iodine-colored hair combed forward and pasted upon his forehead. Fingers of porcelain clutch the pearly beads of what must have been his mother's rosary. He is not the sort of man any gay man would have chosen to become in the 1970's. He is probably not what he himself expected to become. Something of the old dear about him, wizened butterfly, powdered old pouf. Certainly he is what I fear becoming. And then he rises, this old monkey, with the most beatific dignity, in answer to the microphone, and he strides into the sanctuary to take his place in the company of the Blessed.

So this is it—this, what looks like a Christmas party in an insurance company, and not as in Renaissance paintings, and not as we had always thought, not some flower-strewn, some sequined curtain call of grease-painted heroes gesturing to the stalls. A lady with a plastic candy cane pinned to her lapel. A Castro clone with a red bandana exploding from his hip pocket. A perfume-counter lady with an Hermes scarf mantled upon her shoulder. A black man in a checkered sports coat. The pink-haired punkess with a jewel in her nose. Here, too, is the gay couple in middle age; interchangeable plaid shirts and corduroy pants. Blond and shit and Mr. Happy Face. These knew the weight of bodies. *Bill dies.*

. . . Passed on to heaven.

. . . Turning over in his bed one night and then gone.

These learned to love what is corruptible, while I, barren skeptic, reader of St. Augustine, curator of the earthly paradise, inheritor of the empty mirror, I shift my tailbone upon the cold, hard pew.[14]

Will America's Churches Ever Accept Homosexuality?

Richard Rodriguez, the acclaimed author of *Days of Obligation* and an essayist on the *MacNeil/Lehrer News Hour*, is a gay man who has not abandoned his childhood religion.

"In my essay 'Late Victorians' I talked about the effect that the AIDS epidemic has had on homosexuals in San Francisco that I'm aware of, and their intense spirituality," he says. "When one would attend a mass, for example, at Most Holy Redeemer, which is sort of unofficially the gay Catholic Church in San Francisco, there was no mistaking it. You know, my Geiger counter is as primitive as anyone else's, but when one walked into that church on any given Sunday, one was in the presence of the Spirit. The holiness came out.

"I speak as a Catholic, and as someone who believes, a) that life is sorrowful, that there is a great deal of sorrow in life, but b) that the meaning of our lives is revealed through suffering. This is not exactly convenient to secular notions of optimism. But, nonetheless, my sense is that the sorrowful church, the gay church of the last twenty-five years, is really leading the larger population at this point. If you go to a suburban heterosexual parish in Contra Costa County, I dare you to compare Most Holy Redeemer to that church. I dare you to tell me where the experience of holiness is right now in the world."

In past decades, holiness and homosexuality were not often linked. But many religious people in the gay and lesbian community are now building bridges between sexuality and spirituality. In examining this connection, Rodriguez refers to what he calls "the large numbers of homosexuals in the clergy."[15]

Rev. Daniel Kanter, Unitarian Universalist Church, Reston VA

What Rodriguez witnessed was really faith in action, faith understood but not cloned in each individual, faith made public by a radical program in a conservative denomination, faith made visible by a public declaration that all people count and most importantly made meaningful by sheer acts of love.

I believe that churches provide something no government agency or good-deed service can, and I want to call this salvation. Salvation by being there for us, being places where we can bring our needy selves, our aspirations, or questions and dreams, places for rest in calm waters, and letting go from time to time to float. It is salvation provided by being places for us to gather and to find each other and to sit in the mystery of the meaning and purpose of our lives. Our churches are places where everyone paddles and if we trust the raft we can hold on in white water. Our churches are places where we are encouraged to sing whether we can keep a tune or not. Everyone paddles but the current takes us. They are places that ask us to be ourselves and not to "shrink from controversy, sacrifice or change on the path to soulful-ness."[16]

God works at MHR through all the pain and messiness of AIDS. God is experienced in solidarity alongside us in our personal sufferings and tragedies. As Paul Claude says; "Jesus did not come to explain away suffering. He came to fill it with meaning."[17] I do not believe that AIDS and suffering themselves are the desire of the Christian God for human beings. I would not want to worship a God who willed this kind of suffering. I must admit, I have unanswered questions about why such an already marginalized community was stricken and decimated by this terrible epidemic. There can be no doubt, however, that the HIV epidemic transformed Most Holy Redeemer—in a paradoxical way, brought it back to life. I find God at work in the care and love that people at the parish have given to each other and to a much wider community through the agony of AIDS.

Jean-Guy Lussier

MHR stands as a parish worthy of attention. In a climate of dialogue, ingeniousness and collaboration, MHR, through participation of the laity and use of its buildings, has created an outreach program that encompasses everyone, and for whom support, concern and care can be provided. AIDS has forced parishioners and people of good will to pull together in the face of adversity. The same epidemic has brought MHR to the forefront of pioneer models in the way a congregation can care for people with AIDS and their significant ones.[18]

Tony McGuire, Christmas Homily

Recently a sister working with the MHR AIDS Support Group gave this testimony about a person with AIDS. Once the man remarked, "I always felt treated like dirt, until I met members of the MHR Support Group. Now I feel worthwhile. I feel that I am loved." Toward the end of his sickness, he said to the sister: "Prior to this sickness I always thought of myself as a boy. Now I feel like a man." Three hours later, he died.

To me this is a Christmas story. It is the story of the appearance of the grace of God amidst gloom. It is the discovery of a man's life. It is the discovery that human life in its fullness reveals the life of God.[19]

Somehow God brought hope and grace to marginal people in the midst of a holocaust through a very unexpected source, at least from the perspective of the community most catastrophically affected. The God I believe in is a God of surprises, and it certainly was a surprise to the local gay community that its neighborhood Catholic parish became such an extraordinary source of life, of healing, amidst so much death. The attitude of most gay men and women in the Castro towards the Catholic Church continued and often continues to be ambivalent, even hostile, but they recognized that something good was happening at Most Holy Redeemer.

Archbishop John Quinn

The Cross is not the end. Death is not the end. Suffering is not the end. This transfigured and risen Christ takes all suffering and sin and death and gathers them into his triumph. His resurrection means that we have a future, that there is a way out of the tomb. We have a future, which is being prepared by God even in the midst of suffering and death, as Christ's glory was being prepared in the midst of the Cross. And this points out one of the essential qualities of Christian discipleship: hope.

I have seen this kind of hope in some of the faces of persons dying with AIDS. I will always remember Jim Stultz of this parish whom I visited two days before he died. His hope in the Resurrection shone in the way he prepared spiritually for death. Through the grace of his daily prayer and meditation, he carefully brought closure to his affairs on earth and peacefully let go in the hope of the promise of eternal life with God.[20]

San Francisco Examiner

Over the past three years, at both Most Holy Redeemer parish and the highest levels of the archdiocese, the AIDS crisis has forced gays and the church to replace confrontation with compassion.

"If there's a bright side to AIDS, it's the reconciliation between the church and those who have traditionally been alienated from the church," said Dale Meyer, a member of the parish council at Most Holy Redeemer and the coordinator of the archdiocese's AIDS program.

. . . Last August in what many observers see as a turning point in the rocky relations between the archdiocese and the gay community, Quinn presided over a special "Forty Hours Devotion" mass for AIDS victims at Most Holy Redeemer Church.

That prayer marathon will be repeated this week, beginning at 6 p.m. Friday and ending at 10 a.m. Sunday with another Mass celebrated by Quinn.

"Archbishop Quinn is going through a tremendous spiritual renewal over the AIDS issue," said the Rev. Michael Lopes, the chaplain of the archdiocesan AIDS ministry. "He has insisted that we show our compassion and is trying to exercise leadership."[21]

Lopes pointed to a recent article Quinn wrote for the Jesuit weekly magazine *America*, on San Francisco's pastoral response to the AIDS crisis. In that article Quinn repeatedly used the word "gay," a new term in the archbishop's literary vocabulary. . . .

Several long-time church members at Most Holy Redeemer have gone to another parish, while some of the new gay parishioners left when McGuire declined to take a more active stand for gay rights.

But in a parish such as Most Holy Redeemer, where funerals have quadrupled in three years, there's a reality to the AIDS crisis that goes beyond the parishioners' sexual preferences.

"Young people are dying," McGuire said. "A lot of them are from Catholic families. They come out of a religious tradition. They, and people who are very close to them, have started asking, "What's it all about?"

Lopes, the AIDS chaplain agreed.

"All we're talking about here is caring for sick people," he said.

"But it's so hard for people to see that. There's this fear of disease, fear of their own sexuality, fear of death. The most frustrating thing is that people keep focusing on other issues, like 'morality.' "[22]

The parish in response to the epidemic reinvented the Forty Hours devotion. In conversation after a Lenten discussion series, a traditional Chicago Catholic asked McGuire, "How come we don't have the 40 Hours devotion anymore?" McGuire found himself waffling for an answer. "Some of these devotions had become routine activities in a parish and had lost the reason for their origin," he said.

Then somebody else asked, "What was the original reason for Forty Hours?" McGuire racked his brain: "I think it was to pray over a plague of some kind." "Well, don't we have a plague here?"

And so the observance began afresh at Most Holy Redeemer.[23]

In fact the origins of this devotion were not quite what McGuire recalled. Forty Hours began in 1537 in Milan, under siege by the Ottoman armies of Suleyman the Magnificent, who having conquered much of Hungary had his eye on the Mediterranean. Two years later Pope Paul III issued the first papal order recognizing the virtue of unceasing prayer for forty hours:

In order to appease the anger of God provoked by the offenses of Christians, and in order to bring to nought the efforts of the Turks who are pressing forward to the destruction of Christendom, among other pious practices, has been established a round of prayers and supplications to be offered both by day and night by all the faithful of Christ, before our Lord's Most Sacred Body, in all the churches of said city, in such a manner that these prayers and supplications are made by the faithful themselves relieving each other in relays for forty hours continuously in each church in succession, according to the order determined by the Vicar. . . ."[24]

The New Yorker

When I visited [Most Holy Redeemer] church one recent Thursday, the day before the start of its fourth annual weekend of continuous prayer, a knot of men and women carrying candles, crucifixes, and small brass bowls were forming themselves into a rough processional crocodile on the church steps. "Get that oil up there, girl!" I heard a youngish man with a candle say, in a friendly way to a tiny elderly woman wearing turquoise pants. She punched him in the arm and then obediently raised her bowl to chin level, and the procession marched into the church. I later learned that this was a rehearsal for a sacrament of anointing of the sick.

At the front of the altar, a woman with a spiky haircut was tacking up a banner. "The theme for this year's Forty Hours is 'Refresh your People,'" she told me. "We've had four or five years of dealing with AIDS, and we're getting tired, so I'm trying to get across a theme of refreshment, using images of water and wheat—food for the journey across the desert. We're doing the back of the altar in teal, and I've made these teal banners, with wonderful symbolic thingies pasted on with Spra-ment." She stepped back from the banner, and a man carrying a candle studied it carefully. "Oh, it's like wheat," he said, after a pause. "It's fabulous. Absolutely fabulous."

The man carrying the candle, who introduced himself as Thomas Michael, not giving his last name, said, "I'm in charge of ushers for the week-end, and my lover, John, is putting out coffee and cookies to keep people going all night." He was wearing a boldly striped shirt and low-slung black Levi's, and he had a handlebar mustache like an Irish fireman's. "I joined the church four years ago, at the invitation of a friend who's dead now," he went on. "I hadn't been in church for twenty years—since my early twenties, when I confessed that I was living with a man, and a priest threatened me with blanket excommunication. So I withdrew, and I was *gaaay.* Now I'm back. Both John and I will be taking a shift to pray in the church this weekend, and on Saturday we'll be anointed. Six months ago, John got shingles. I started drinking heavily, because I didn't want to know, and then one morning I woke up with a hangover and said, 'Let's quit running away and have the test and fight the S.O.B. down to hell.' I don't care what anyone says, nothing prepares you for the moment when the doctor tells you, 'I'm sorry. You're HIV-positive.' I know that unless something comes up we're going to die—if not from AIDS, from some complication."[25]

As we watched a man in a small cherry picker, trailing a banner of teal, rise hydraulically to the ceiling, Thomas Michael added, "This is the place where I've let a lot of people go."[26]

Tony McGuire, homily, opening of Forty Hours 1987

The names which are read at the entrance of the church are an indication of the increase of the numbers of people who have died in our community in the last year. Death has brought a deep sense of loss to all of us, especially to family and loved ones. I received several letters from mothers who expressed their loss in poignant phrases: "It has been a terrible loss of my son. He will remain in our hearts forever." "I am writing to you because my heart is totally broken and my spirit is wounded."

The other side of this sense of loss coming from increased death is that it has helped our community more consciously choose life. This is the theme which our banners proclaim, choose life, not the life which comes from the relentless pursuit of power and possessions, not life in the fast lane, not life which is only skin deep. But life as God reveals it in his word today. As the Jewish people entered the promised land, the Lord commanded them: "Choose life, then, that you and your descendants may live, by loving the Lord, your God, keeping his voice and holding fast to him." Those who are choosing life are leading us to find life at the center, life from discerning the Word of the Lord in our lives. We want to grow in this life through prayer and contemplation, through our outreach as a community, particularly this Forty Hours and through the Eucharist which unites our contemplation and action.

As a community we are discovering again the importance and power of prayer . . . : a man from our parish with AIDS is offering his suffering for the safety of the Pope; a small group of people come into the church on Friday night at 3.00 am and pray for those who are cruising in the neighborhood. . . .

We are also discovering renewed life in community. One dying man used to come in a wheel chair every Sunday. At the sign of peace, the old ladies would hug and kiss him. When he was getting weaker, his mother suggested that he not come. He said, "I can't pass up all those hugs." In another woman's case, her son died. After the Mass, all his friends gathered in the rectory dining room for wine and cheese. At the end I was in line to say goodbye. She said, "All you people do in California is hug and drink white wine." (I suppose we'd be OK, if that were all!)[27]

Hundreds of letters came to McGuire and the parish as a result of the publicity the Forty Hours received in the international and local media. It had opened the door for much reconciliation. McGuire tells the story of a gay former Catholic religious brother who had not been in church for twenty years. He happened to walk into the church during the Forty Hours exposition of the Blessed Sacrament after the bars closed at two a.m. He talked to McGuire, who invited him to come back for the 10 a.m. mass that morning. He came, and was shocked to see the changes in the liturgy since Vatican II. Hence an encounter after the bars closed enabled this ex-brother to come back to the Church. Later, on becoming HIV positive himself, the people at Most Holy Redeemer accompanied him in friendship over the last years of his life.

Tony McGuire

... Don Lattin wrote a very positive article in *The Examiner* about what was going on in the parish. As a result of the article I received a letter from a man in San Quentin who said, "When I was a young man, I developed TB and was shunned by everybody including my own relatives, and so I know what the AIDS guys are going through. Through the years I have seen many examples of real charity, but never have I seen any as great as the work of your parish."[28]

Forty Hours also provided the impetus for MHR to work with other churches and other traditions in the Castro. There was a charismatic prayer service attended by prayer groups from all over the diocese. Then there was the rosary, interspersed with Marian hymns and solo instrumentals. There was also the mass of anointing the sick, a Taizé-style prayer service around the Cross, and a communal sacrament of reconciliation. The Taizé prayer was the most ecumenical of the services attached to the Forty Hours. Ministers and priests from other churches were invited to participate. McGuire says one year a group of Druids attended: "I remember these druids dressed in black and white from down the peninsula. The Sisters of Mother Teresa would always go and get blessings from everybody. I always wanted a picture of the Druids giving the sisters a blessing!"[29] Day and night the Blessed Sacrament was exposed, a sign of God's presence and mercy. Every year the Forty Hours began with a preached retreat, over several nights. Certain nights were declared nights of fasting and prayer in the homes of the parish. A special prayer was composed and published on cards, distributed to everyone attending the devotion:

Blessed are you, Lord of All, giving new life and health to those who call upon you.
   Usher in your kingdom and manifest your power to heal those with AIDS.
   Blessed are you, Lord of Wisdom, who push back the borders of darkness and disease.
   Enlighten those who search for a cure for AIDS.
   And strengthen those who care for our suffering brothers and sisters.
   Blessed are you, Lord of Love and Peace.
   Be with the families and loved ones of those who live with this disease.
   Touch us all with your love and make us instruments of your healing.

Blessed are you, Lord, in this Sacrament of your Body and Blood.

Let us receive with joyful thanks this true and living bread from heaven, your reconciling light and life throughout the ages. Amen.

Tony McGuire, closing of Forty Hours, 1987

Richard Rohr used the adjective *sober* to describe our community. (He wasn't at the party after the Forty Hours!) He meant *sober* in the sense of serious, reflective. Some of the visiting priests over the weekend also remarked on the attention the community gives to preaching here. There is a search for meaning and understanding; a quest for a deeper grasp on life. Hence, the theme *CHOOSE LIFE* seemed so apt for this year.

This week began with a very challenging, provocative retreat by Richard Rohr, O.F.M. Like a true Franciscan he spoke from the edge, looking with a prophetic eye at the assumptions and foibles of main-line Catholics and middle-class Americans. . . . Mary Archer made the good comment: "He forgot to mention the greys in the gay and grey combination."

After two days of prayer and fasting, we began the Opening Mass of the Forty Hours with the sobering, plaintive reading of the names of those who died in the past year. The impact was powerful and the scroll inscribing the names became an icon for the weekend. As the balloons lofted above us, we handed over to the Lord those 240 dear ones and sang out for them as for ourselves: "Jesus, remember me when you come into your kingdom." The banners, (DID you say "Jungle of banners, Father?"), made by Juliana, the Banner Baroness, expressed to all the visitors the great variety which we live out as a community, trying to CHOOSE LIFE as God wills for us.

As in years before we were graced with visitors from beyond our parish: priests, religious, laity, the visiting charismatic groups, our fellow Christians who organized the ecumenical service. . . . We even had a man in a wedding dress with rabbit ears at the Sunday coffee. Did anybody decide which banner he stood under? (Life in the Castro.) One disturbing intrusion was the increased number of media persons invading our prayer moments. . . . We had our glories and our glitches. The poignant moments included the early morning *Lauda Sion*, the Mass of Anointing of the Sick which was so heartfelt and consoling. I had a visitor from Ireland who happened into the church for the Mass. She said that she had never seen anything like that since she had been in Lourdes. The moment which touched us all so deeply was the prayer around the cross. At the end, a black man emerged and summed up our inner groanings by singing from deep within his soul the Our Father. It combined the lament of the blacks with our lament and placed them both at the foot of the cross of Our Most Holy Redeemer.

Glitches we had as well, and causes of amusement: the Melkite deacon's bonnet, Joe Hedley chasing the Archbishop around the sanctuary with the humeral veil. And would you believe, I forgot the words of the Hail Mary? (Anthony, sit in the corner!)

The final Mass continued that very reflective mood, especially in the words of the Archbishop which helped us see the death around us in the light of Christ's death and resurrection. . . .

At the end of the day, as I was kicking back in my room, I got a call from Coming Home Hospice. Dan Bova's parents called to ask me to say the prayers of the dying over him. When I arrived there, I could hardly see the print on the page of the prayer book. My eyes were filled with tears. But they were not the tears of sadness or despair, but a welling up sense that God was in the midst of this. I have known Dan for two years. And accompanied him along the way of his sickness, first in his home, then in Hospice. His wonderful parents have become a part of our community. As his body got smaller, his ears seemed to get bigger. He seemed to be all ears as we gathered around his bed: his parents, Joan Healy from the Most Holy Redeemer Support Group, and I. We prayed over him, and cried over him, and turned him over to the Living God as we had done the other 240.

It was the perfect end to the week. That is our call as a community: to help those who are dying to suffer in dignity and to die in peace. May the Lord strengthen us by His Word and Sacrament and by our life in community to measure up to the task ahead of us.[30]

James Hanvey

"A community [MHR] was suffering and in pain. It was also a community discovering a new liberation and strength. Somehow they were finding a compassion and joy and appreciation of life which was not there before despite all the celebration and parades."[31]

George Higginson

I had just lost a friend from AIDS. Jim Stultz said, "You've got to come to the 40 Hours," so I went to the Healing Mass. I was going through mourning, as it was the first time I had lost someone from AIDS.

I sat there way at the back of the church, and this woman came into the pew, put her hand on my shoulder and did not say a word. I will never forget that moment. It was as if an angel had come. I learnt later her name was Marie Krystofiac.

She was one of the leaders of the older generation reaching out to the gay people. She was the one who stepped across the aisle, and gave permission for others to follow. She became a greeter and it was wonderful. You came in and there was this little old lady who reminded me of my mother, you know, greeting and hugging everybody—she did not care what they looked like, you know. I will never forget.[32]

Michael Vargas

We offered something to each other because of the peculiar nature of this parish. It might not have happened elsewhere. It didn't happen at Mission Dolores.

Part of it was a mutual adoption between two very different communities. We became surrogate family for each other in the absence of our natural families.

My experience of the last fifteen years was more like my grandmother's than my parents. I've seen my peers health go down and die; my parents haven't had that experience. Watching person after person die. This hasn't impacted their spirituality or faith life. It affects my grandmother; we could talk about this.[33]

Kevin Ballard

Marie Krystofiak, she was a wee bit of everything. Her son had been in high school with me.

She really reached out to the gay community and she was on all the parish groups. She was full of joy and reaching out. My Mum had the same attitude.

The older ladies almost got into a competition! Marie was so popular. They all began to look at the gay men as our boys. A lot had to do with Mary: these were the ladies that said the rosary. All children were Mary's children, and so they were also their children. They were gifted with being motherly, they were mothers and grandmothers and their children were far away. "Well, here is a man who needs a mother." The old-time men who had not been scared off also came around.[34]

Bob Werkheiser

I met this very petite lady one evening after Saturday Mass in 1978, standing on the corner, across from the church, as she waited on a Muni bus to take her up the long hill to her home on Caselli Street. Many times I had seen her at church, moving about the Castro, or standing before the Blessed Mother's statue in front of the church, saying her prayers and repeating her petitions of intention for those she loved. I gave her a ride home. I later learned that she had been recently widowed, freeing her up from a role as homemaker, mother, and caregiver of her ill husband, allowing her time to take a more active role in the church community—for which she possessed a passion.

We continued to run into each other at church or in the neighborhood, to have a cup of coffee, share lunch or dinner, and tell our stories, later realizing that we had created a strong bond and support for one another.

Changes were taking place in our Church and the neighborhood that we had known. We had a new pastor, music director and choir,[35] and many different faces in the church community. We were both new to taking an active role in the activities of the church. We both joined the Liturgy Committee, meeting each Tuesday evening to read the scripture for the following Sunday worship, attempting to interpret God's message and themes to incorporate into our Sunday liturgy.

During this period, the newspapers were featuring articles about gay men who were becoming ill and quickly dying from a new disease, later to be called AIDS. Whatever this illness was, most of the victims did not perceive that a church would care about them, and many of their parents would not want anything to do with this problem of their children, that was brought on by a different lifestyle.

Marie Krystofiak's immigrant mother had been a housekeeper to the nuns at our convent, long since closed because there were no more children in the parish. It was at a Tuesday night meeting that Marie asked Father McGuire if there was something we could do for so many ill people in our neighbourhood. And would it be possible to convert the convent into a care facility? Hospice was just becoming familiar.

The seed was planted. About a year and half later, Coming Home Hospice became a reality, providing sixteen private rooms and a safe place for guests, with caring people, to walk their final journey with them. Marie worked the phones, visited each patient with a huge smile, hugs, prayers, and company. Her kitchen table was filled with notes, phone numbers, lists of things to do, assignments for cookies that needed to be baked, someone to work the booth at the Castro street Fair, greeters for Masses, parents to reconcile with their children, and creating "almost like an evangelist," real faith journeys for everyone she touched.

Each Sunday, she stood at the back of the church, greeting everyone she knew, and did not miss a new face, remembering every name—she called everyone "my love," and threatened to come after them if they didn't show up next Sunday. Her newfound mission was a seven-day a week job. And many evenings were filled with tasks, meetings, or middle of the night calls from Hospice to help someone move onto a new life filled with peace. She never failed to say, "I'll be right down."

I can hear her now, out of frustration saying: "What's the matter with these people? Don't they know that there is only one God and that his love is unconditional? Why don't they get their acts together?"

Marie was a best friend who helped me on my faith journey, taught me all there was to know about football as we watched every 49'er game. We also enjoyed our trips to Reno, playing the slots long into the morning hours.

She is worthy of this honor and we know that her new role is as passionate as her former.[36]

Mary Geracimos

AIDS had a terrible effect on the parish. Going to the Hibernia Bank on Monday mornings, I now saw young kids with canes; I remember one in particular, no more than 21, trying to walk across 18th and Castro with two canes. It broke my heart. He was emaciated.

The Castro became like a leper colony. It wasn't long since they'd been dancing on Monday morning.

This is when the church started to grow. Before, it was party time, and when AIDS came people got scared—and when you're scared you go to church.

The parish kind of pulled together—gay and straight, old and young, the Support Group. We had Meals On Wheels here; we had the Gay and Lesbian Outreach.

But it broke my heart to see the young men with AIDS coming in. What I found hard was putting all the deaths in the registry. I remember five AIDS-related funerals in one week. It wasn't like that every week, but there were a few every week. I was especially affected as I have two sons around the same age.[37]

In the early days of AIDS, the best and most current information about the disease was printed in the bulletin. A 1984 bulletin says the San Francisco Department of Public Health reported 54 new cases of AIDS in July, the most ever in a single month, up to that time. As of July 30th, 439 Californians had died. "This deadly syndrome is spreading rapidly. The suffering at every level — physical, emotional, psychological — is intense. With the compassion of Jesus we wish to reach out to parishioners suffering from AIDS. We continue to pray at every Mass for persons with AIDS. Perhaps there are other ways of assisting. So, if you are a person with AIDS, or know someone with AIDS who would appreciate a visit, or some other assistance, please let us know. Contact Sister Cleta at the Rectory."[38]

The parish was blessed to have parishioners with expertise in the field — people like Cliff Morrison, a gay clinical nurse specialist who became well known in the city for starting and running the AIDS ward at San Francisco General Hospital.[39] Morrison spoke about AIDS at every mass one weekend. McGuire introduced him in the bulletin by telling the story of a young Gulf coast fisherman who viewed with anxiety the arrival of Vietnamese fishermen. They were refugees who wanted to continue fishing, which was all that they knew how to do, but many U.S. fishermen threatened them, even beating them up, seeing the Vietnamese as competition who undersold them. One young U.S. fisherman, shocked by the threats but also frightened for his own livelihood, wanted to meet one of the Vietnamese fishermen. On meeting him a relationship began to flower. "This story, a beautiful application of today's readings, reminds us of the central commandment of love to which Jesus calls us. At the Masses this weekend, Cliff Morrison from SF General Hospital, and a member of our parish, will speak about the experience of people with AIDS who in our day are generally rejected by others, though they are in desperate conditions."[40]

Morrison also offered a program for parishioners interested in helping persons with AIDS. In this he was helped by another parishioner, Bill Nelson, a nurse on Ward 5B. Other parishioners such as Dale Meyer, who headed up the Catholic Charities response to AIDS in the city, also were able to share their expertise with the parish.[41] Fittingly, Morrison was one of the people invited back by the parish to speak at the mass celebrating its Centenary. Morrison spoke of how AIDS changed everything in the Castro, and for Most Holy Redeemer Parish.[42]

In my searches of the parish Record of Interments for this period, I find that in 1980 the deaths in the parish are all of older people, aged (in order): 108, 95, 82, 80, 86, 92, 76, 72, 74, 82, 61, 64, 75, 59, 72, 82, 85, 54, 92, 83. By 1985, the ages of the deaths read (again in order): 42, 40, 42, 29, 27, 45, 43, 62, 82, 84, 39, 59, 102, 39, 35, 32, 33, 39, 37, 51, 57, 88, 81, 48, 61. The impersonal data give stark statistical witness to what happened in the years in-between. The younger deaths in 1985 are of men and almost exclusively due to AIDS.

Tony McGuire, in the MHR bulletin

To celebrate this Feast of the Baptism of the Lord, a young man who has AIDS will be baptized. Normally adult baptisms take place at Easter, but because of the sickness, this baptism will take place at the 10:00 a.m. Mass on January 10th.

The one being baptised is Gary Niksich, 37, from Kirkland, Washington. Gary came to San Francisco in 1978 and in 1980 joined Michael Scollard to open a beauty salon on Potrero Hill.

Michael sang in the Most Holy Redeemer choir and talked to Gary about the Church. With a friend of his who had AIDS (Gordon DeMattos), he came to Church for the first time since he was a child. His reaction was: "I felt that I had been to Church for the first time. I felt a oneness, a warming experience. The Mass was a beautiful experience. . . . The greeter made me feel so welcome." He continued coming to Church with Gordon for a year. Then when Gordon died he did not come back.

He himself was diagnosed with AIDS in July of 1987. The social worker at Pacific Presbyterian Hospital suggested that his mother call the Most Holy Redeemer Support Group. One of the coordinators and a volunteer came and brought along a picture of the Virgin Mary. While sick in the hospital he derived great strength from the picture of Mary. Little by little he was being challenged to a personal faith in Jesus.

Previously coming to Church had been like going to a show. He was not a real part of it. Now he wanted to be a part of the community. He talked about faith to the volunteer who had shown great faith in his work. He asked the coordinator about Heaven and what happens when a person dies. She talked about the afterlife in such a beautiful way that he almost felt it.

He became more and more convinced that Jesus loved him. Prior to that he felt that because he was gay, he could not be loved by Jesus.

"When somebody loves you, you love him back. Jesus has filled a place in my life that no one else ever filled before. I know that He loves me. I know that he will forgive me if I've ever done anything wrong. I ask for His forgiveness all the time."

In reflecting on his baptism, Gary sees it as a way of formalizing his relationship of faith and love with Jesus. As Jesus' experience of sonship with the

Father was proclaimed at His baptism, so Gary's experience of loving union with Jesus will be manifest in the sacrament of Baptist. He will become formally a member of the Catholic community. He says, "I am really happy about this. It's not a decision I made lightly."[43]

Tony McGuire, homily

The other day I came to see a man dying in hospital. With him were his partner and his family. After the anointing in which all participated, I read over him the prayers of the dying, . . . after the prayers, there was like an explosion in the room.

He called out to his partner, then to his mother and father and to his brothers. Each of them had the opportunity to comfort him, to reassure him of his or her love and to ask pardon for any obex in the way of that love. Each came and hugged him and held him. I am not sure of all that was happening, but I felt that the anointing and the prayer helped him experience the presence of Christ calling him home and proclaiming his forgiveness.

He experienced the compassion of Christ present in the Sacrament and in the small community gathered around him. This is what Jesus reveals to us today in the readings. By His words and deeds, by His very person, He reveals to us the inner quality of God who is compassion.[44]

In the same sermon, McGuire spoke of the RENEW small faith communities which the parish initiated that fall. They provided an opportunity for members of the parish to come together and experience renewal and support in a smaller, more intimate context. They served, and still serve, as a kind of base community for parishioners, rooted in faith. And those who were HIV-positive found in them interpersonal support that helped them meet the challenges of their disease. They too brought the parish community together during the AIDS crisis in new and previously unthinkable ways. I can think of no other institution in the Castro capable of the same accomplishment.

Kevin Ballard

I remember a Sunday Mass when a family came from Wisconsin, as their son had come out to them and told them he had AIDS and was gay. They would look totally frozen in the church and were surrounded in the now-packed pews. They seemed to be filled with shame for religious reasons. My mother and her friends would single them out at coffee and work on them. They would cut off the woman and get at her.

I remember when Tommy's mother visited. Tommy was from Tommy's Florist, this nice quiet guy, people went to him. God seemed to be focusing people on what they had in common and using humor to do it. The old ladies surrounded his mother, and they would say what a nice young man Tommy was.

"You did such a good job with him." "He helps me with my groceries." I can re-member, as my mother would drag me over to talk.[45]

Ruth Garner, mother of John

John was a physician, he was 36 years old. He was a very dynamic person, an avid skier; he had a private pilot's licence. He was a very contributing person to society.

His homosexuality was a part of him. I believe when *Coming Home Hospice* was dedicated here not long ago, the Archbishop, John Quinn, spoke eloquently about how we are not dealing with a lifestyle but a disease . . . with young peo-ple dying. That is what the parish has furnished, not getting into moral views of what Catholics might justly believe homosexuality is.

This is a thousand diseases. It is a spiritual disease. It is a medical disease. It is a family disease. It affects everyone. What other disease carries such a stigma or disrupts so many lives?

At my age to lose a child you have to reorient your thinking. It's not in God's order usually to lose your children. And so many of them.

This disease is decimating a whole generation of people. This has to be looked at. My experience has been an outpouring of care and love, both in ma-terial ways and in spiritual ways, as far as Most Holy Redeemer parish is con-cerned, with the pastor and the support group. The people in the parish all show-ing their concern.

And then again, I think the church has to be a leader. What we're really talk-ing about is the homophobic prejudice that is in almost all society. That has to be set aside. This is the plague of this century. I do believe that the church is one of the origins of homophobia, but at least that is not true in this parish. Or in this city to some degree. There has been a tremendous outpouring of love and con-cern.

Look at the hundreds of volunteers; who come to people in their homes, take people to the doctor, come and clean homes. I don't know any other place I've lived where there would be all this genuine concern. You can have concern, but when you back it up with your own time in coming to do all those things—now that is the most touching thing about this city.

I'm not saying you don't go through the gamut of "Why my child?' or, "Isn't this a terrible thing?", but you are so caught up in their daily care. This is a dis-ease with a daily crisis in their care.

My son unfortunately had severe dementia. He had 24-hour care for fourteen months. He had the support of his brothers and sisters who were here nearly con-tinuously.

It's devastating for many parents to accept it. Because as your child is grow-ing up, you have a vision of what that child should be, particularly male chil-dren, thinking they will be married and have children. It's very difficult at times. But if parents can get past that feeling and see this is still their child.

I guess my feeling is there's a whole range of how society acts. It's very difficult for a young person to survive without the support of their own people. Very often it's almost an explosion of their being able to come out, that society has to some degree accepted them. People in a great many areas are still ignorant about what being gay is.

I think my greatest fear was that John wasn't going to be loved or have love in his life, and that wasn't true at all. He had friends in both the gay and straight community. [Being gay] was his sexual orientation. But it wasn't his whole life. It just wasn't, and I think that is true of most young people. You don't immediately think of a heterosexual person's mores.

I feel that God created my son the way he was. I know he was a good living person. Everyone loved him. He was a good contributing person in his profession. It was difficult for him at times to accept his homosexuality. I believed he would have wished it to be different, but as humans we have to accept what we are.

I don't think AIDS is any condemnation of gays. I think it's proven this disease will spread among the heterosexual population as well.[46]

When I worked as the parish deacon for a year in 1990, AIDS was still terrifying people, still a devastating killer in the parish. I presided at funerals of people I had known. I saw first-hand how AIDS brought very different people together in a common purpose and meaning. In some ways, I suppose, war often has the same effect in uniting a country.

Donal Godfrey

This morning I was mystified when I received a letter from Germany, because I had no recollection of the person identified on the back of the envelope. The letter read:

"Dear Mr. Godfrey: As a friend of Mr Arthur Diaz, I want to inform you that he died on November 22nd in Bonn, Germany. I invited him for a visit to Germany in September, where he got sick from an AIDS complication. Probably the funeral will be at Bonn next week. He often mentioned your help to Mrs. Anna and him in the past. Yours sincerely," etc.

Arthur was the only person in the world who still loved "Mrs. Anna," a woman now in her nineties. I wonder what will happen to her? I met Arthur because, although not a Catholic himself, he brought Mrs Anna to Most Holy Redeemer Church for mass on some of the occasions when I was presiding. Arthur suffered a lot during his short life, partly because he was gay, but also because he was HIV-positive. When I met him for coffee I was always conscious of his joy at life, his simplicity, dignity and concern for others, even when he himself was dealing with this life threatening disease. He talked openly of his intimate relationship with God in ways that made me feel very humble.

Arthur is one of hundreds of young men from that parish who die each year. I never knew quite what to say to the parents, families, lovers, and friends at their funerals and memorial services, but I was always conscious of being held, loved, and supported by the community of that parish.

Recently a fellow Jesuit asked me what gave me hope these days. I find hope in prayer certainly, but I also find hope through communities like that parish.[47]

AIDS encouraged, even required, cooperation among church and secular groups and city agencies. The parish made its facilities available to many groups for meetings and activities related to AIDS. The foremost example of collaboration with an outside agency was the conversion of the parish convent into an AIDS hospice, "Coming Home." The building, formerly home to the Sisters of Charity, B.V.M., who staffed the parish school from 1925 to 1979, stands directly opposite the rectory. It still bears a cross over the door, the lettering "Most Holy Redeemer Convent," and the windows in what was the chapel display doves, the emblem of the Holy Spirit.

The convent had been used by a motley assortment of groups since its closure. It had been used by the Jesuit Volunteer Corps and housed refugees from Central America. McGuire wanted it used for some purpose that was the parish's own. A subcommittee of the parish council studied possible uses of the property. Someone suggested it might serve as housing for seniors, and McGuire remembers someone else objecting: "No one will live in those cells. You'd have to be a nun or close to death!" The offhand comment conjured up another possible use, the one that in the end was implemented.

Four alternatives were considered by committee. "Wellderly, a transitional housing program sponsored by Diamond Senior Center; another was a shared retirement home for religious women, and the third was to use it as a youth shelter."[48] The fourth proposal, however, was the one accepted, and in November 1985 the convent was leased to Hospice of San Francisco. Coming Home Hospice is a testament to the parish's resourcefulness in responding to AIDS and its stature among the institutions of the larger civic life. Such cooperation operated out of a different model of church, one that was impossible before Vatican II.[49] The hospice was not an effort of the Catholic Church to respond to AIDS. It was a parish church working with the secular community to face the crisis together.[50] In a homily, McGuire described the Coming Home hospice as "a sign of love. . . . It is an enterprise which has brought out the best in many groups in this community. It has mobilized bingos and dinners and tea dances and open houses. It has opened purse strings of foundations and of city commissions. It has brought out volunteers to paint and hammer and clean. It has helped people grow."[51] Without the support, provision of the building, money, work, and enthusiasm of the people at Most Holy Redeemer the hospice could not have been opened. (Nowadays it is run [by California Pacific Medical Center] independently of the parish; in recent years the connection to MHR has faded, nearly to the point of vanishing. Nearly all of the patients being cared for at Coming Home now are dying of something other than AIDS.)

McGuire and the parish council asked the congregation to vote on the hospice proposal. Two hundred sixteen voted in favor; 29 were opposed. McGuire, very much in favor, had the final say as pastor, but the parish council was also unanimous in its support. Parish volunteers worked on the construction, headed up the weekly bingo and other fundraising efforts, and assisted with the running of the place after it opened.

Hospice care was first introduced to the United States in 1974 as a way to allow people to live the final part of their lives in dignity, the emphasis being on patient care and pain control, without the use of extraordinary means to prolong life. Coming Home was the first hospice in the world established specifically for AIDS patients. Physicians, hospital administrators, and government officials from around the world came to visit in the years after it opened, to observe and study the innovation.[52] Elizabeth Taylor made a private visit to each of its fourteen residents.[53] Archbishop Quinn was a regular visitor, as of course were the clergy, staff, and parishioners of Most Holy Redeemer.

One imagines those early hospice patients might have fatigued of the more ceremonial visits and welcomed someone with whom they could dish Elizabeth Taylor's wig.

Randy Calvo, homily, Easter 1991

I repeat a story told once before, a story of this parish which bears retelling.

About four years ago, there appeared in the London *Tablet* an article about the AIDS epidemic and Most Holy Redeemer parish. The article described the efforts of the Support Group to provide practical care for those sick with AIDS; it mentioned the parish gathering in prayer for the Forty Hours; it talked of the pain and death that this disease has brought to this community. But the writer also mentioned that he was struck by a practice he observed by many of you parishioners here in Sundays. What do you think that was? Besides Mass here, what else happens on Sundays?

Sunday brunch!

It struck this visitor from London that, in the midst of the suffering and dying, in a place, which many have described as the epicentre of the epidemic, people could still join together in a meal that reaffirms friendship and life. To him it was unmistakably a sign of life amid death, a sign of hope.

Sunday brunch in this parish is a kind of Easter sacramental flowing from the Sunday Eucharist. And this morning we gather around the Lord's Table to share the meal that forms the basis for all the other meals that affirm our faith in life and faith in love. We come to this Easter feast to celebrate life arising from death; we celebrate the resurrection of Jesus Christ.

We in this parish come to this Easter by way of the cross of Good Friday. We in this parish have gone through our own dying in many different ways. Some of us have watched loved ones and friends get sick and die. Others live with HIV infection. Some have had to wrestle with rejection and loneliness and others with addiction. I say this because we in this parish come to this Easter celebration not with faith shallow, not with faith easy, but one that rises from the depths of our own experience of dying in a thousand different ways.

It is the faith of the beloved disciple described in the Gospel we've just heard. Two disciples ran to the tomb, one looked in and saw an empty tomb. And he believed.

We in this parish can sing with full voice the Easter song "Alleluia," because its conviction arises from deep within us. For here in this community we have walked at the edge of death and life, confronting both as life and death mixed in a paradox of dying and rising.

The disciple whom Jesus loved ran to the tomb, looked in and saw an empty tomb. And he believed. A couple of weeks ago I got a letter from someone whose lover died about four years ago, and I celebrated his memorial mass. He wrote to tell me that he had recently been diagnosed positive with HIV and that he had just told his parents, and that this was traumatic. He also said that in the past four years all his closest friends had died. He said, "Hard to believe I'm the last of the gang."

What he said reminded me of words of a song from the musical *Les Miserables*:
"There's a grief that can't be spoken
There's a pain that goes on and on
Empty chairs at empty tables
Now my friends are dead and gone."

"Empty chairs at empty tables." In the past five years I have stood at this table of the Lord and have watched a place in a pew become empty through death. I know who were in those places: Jim Stultz, Rick Cotton, Ken Vargo, Larry Glover, John Lococco, Bill Wilde, Mary Archer and Roberta Snell, David Posey, Larry Parsons, Sam Sharp, just to name a few. Their names along with scores of others who have died are written in that scroll we have carried in procession to commemorate them today.

"Empty chairs at empty tables." An empty place in a pew. An empty tomb. On this Easter morning we are called to have the faith of the one Jesus loved: the one who ran to the empty tomb, looked in, and believed. Empty chairs at empty tables, an empty place in a pew, and the empty tomb are not the same; but all call us to the same faith, faith in the risen Christ.

We in this parish come to this Easter in this faith; a faith that has not always been easy, one that has been tried, but a faith that remains a lifeline to this world. It is a faith which enables us to go to brunch on a Sunday.

So let us brunch. I know it may sound hokey—"Let's have brunch." I know it may sound contrived to say, "Let's have brunch" as an Easter saying, but our church has always associated Easter faith with a meal. Just listen to one of our ancient texts, from an Easter sermon of St. John Chrysostom:

"Let's all then enter the joy of the Lord!
Both the first and the last and those who come after, enjoy!
Rich and poor, dance with one another,
Sober and slothful, celebrate the day.
Those who have kept the fast and those who have not,
Rejoice today for the table is richly spread.
Fare royally upon it. Let no one go away hungry.
All of you, enjoy the banquet of faith!
All enjoy the riches of the Lord's goodness."
So let there be brunches on every Sunday. May it flow from the faith we share at Eucharist. May it be a foretaste of the eternal banquet promised when we will join those who have gone before us in faith—join together in the Feast of the Risen Lord.[54]

Another priest who was very much a part of the MHR community, and who attended those dying from AIDS at the hospice, was Fr. Tom Hayes. Hayes lived at Most Holy Redeemer; his official ministry was as AIDS Chaplain for the San Francisco Archdiocese, until his religious congregation, the Oblates of Mary Immaculate, assigned him to a parish in Oakland in September 2000. From *American Catholicism*:

Most of Hayes' time is spent ministering to dying young men and the rest to providing pastoral care to a Catholic population whose position within the Church is ambiguous, to say the least. First meetings are often at the deathbed, when a gay man who has been estranged from the Church decides to make a last-minute reconciliation. "His partner and friends will usually be there when I come into the apartment," Hayes said. "You often feel a great coldness. There is a lot of anger toward the Church on the part of the gay community." "Sometimes," he admitted, "It can be a terrific strain."

Each fall, Most Holy Redeemer has a Forty Hours' devotion for AIDS victims. The church keeps a scroll with the names of parishioners who died during the previous year. At the closing ceremony, members of the congregation read off the list of new names. "Each reader does ten names," Hayes said, "one reader after the other. The list goes on and on. It's very wrenching." Archbishop Quinn always made a point of attending the closing liturgy, a gesture that was much appreciated in the parish. The one year he had to be in Rome, the ceremony was rescheduled so he could attend.

Hayes has a dry humor and a store of Felliniesque tales of life at the parish. But except for the rate of funerals, he insists that Most Holy Redeemer is for the most part a normal parish. "We're very participative," he said. "There are a number of former priests and nuns who know a lot about their religion and the liturgy. Most parishes have trouble recruiting lectors or choir members, but we have a yearlong waiting list. And I do think gays often have a more highly developed affective and intuitive side. We have a lot of artists and designers," He smiled. "When we decorate, we *decorate*. Wonderful asymmetric stuff that you'd never see in the average church."

I asked how he measured success. "When people begin to center their lives on the reality of their love by Jesus Christ and know that they're accepted and loved by this parish community, and that they're part of a world-wide community of love and faith." It is an answer that could easily sound trite and practiced, but Hayes said it with real conviction.[55]

Most Holy Redeemer was saddened when Hayes was sent to Sacred Heart Parish in Oakland. No one was appointed by the archdiocese to fill his place as chaplain for people with AIDS. At his final mass and going away party on September 24, 2000, there was a huge card with hundreds of signatures and a present of cash for the parish he was going to. His usual dry wit was shown in the morning's homily. It's often said, he began, that San Francisco is pure theatre, big, bold and exaggerated. Well, he said, then Most Holy Redeemer is the IMAX of it all!

Tom Hayes

[MHR] is big, brassy and in-your-face Catholic. What good is faith if we do not live it out, but only keep it to ourselves, as St James says in the reading.

This community takes this to heart in a distracting world. In the late eighties and early nineties many people came to MHR to study models of compassion and concern regarding HIV infection. This community is renowned for putting faith into action. Living in a world in which we meet people who are accidents waiting to happen, I commend you deeply as a community deeply rooted in faith. We must make good things happen. St James would like this community as we have a practical faith.

Once I got a call to Judas Street, not to a good section of the city, a woman of no religion wanted her son who was dying of AIDS to receive "just a plain baptism!" I didn't know what this was, but figured I was as plain as she could get. It was a tragic family, the father just out of prison the day before, the woman was distraught.

The young man, I have to ask him one question: "Do you believe in Jesus Christ as your Lord and Saviour?" He said, "No problem." He said it again. I never heard that in the RCIA. It seemed to fit into the ambiance. I asked his mother for water. She came back with a green-stemmed martini glass. I baptised the young man.

God is someplace in this realistic mix of life. Grace appears in mixed places. It was an interesting experience. So if you see a lady with a green-stemmed martini glass, you know she came from San Francisco.

People become the experience of grace. I give thanks for the blessings each of you have been over the past twelve years. Forty percent of this community have died since I came here. Their names are on the scrolls. No pope or king has ever seen what I have seen looking out of my window. [General laughter and applause.] [56] Being part of this community has been the most challenging, frustrating, rewarding experience of my life and I thank you for that.

I want to close with a prayer and a wish. St Paul says: "I give thanks to my God every time I think of you. I rejoice at how you have helped me promote the Gospel." I pray your love may ever more and more abound so you may value things that really matter up to the very day of Christ.[57]

McGuire left Most Holy Redeemer in 1990. Like hundreds of other San Franciscans working with people with AIDS, McGuire needed a sabbatical. Death, among young gays who just returned to his Castro District church and elderly parishioners who never left, is always knocking at the door of Most Holy Redeemer. The Irish priest from the Mission district of San Francisco was off to a very different life: a sabbatical in Hong Kong, where he would learn Chinese, later to serve the Asian community in San Francisco. Currently McGuire is pastor of St. Matthew's parish in San Mateo. He was replaced as pastor by Fr. Zachary Shore. One of the first issues Shore had to confront was AIDS, just as McGuire had been compelled to do upon his own arrival at MHR.

Zachary Shore

I learned, to my great surprise, about AIDS, the Coming Home hospice, the Most Holy Redeemer Support Group. I had no knowledge about AIDS. I was not aware that those with AIDS, regardless of what parish they lived in, wanted to see a priest from Most Holy Redeemer church because they knew we would be understanding of gay people with HIV.

I remember visiting a gay man at the Coming Home hospice who kept asking his mother and his parents to come and visit him from New York. His mother kept making excuses so he asked me to phone. I said to her, "Your son is dying and wants to see you." She said, "We cannot come out. My husband has a bakery and he gets up very early." I had to tell the man, "I'm sorry, but your parents don't seem able to come out."

He asked me to try again. I phoned and said, "You know, your son is dying, and he is really desperate to meet you one last time." His mother said to me, "We have the casket picked out and we have his clothing ready for his funeral, but neither of us can come out." I just thought, how cold.

I remember another hospice resident whose mother did come from New York to visit. She left her gay son $500 and told him never to call or bother them again.

Many times over the years I heard those with AIDS say that this parish is their family, because their natural families did not want anything to do with them.[58]

In the early years, Shore commonly presided at two or three AIDS-related funerals each week. Over time, the funerals declined dramatically, owing chiefly to the development of medications that interfere with, but cannot entirely arrest, HIV's destructive effect on the immune system. Some parishioners living with AIDS actually found it hard to adjust to the new prognosis that their lives would not end as soon as they'd expected. I was surprised and delighted to see parishioners come back from death.

The changes in Most Holy Redeemer caused by the epidemic have been too deeply wrought, the lessons too deeply learned, to be undone, unlearned. Even in this brave new world of not-always-fatal AIDS, we remain a community where very different cultures unite around the table of the Eucharist. In MHR the words of Richard Smith have been lived out: "The AIDS epidemic is a moment when the gay community and the Catholic church come together in the face of immense human pain. We can hope that, without abdicating their respective identities and values, these two cultures can nevertheless find a common ground on which to meet. In this tragic moment, may the structure of war give way to the structure of dialogue. May extravagant compassion be extended, profound truths be shared, rich stories be told, and amazing discoveries be made about the vastness of love and life."[59]

NOTES

1. A letter appeared in the *Bay Area Reporter* (signed Ray Reuter, January 31, 1985): "I have often been a critic of the Catholic church and especially of SF's Archbishop Quinn. But I have to eat a bit of "humble pie" and give credit where it is owed. I just learned that the Catholic parish in the Castro, Most Holy Redeemer, started a food drive and money-raising campaign for the AIDS food bank. Since Thanksgiving, I am told, my Catholic neighbors have donated a number of food baskets to the Food Bank plus somewhere around thirteen hundred dollars in cash. They are supposed to carry on their work for the AIDS patients all year. As a Gay man I feel that AIDS is an open sore in the flesh of all of us. I bite my tongue and thank my neighbors at Most Holy Redeemer for their help to my brothers who are suffering from AIDS." This outreach had begun the previous year. In the MHR Parish Council Minutes for November 12, 1984, Dale Meyer reported to the Council that $580 had been raised for an AIDS holiday food bank. The minutes for October 8 report the Gay and Lesbian Committee hoped to cooperate on this matter with the Parsonage, an Episcopal Ministry in the Castro for gay and lesbian people, and with MCC.

2. Anthony McGuire, "Our Roots: An Interview with Reverend Anthony McGuire about the beginning of Most Holy Redeemer AIDS Support Group," in *Spirit, Our Stories,* vol. 1 no. 10, December 1997; 1, 4. At a parish town hall meeting in late 2006 there was once again talk of the Support Group changing their name. At the meeting chaired by Nanette Miller in late 2006 reasons given for the proposal were the need to be able to find suitable funding and also the need to care for elders.

3. See Sam Whiting, "Where History Was Made: Thirty Years of Gay Pride," special section of the *San Francisco Chronicle,* June 23, 2000. Writing of the Star Pharmacy, Whiting says: "498 Castro Street. In December 1981, AIDS poster boy Bobbi Campbell posted in the display window the first notices describing the 'gay cancer' that was to plague the Castro. Star Pharmacy closed in 1985, and the window now belongs to Walgreen's. Ironically, a few years later this location set a prescription sales record, noted by a plaque on the wall." Until its sale, Star Pharmacy was part owned and run by longtime MHR parishioner John Squeri.

4. *The Castro*, KQED. The Van Ettens, a couple (Thomas took Robert's last name), were later MHR parishioners and worked with the AIDS Support Group.

5. Anthony McGuire, "Response to AIDS: Prayer comes First"; "Comment" in *San Francisco Catholic,* June–July 1987, 13.

6. February 4, 2001 interview by author.

7. Peggy Green, "When You Choose to Live: an interview by Peggy Green," early Most Holy Redeemer Support Group newsletter, July 1990: 1, 3.

8. "Many HIV-positive people use the words spiritual and spirituality more comfortably than many students of divinity. Their experience of having to contend with the basic issues of their sexuality and their mortality has led them to acknowledge a dimension of their own reality quite distinct, though not separate, from their bodies and their psyches: the dimension through which they discover the meaning of their experiences, determine the direction of their lives, anticipate the future with hope, become reconciled with the past and reach out to others in service and love." Robert Doran, S. J., *Compass,* November 1990. Fr. Doran played the key role in initiating a Catholic AIDS ministry in Toronto, specifically with the monthly healing masses at Our Lady of Lourdes parish. Studying at Regis College of the University of Toronto at the time I was present at the first meeting at his apartment, which began this ministry.

9. Tom West, "Reflections from Tom West, O.F.M.," *MHR AIDS Support News,* vol. 1 no. 2, June 1995. These days with a thankfully better prognosis for people living with HIV, the Support Group has moved to other areas of ministry. For instance, it initiated group support for gay men in midlife, "Mid-life Gay Men" (MGM). In such ways the parish continues to initiate new ministries for gay people. (John Brennan, "New SF Group forms for gay men in mid-life," *The Slant,* vol. 12 no. 10, October 2000.)

10. Sections of the National AIDS Quilt have been displayed at MHR on various occasions.

11. Arpin moved to San Francisco from the East Coast after his diagnosis with AIDS. I knew Fr. Bob personally as a fellow parishioner and presider at Most Holy Redeemer. He experienced a reconciliation with the institutional Church when, in failing health and what were to be the last years of his life, he was invited by Fr. Zachary Shore to preside at MHR on a fairly regular basis. For those many in the parish also living with HIV disease, Arpin's presiding was greatly healing. Catholic gays with HIV felt a great kinship with a priest who so publicly identified as gay and having AIDS. Arpin wrote a book about his experiences *Wonderfully, Fearfully Made*, quoted here and elsewhere. He died at the age of 48 in 1995. Two hundred mourners gathered at his funeral at Most

Holy Redeemer to celebrate his life. See Susan Ferriss, "S. F. Mourns Gay Priest Who Saw No Bounds to Love: Rev. Robert Arpin Spoke Out About Living with AIDS," *San Francisco Examiner,* May 28, 1995, C1: " 'I never heard him apologize once for his gayness, for his disease, or for his life,' said Rev. Tom Ryan, a priest at St. Ambrose in Berkeley and a member of a priest's support group to which Arpin belonged. 'He said, "No one can tell me how to love. God gives me the gift of how to love." As a gay Catholic priest, he showed himself to be the Christ inside of us.' "

Two other priests with HIV have also been associated with the parish: John McGrann and Paul Paradis, S. J., who presided regularly at MHR in the 1980s. McGrann, was also open about being HIV-positive; even now, there are only a handful of Catholic priests willing to disclose such a diagnosis. McGrann wrote in the parish bulletin of February 7, 1993: "Hopefully my 'telling the truth' can help others to do the same, and we can continue our support of one another in the name of Jesus." McGrann was founder of Kairos House, which stood within the parish boundaries, a resource center for caregivers of people with AIDS. From the Kairos House brochure: "Giving care to persons with HIV infection raises issues of suffering and mortality that many are reluctant to address. Caregivers who become too busy or too isolated to explore these issues and share their emotional ups and downs often become exhausted. If caregivers don't take care of themselves, they eventually become incapable of caring for others." Fr. McGrann presided at funerals and other liturgies at MHR. I remember attending the funeral of a gay man with AIDS at which McGrann presided, and hearing him speak of his dissent from the institutional church and his belief that God does indeed bless loving gay relationships.

12. Jean-Guy Lussier, C.S.C., "The Roman Catholic Archdiocese of San Francisco and its response to the AIDS epidemic" (M.A. diss., Graduate Theological Union: Berkeley, 1989), 139–45.

13. Donal Godfrey, "A Church Living with AIDS." *The Month,* February 1996, 61.

14. Richard Rodriguez, *Days of Obligation: An Argument with My Mexican Father* (Penguin Books: London, 1993), 43–47. Richard Rodriguez beautifully describes one such ritual at MHR in his book *Days of Obligation.* Rodriguez moved back to San Francisco in 1979.

15. Colleen O'Connor, "Will America's Churches Ever Accept Homosexuality?," http://www.gracecathedral.org/enrichment/features/fea_19990801_f03_right.html.

16. Daniel Kanter, "Sermon: Visions of the Church," preached at the U. U. Church of Reston, Virginia, March 4, 2001, available at http://www.uureston.org/minister/sermons/guest/kanter.htm. Kanter quoted the Rodriguez passage about the commissioning of the AIDS Support Group in a sermon, and gave Most Holy Redeemer as an example of a parish that he says teaches him how to love:

17. Paul Claude, quoted by Anthony McGuire in his introductory remarks for the opening of the Forty Hours devotions at the parish. Undated and unpublished.

18. Lussier, 158.

19. Undated and unpublished.

20. John R. Quinn, homily delivered at MHR on the Feast of the Transfiguration, August 6, 1989, unpublished. Quinn also spoke out against recent violent attacks on gay people.

Jim Stultz, cited by Quinn, wrote a moving article in *America* magazine, "Towards a Spirituality for Victims of AIDS," 28 June 1986, 509-11: "Within the church there has been prejudice against homosexual people. But the AIDS epidemic has created a role for homosexuals in the church and in Christian life. Those who have contracted AIDS or ARC have an opportunity to share in a special way in the redemptive life of Jesus and of His church. It is urgent that they be helped to understand this opportunity and to seize it."

21. In April 1985, Quinn appointed Fr. Michael Lopes, O.P, to serve as the first Roman Catholic archdiocesan chaplain to AIDS patients and their families. Other priest chaplains to the AIDS community in San Francisco include Leo Hombach, S.J., and later, Tom Hayes, O. M. I., who for years resided at Most Holy Redeemer.

22. Don Lattin, "How AIDS brought gays and a parish together," *San Francisco Examiner,* July 28, 1986.

23. See Anthony McGuire, "Response to AIDS," 13.

24. "Forty Hours Devotion," *Catholic Encyclopedia*, 1909.

25. Thomas Michael, whose family name was McCormick, did indeed die from AIDS complications just as he had predicted in *The New Yorker*. I attended his funeral five years later. In a packed church we listened to many people, gay and straight alike, describe how Thomas Michael had touched their lives. I was impressed at the ability of the community to both cry and laugh during the service. It truly was a celebration of his life.

26. Anonymous, "Devotion," in "Talk of the Town," *New Yorker,* August 29, 1986.

27. Unpublished.

28. Most Holy Redeemer bulletin, Sunday, August 19, 1986.

29. February 4, 2001 interview by author.

30. Anthony McGuire, "Forty Hours Devotion: Pastor Muses the Morning After," letter to the Most Holy Redeemer Parish community, September 1987.

31. James Hanvey, S.J., *The Tablet,* April 4, 1987. Hanvey attended MHR during a summer spent in San Francisco.

32. George Higginson, interview by author, tape recording: San Francisco, April 25, 2001. Marie and the other elderly women in the parish like her remained pious and traditional Catholics, yet were able to reach out and embrace the gay community and those with AIDS with love. If such a transition was possible for them, there is hope it will also be possible in other parishes and in the wider communion.

33. Michael Vargas, interview by author, tape recording: San Francisco, October 5, 2001.

34. October 22, 2001 interview by author.

35. John Oddo, an openly gay man, had been hired as Music Director under Moriarty as pastor, owing to the influence of gay deacon Laurence Rolle.

36. Bob Werkheiser on accepting the award given to the late Marie Krystofiak at the "In-Kindness Awards" ceremony held by the Most Holy Redeemer AIDS Support Group, October 28, 2001.

37. February 20, 2001 interview by author.

38. Most Holy Redeemer bulletin, October 28, 1984.

39. See the description of Cliff Morrison by Randy Shilts in *And The Band Played On: Politics, People, and the AIDS Epidemic* (St. Martin's Press: New York, 1987),

355: "Cliff Morrison, a gay clinical nurse specialist, organized and designed the ward as he saw fit, because the more important hospital administrators all seemed rather embarrassed by the ward and the disease. The thirty-two-year old Morrison was a dedicated idealist who disliked the hierarchical doctor-nurse-patient model that dominated hospitals. Doctors would not run this ward, he would; and he wouldn't even call himself head nurse, preferring instead the less authoritative moniker of 'nursing coordinator.' . . . When Cliff Morrison and Dr. Paul Volberding, the AIDS Clinic director, cut the ribbon for the opening of Ward 5B on that Tuesday afternoon, Volberding was amazed that hospitals elsewhere, particularly in New York City, weren't planning similar wards."

Shilts also describes how Morrison instituted then unorthodox policies in Ward 5B. Up until this time an ailing man's biological family had been given all prerogatives in deciding who saw a patient in a critical care unit: "However, an unseemly conflict had arisen recently when one patient's mother marched into her dying son's room and ordered out his longtime lover. 'I'm his mother and I don't want any faggots in this room,' she announced brusquely. 'And I don't want any of those nurses who are faggots. They did this to him.'

"The patient broke down crying but was unable to speak because he was on a ventilator. A few days later, he died without seeing his lover again.

"Morrison announced the new 5B policy: that all patients designate their significant others who would have visiting privileges. As far as Morrison was concerned the definition of the American family had changed. It should be the right of patients to define their families, not the right of the hospital." (395)

40. McGuire, Most Holy Redeemer bulletin, October 28, 1984.

41. Dale Meyer was asked by Archbishop to assess the AIDS needs of the city in order that Catholic Charities could provide services in areas that were being overlooked. The Peter Claver Community, which provided housing for homeless people living with AIDS, was one result of this inquiry. Meyer told the Archbishop privately that he was an out gay man and that he did not want to work for the diocese unless that was acceptable to the Archbishop.

42. *And the Band Played On,* 377: "[The Castro's] collective concern fuelled the most dramatic shift in behaviour since the contemporary gay movement was forged in the Stonewall riots of 1969. Non-sexual social alternatives thrived. A half-block off Castro Street, the Castro Country Club flourished, offering gay men a relaxed, alcohol-free environment in which they could play Trivial Pursuit and canasta away from the heavy cruise scenes in gay bars. Gay Alcoholics Anonymous Groups proliferated in church basements of gay neighbourhoods throughout the city. Weekly bingo at Most Holy Redeemer Church, two blocks off Castro Street, found an untapped market among gay men, who started crowding the church basement every Wednesday night." The Castro Country Club was founded, and at one time owned, by an openly gay parishioner at MHR, Joseph Healy; Healy has since become a priest in the diocese of San Francisco. Gay AA meetings meet in the old Most Holy Redeemer School cafeteria and in the Ellard Hall beneath the church.

43. Most Holy Redeemer bulletin, January 10, 1988.

44. Undated and unpublished, provided to author by McGuire.

45. October 22, 2001, interview by author.

46. Transcript of Dutch television documentary about Most Holy Redeemer. I borrowed the video tape from Anthony McGuire; unfortunately the credits were not taped.

47. Donal Godfrey, "Lifelines," *AMDG*, Dublin, 1996, 20.

48. Anonymous, "Hospice to Lease Convent," *Parish Herald, Most Holy Redeemer Catholic Church,* August 15, 1985, 1.

49. Another example of MHR's collaborative charism was an interfaith conference on AIDS held at the parish and other venues in San Francisco in 1999. Representatives from Catholic, Buddhist, Jewish, Islamic, Native American, Protestant, Orthodox, and Hindu traditions attended the conference: "A Call to Oneness: A Conference on Compassion and HIV/AIDS Disease."

50. Anthony McGuire, "Life Begins at 80," a talk given to the parish community as part of the Centennial celebrations, June 15, 2002.

51. Anthony McGuire, quoted by Lussier, 151.

52. See Tammy Hyun Joo Kresta, "S.F. Hospice Shows Others the Way; Home-Style Care for AIDS Patients Is Model for World," *San Francisco Examiner,* October 18, 1993, A4.

53. Rand Richards, *Historic Walks in San Francisco* (Heritage House Publishers: San Francisco, 2002), 6.

54. Unpublished sermon provided to author. One person who attended the service told me there was not a dry eye in the church that morning. Calvo received a good number of letters after his sermon, including one dated April 1, 1991: "I am writing to let you know I attended your celebration of Easter the other day at MHR. I have attended many previous services at MHR and am always rejuvenated in spirit and of course with the Lord.

"Somehow this last Sunday upon hearing your superb homily it touched me very emotionally. During that time you made me reflect on my personal goals, my parents and family, my close friends who have left me, and especially my own existence. You see, I also had received the news of being positive. Hearing you brought spiritual strength and comfort which lies ahead. You've made me more aware of accepting the unfortunate and not feeling guilty. Your message is so real, so soothing, and yet positive in the path to live. What lies ahead for me is in God's hands, and knowing that gives me strength in my work and personal goals. I want to thank you as you've touched me as a sign from above."

55. Charles R. Carroll, *American Catholicism: The Saints and Sinners Who Built America's Most Powerful Church* (Times Books, Random House: New York, 1997), 352–53.

56. Hayes is referring to the fact that the rectory looks out over Collingwood Park, notorious as a cruising-place at night where gay men meet. Again, in a homily on Trinity Sunday, July 18, 2000, Hayes declared that MHR stands for something in the neighborhood—it makes a statement: "I live in a board-and-care home next door. I look out of the window. Next week I will talk about what I see after dark! I see the Marian shrine being explained to a child, I see a drunk holding onto bars for security and getting a sandwich at our door, visitors getting an explanation of the restoration

project, four or five guys—one guy is loitering. He has spray-on black pants! He crosses himself. Aren't Roman Catholics interesting people? . . . MHR is a sign of faith. As a community we bring life to the marketplace, from this Eucharistic life. We need to share it so others can be invited to come in. . . . This is our Support Group. Our God is a community of persons united in love. We are bound together as a community of faith. This faith will send us home to the heart of God."

57. Unpublished homily, September 24, 2000.

58. Zachary Shore, interview by author, tape recording: San Francisco, February 22, 2001.

59. Richard L. Smith, *AIDS, Gays and the American Catholic Church* (The Pilgrim Press: Cleveland, 1994), 135.

Chapter Four

Father Zachary Shore

Zachary Shore grew up just over the hill from MHR in Noe Valley, and began his adult religious life as a De La Salle brother. After leaving the order, he was ordained a priest in 1981. Shore was appointed pastor of Most Holy Redeemer in 1989, but in an unusual arrangement, spent six months as co-pastor with Tony McGuire until July 1st of 1990. The understanding with Archbishop Quinn, perhaps from a reflex to protect the little parish that had taught him so much, was that Shore would get another assignment if he and MHR didn't suit each other.

Here I consider Shore's pastorate only from the perspective of the continuing integration of the gay community into the life of the parish.[1] By 1990, Most Holy Redeemer was most definitely the Roman Catholic Church with the largest percentage of 'out' gay parishioners in the world. Gay people themselves sometimes find it "too gay." They may come to Most Holy Redeemer to reconcile their sexuality and their faith, and if they succeed, they may no longer need Most Holy Redeemer. They may switch to a more "ordinary" parish, closer to home, or with a bigger choir, or more or less ethnic diversity. If they fail, they may give up Catholic worship altogether.

No human community remains static, and certainly Most Holy Redeemer changed over the course of Shore's time as pastor. So did Shore. A relative innocent to the complexities of the Castro, he had much to learn from McGuire and the parishioners about the local culture, about AIDS, about the ways in which the gays and the grays had found common ground. Kind and unassuming by nature, Shore found himself able to relax and become comfortable, for instance, with being hugged by parishioners, which at first made him nervous. Hugging was part of MHR's vocabulary, he realized. He learned to be pleased the parish found him so approachable, and eventually sustained dozens, sometimes hundreds of hugs every Sunday.

The parish warmed to Shore's easygoing manner, found him personally compassionate and nurturing. Lisa Middleton, a transgender parishioner, remembers going to him for confession:

> I went into the church on a Saturday afternoon. I sat in the pew for a while and then I went in and had confession with Fr. Shore. I am not one who goes frequently, but it was a wonderful healing time.
>
> It was incredibly long. I felt I could tell the truth. I told him what I was going through, what I was trying to do. At that time, I was still living as a male. I was up here for work, but at some time in the near future I would be coming out, and that was nice to be able to say. He gave me some advice on getting into the parish, suggesting I start with one of the quieter masses such as the five p.m. Saturday mass.
>
> I felt I was around people I could be comfortable with. I wanted to hide [in the back] pew and I did that for about two or three years. The church had been remodeled. I was at the back of the church, but now at the ten a.m. mass. I just stayed there and tried to find a peaceful place for me, and it was just a little over a year later that I came out as transsexual here at work. I was still living as a man. My work hours were as a male and everything else I did from the moment I left work until I came back to work was as a female. That was unbelievably stressful. MHR, the people there, were a wonderful place to go every Sunday. I prayed for help to get through that week and I did. There were an awful lot of people that helped me. I started getting more active in church.

For many years while Shore was pastor, a sign outside the church proclaimed: "God's inclusive love proclaimed here. We welcome and affirm all people, the people of every race, gender, sexual orientation and place of national origin." And for the centennial observance in 2001, banners were placed on lampposts in the neighborhood representing MHR's bell tower, reading: "An inclusive Catholic Community." Even so, the parish shares some of the limitations as well as the strengths of the neighborhood. The Castro, like the parish, although changing yet again, still remains largely male and gay, which some women at Most Holy Redeemer find frustrating. Christine McQuiston had lapsed from the Church for many years, before she discovered Most Holy Redeemer. Not many women I interviewed seemed to agree with McQuiston; but then, women who do, might find it difficult to stay:

> When I was telling you how coming to Mass was aggravating Zoe [McQuiston's partner] more than it was nourishing her, it has more to do with misogyny and other kinds of exclusion on the part of the church than just homophobia. The shadow side of the "gay community" is the sexism that manifests on both sides of the gender coin. Put the misogynistic tendencies of a large community of gay men together with the institutional misogyny of the church, and you have a sit-

uation that is neither psychologically nor spiritually supportive for women. I'm sorry to say, but this is the real shadow side of the MHR community.[2]

Like McGuire, Shore was never judgmental about his parishioners' lives, enjoyed the neighborhood's diversity rather than feeling threatened by it; but in other respects his style was very different from Father Tony's. The parish music director, John Oddo, captures it succinctly:

> Well, Tony and Zachary are very different people, and I think one of the good things Zachary has brought to the parish is that he is kind of innocent. I think of the baptism we did of the first child of a gay couple. Tony would not have done that; at least in the way we did it.
>
> Under Zachary the parishioners have been able to do some things on their own. It has been good. We have dances now; we have same-sex couples dancing together now. That is a big change. That would not have happened under Tony. There was a St. Patrick's dance but that was for the old guard.
>
> It is about letting the parish be what it would be if you let it be what it was. Zachary's gift to the parish is allowing us to be ourselves.[3]

Shore's laissez-faire management style allowed parishioners to take certain initiatives McGuire might have stalled. Unquestionably, McGuire had a gift for embracing diversity, and brought about a tremendous transformation in the parish. He was, however, more aware of church politics and always had an eye on the line between what might and what might not be acceptable to the archdiocese. There were times when McGuire judged the time was wrong for some gesture his gay parishioners wanted to make—the incident of the lector announcing a gay couple's anniversary, for instance. McGuire felt the time was not yet right for such public acknowledgments of gay relationships, even though they were *de facto* acknowledged by him and everyone else in the parish. Under Shore as pastor, however, gay partnerships were almost routinely acknowledged. The entire congregation applauded when among the announcements before mass one Sunday was congratulations on the thirtieth anniversary of Ken Dunphy and his partner Richard. I doubt Shore was responsible for the announcement, but he didn't object to it. Father Shore did not compel: he allowed.

The baptism of children being raised by gay couples took place publicly at the ten a.m. Sunday liturgy. McGuire was never presented with the issue: in his time, no gay or lesbian couple had come forward with a child to be baptized. Adoption or co-parenting arrangements resulting in families headed by gay couples were rare then, even in San Francisco. One gay couple, Dan McPherson and Kevin Gogin, active MHR parishioners while McGuire was pastor, did adopt a daughter, Sarah, in 1988, but she was quietly baptized outside the parish

at St. Ignatius Church. Sarah's regular presence with them at mass got the
parish accustomed to a new kind of family, Catholic and gay. As deacon at Most
Holy Redeemer then, I remember the love and attention Sarah received from
the congregation.

Rob Lane and Don Propstra's adopted son Timothy was baptized at a regular liturgy in the parish on October 21, 1990. Lane is Catholic and Propstra
Protestant. Since a Catholic Church service was an impossibility, they'd held
a commitment ceremony at a Unitarian church, with a reception following at
the Fairmont Hotel. Over the years, a number of MHR's gay and lesbian couples have held weddings or commitment ceremonies, occasionally with a
Catholic priest taking some prominent role, but never a priest from Most Holy
Redeemer. Some MHR priests would attend the post-ceremony receptions;
other priests might attend the services simply as friends, careful to take no
role that could be construed as "official" and which might compromise them.

Lane and Propstra wanted their son brought up Catholic and baptized in
church. As Rob Lane tells it,

> My family, all Catholics, all came to the [commitment] ceremony. Then the next
> day, a Sunday, they had a mass with Tom, my priest friend from the East Coast,
> who had also come to attend our commitment ceremony. . . . We scheduled a
> brunch for after mass, at which stage we were going to tell them that we were
> expecting Timothy. It went well; after all, we were now married!
>
> Timothy arrived one month after our commitment ceremony. It was hectic. Fr.
> Shore did not really know us at this stage, but he agreed to meet with us.
>
> He had a lot more to say than I expected. Father said, "Well who is going to
> take care of this child?" He got into all these kind of questions. It was his first
> time dealing with anything like this. It threw Don off; the questions were intim-
> idating and investigative by nature. Deep down, I was hurt and confused, ask-
> ing what the hell this was all about, not feeling totally comfortable about what
> we had done. But also as new adoptive parents, there is a certain amount of a
> defensive mechanism that adoptive parents put up to welcome their child for the
> sake of the child, and if you are a gay man, that is added to with all the church
> stuff. However, at some point Father Shore changed. I think he just started to
> think in terms of the child.
>
> So Timothy was baptized at the main Sunday 10 a.m. Mass. Kevin and Dan
> [Gogin and McPherson] were the godparents. We had a big party afterwards. We
> were new at being parents, new at being gay parents, new at being in a commu-
> nity and standing up in front of it. We had no role models around us of men hav-
> ing children so that was new. . . . I remember the parishioners being very excited
> at the time, people clapped. There was a lot of positive reaction. . . .
>
> For some parishioners however there was an uneasiness about the situation.
> Some men of the parish would not tolerate noise [i.e., the noise of children],
> they were not used to it.[4]

Timothy Lane-Propstra was baptized at Most Holy Redeemer, just as the child of any married couple in the parish would have been, as part of the ten a.m. on a Sunday morning. At the end of the ceremony Shore said to the congregation, "I give you Timothy." People clapped and clapped for a long time, becoming emotional.

At Shore's going-away party in 2002, the groundbreaking event was remembered. Even Timothy spoke. As the gay newspaper *Bay Area Reporter* relates, in part:

> Shore related that after the baptism he got a phone call from the bishop.[5] "One of the parishioners had complained about the hoopla. 'What hoopla?'" Shore claimed he said, his voice lifting into an upper register of feigned innocence.
>
> One of the last speakers was Timothy himself, who's now 11. "I'd like to say thank you to Father Shore for being there my whole life."[6]

While this sort of baptism has become an unremarkable part of the life of Most Holy Redeemer, it remains rare and in many places unheard of in other Catholic parishes. Lane and Propstra now have two other children, Lindsey and Christopher, also baptized at Most Holy Redeemer.

The relationship of the parish to the diocese also changed under Shore, especially when Archbishop William Levada replaced Archbishop Quinn, upon Quinn's early retirement. Levada took an aloof, hands-off approach to the parish, and did not visit MHR for over a year. Levada involved himself in a public dispute with the Sisters of Perpetual Indulgence[7] and took political positions, which were perceived as anti-gay, or at least insensitive to the community, having serious negative effects on the life of the parish.

> During the 1990's, the Archdiocese engaged in several public policy disputes in its efforts to clearly articulate and uphold the Church's teaching on marriage and sexuality. The Archdiocese consistently opposed attempts to place "domestic partners" on the same level as married couples. In March 1996, Archbishop Levada publicly opposed the Mayor of San Francisco's "recognition ceremony" for same-sex marriages ["domestic partnerships," actually]. In 2000, the archdiocese supported a state ballot initiative that stipulated that the state recognizes only marriage between a man and a woman.[8]

Without comment, Levada did not visit the parish's annual Forty Hours Devotion for AIDS, until in November 2002 he asked to be invited to the closing Forty Hours mass. Quinn made many private visits to gay men close to death from AIDS. No one has related such a story to me about his successor.

Some parishioners were content that Levada stayed away; at least he left the parish alone. Most however were disappointed, if not upset, that what the

new archbishop had to say to and about the gay community was so over-
whelmingly negative. Relations were strained, and everyone felt it.[9]

> We hold Levada at arms length. We don't know if it is safe to let him closer. My
> impression is he would like us to disappear and go away—but he hopes we
> won't make too much noise if he doesn't pay attention to us. Levada has never in-
> tervened. I was involved in the Restoration project when he came to re-dedicate
> the church. There was a knocking [at the church door] as part of the ritual, and
> I had a fleeting thought to myself: Do we really want to let him in?
>
> It was also very powerful to see him anoint the walls of the church and the al-
> tar. In some ways it said, we do have a place here. We are still a church of the
> diocese. I was ambivalent about it all.[10]

The far-off Rome World Pride millennial celebration in 2000 became a new
source of friction. A world gay pride event in Rome was unwelcome to the
Vatican, from whose perspective it was an insult to the jubilee year observing
the two thousandth anniversary of the birth of Christ. Millions of pilgrims
would be visiting Rome at exactly the same time as the gay pride event. Archbishop Levada's office sent TV-broadcast videotapes of the San Francisco's
gay pride parade to the Vatican, presumably as an aid in projecting what sort
of spectacle a major gay parade in Rome might be. Levada was quoted saying: "When asked [in Rome] in a conversation about the annual Gay Pride
Event in San Francisco, I said that I personally had not seen it, because I usually go out of town. I said that there were reports of public displays of nudity
that were offensive and displays of costumes that ridicule Catholic leaders
and members of religious orders."[11] Appalled by the news coverage of the San
Francisco parade—the Vatican took its case to the city of Rome, asking au-
thorities to ban the event. Rome Pride went ahead as scheduled, although
there was a rerouting of the parade owing to the Vatican pressure. Certainly
Levada caused deep offense to many MHR parishioners by sending the news
videos. The Van Ettens, for instance, were enraged and took the matter to the
next parish council meeting. The council spent an hour discussing the matter,
then came to a consensus to ask parishioners to write to the archbishop expressing their feelings on the issue. A flyer placed in the June 11 bulletin
stated:

> Next month's World Pride Celebration in Rome was planned and scheduled so
> it would not conflict with other events in the Eternal City and not offend the
> Vatican. Recently the Vatican has voiced its displeasure with the Celebration,
> saying it is inappropriate to be held in Rome during a Jubilee Year. Archbishop
> Levada's office has provided Rome with a videotape of San Francisco's Gay
> Pride Parade (Channel 20, 1998). Also sent was an *NBC-TV Extra* feature on
> the Sisters of Perpetual Indulgence, including footage of them in a public pa-

rade, and scenes from a June 1994 public street demonstration showing gay men dancing naked, and the next day's gay Pride Parade, also with scenes of public nudity," according to Maurice Healy, a spokesman for the Archdiocese of San Francisco.

Since Archbishop Levada's arrival in San Francisco, there has been infrequent communication between him and the parish. The Parish Council believes that the time has come for us to communicate in a new way with the Archbishop.

We ask for your help in writing the Archbishop a brief letter focused on two points: in the spirit of reconciliation, 1. How do you feel about the Archbishop's actions regarding the World Pride Celebration, and 2. Regarding his recent actions, what do you need of him as a leader of your local community?

. . . Bring your letter to mass next weekend, where it will be collected for delivery to the Archbishop.

That Sunday, Pentecost Sunday, Ric Meyer got up before the 10 a.m. assembly to address about the situation and encourage letters to the archbishop to be brought to church the following Sunday.[12]

Not everyone in the parish was in favor of a confrontational approach. Ellen Grund, a parishioner in a committed relationship with an Episcopal woman priest, wrote a letter to the parish council, which presents the ongoing dilemma of MHR well:

Ever since our last meeting, I have been uneasy with the Parish Council's endorsement of a letter writing campaign to the Archbishop. After a few days of thinking it over, I realized that this issue and our response are both worthy of more than the brief, hurried, and sometimes heated attention we were able to give it at our last meeting. The sense of urgency brought to our attention by our guests may have moved us into action before we had a chance to fully digest the issue. I urge Fr. Shore and the Council to step back and collectively weigh the possible ramifications of our actions before we proceed further.

We are blessed with a supportive pastor, a beautiful church, and a tremendously loving community. We are also blessed that the Archbishop has supported the restoration of MHR and Fr. Shore's ministry here. Please consider the potential cost of this direct confrontation as a parish. As church history will attest, change is painfully slow and a letter writing campaign is unlikely to speed it along. I fear if we push too hard as a parish we risk losing the blessings we do have. In essence, MHR could be "martyred for the cause"; and the inclusive love of Christ will be greatly furthered by continuing to thrive as an inclusive parish. Yes, this is a battle we need to fight, but perhaps not on this stage.

Since Sunday I have heard from several parishioners who were confused by the request because they were not aware of the World Pride event or the Archbishop's response, and therefore did not feel they had adequate information to write a letter. Others expressed anger toward the method of using a letter writing campaign. Still others felt the effort futile, given the many letters that have been written to the Archbishop before. There also seems to be a lack of parish consensus about how to, or even if we should, deal formally with this event as a parish. Given these problems, we are unlikely to collect letters that accurately reflect the parish as a whole.

Let's use the collection of letters on Sunday as an opportunity to better understand our community. Then a parish meeting can be held to openly discuss this issue, much as we did when Gramick and Nugent were silenced by Rome. Since any action we take at the parish level impacts the entire community, perhaps we should allow the entire community to help decide what action to take. At a minimum, I urge the Parish Council to meet again to discuss this further before sending the letters to the Archbishop,

Peace,

Ellen.[13]

Thomas Van Etten wrote in response:

While it is important to affirm our supportive pastor, our beautiful church and loving community . . . I oppose "closeting" our feelings regarding the abuse that we Roman Catholic Lesbian/Gay/Transgender people experience from the Roman Catholic Hierarchy. To remain silent is to collaborate in our own oppression by restricting our basic human right to follow our own conscience!

While discerning Ellen Grund's concerns, I cannot in good conscience condone her approach. I will never accept crumbs at the Banquet. Too many of my 56 years of life experience scream at me over and over again that "silence=death."

May I quote please from a wonderful book published in May 2000 by the University of Chicago Press authored by Mark D. Jordan. "One effect of the church's official discourse about homosexuality is just to keep dissidents busy rebutting them. Instead of building alternative forms of Catholic community, we spend our energy trying to explain, once again, why the latest Vatican pronouncement is unscriptural or self-contradictory or antiscientic. That's the sinister genius of Roman Catholicism: to prevent lesbians and gay people from being church; so that we are always reacting to something that we are not part of in an integral and intimate way."

If we remain silent we will never achieve equality in the Church that we all seem to love.

God Bless each and every one of us,

Thomas Van Etten.[14]

One hundred twenty-five letters to the archbishop were delivered to Most Holy Redeemers by parishioners that Sunday—a substantial number, though it represented less than a third of those attending mass. Quite apart from their (unknown) eventual effect on the archbishop, the letters are revealing about how members of the MHR congregation perceive their relationship with the institutional Church. Christine McQuiston's partner, Zobrieta (Zoe) Puckett, wrote:

I have attended services at Most Holy Redeemer Church for the past five years, along with my life partner and her mother. During my childhood I attended the Church of Christ, where I received baptism in Jesus Christ. . . .

Not everyone knows that he or she is gay or lesbian during childhood but many do. I know that I certainly did, although I had no words to describe why I felt the way that I did. I came from a closed society where even today there is much censoring of literature and other media. There was no gay or lesbian community so no one "infected me with lesbianism." It is simply how God created me.

The images that you submitted to the Vatican about the gay community are extremely prejudiced. You could have chosen to balance the images with pictures of PFLAG [Parents and Friends of Lesbians and Gays], marching thousands strong and fully clothed. You could have included photos of the numerous contingencies of marching gay and lesbian professionals, such as firefighters, police officers, and healthcare workers, who also march with their clothes on. I could name hundreds of other marchers, including the Most Holy Redeemer parishioners, who march in the parade with pride and dignity. The news media targets those within the gay community who behave provocatively and it exploits them to get more viewers. Unfortunately, those tactics usually work. Why did you behave like the press does? As an overseer of a predominantly gay parish, you could have come to our parish and met some of our members, in order to have been able to accurately depict us as we really are.

Do you honestly think that Jesus would have approved of the way you depicted gays and lesbians, by submitting only negative images to those in Rome, already sick from fear of us? Why did you neglect to say anything positive about us? Will the holocaust that you are helping to bring into the world be any less tragic than the Jewish Holocaust? In twenty years, will your church be compelled to apologize to gays and lesbians for its failure to act, as the church so recently did to Jewish people? These questions haunt me now. Perhaps they will haunt you in the future when you witness the destruction that you are helping to create. Over the past year, hate crimes against gays and lesbians has increased by 85% throughout the United States. Can't you see the writing on the wall? . . .

Finally, please realize that the behaviors [in gay men and lesbians] that offend you so greatly stem from a childhood of being shamed because of their sexual identities, even if they don't realize that they are gay or lesbian at the time. When you tell a child that he or she is a flower, they will grow up as a flower. When you tell the same child that he or she is a weed that needs to be pulled out of the garden, that's just what you get. Is it any wonder that some gays and lesbians act out the negative images about homosexuals that they have been exposed to during childhood? It is estimated that there are over 125,000 homeless gay, lesbian, and transgender youth in the United States and 80% say that homophobia forced them out of their homes, putting them in harm's way. Your actions compound the problems that these children already face. Children absorb what we release like sponges absorb water. When you release your fear-inspired images of homosexuality, please be aware that children are present.[15]

These letters were bound together and Father Shore brought them to the Archbishop, along with Les Young, president of the parish council. Shore relates it as a cordial meeting lasting about an hour. The archbishop promised to read the letters and wanted to discuss their content at another, later meeting, which was arranged at the MHR rectory in December. Around fifteen parishioners were invited, gay and non-gay. Levada arrived with a folder, seemingly prepared to give a talk; however, the parish was able to set the agenda by starting off with a time of prayer. Afterward Shore welcomed Levada, Bishop Wester, and Sr. Antonio Heaphy PBVM, from the Chancery Office who had accompanied them. Shore also thanked Levada for coming and introduced each parishioner present, telling Levada something about his or her affiliation with the parish. Jim Gunther, present with his male partner Jamie Cherrie, then said to the archbishop: "We don't really know you. We read a lot about you, but we don't really know who you are. Why did you become a priest?" Eyes darted nervously around the room, everyone wondering where the question could possibly lead. The archbishop began to talk about his vocation to the priesthood, his parents, his schooling, and then in turn he asked Jim: "What do you like about the Church?" Gunther then spoke about the Church's structures, history, and traditions. Another parishioner began talking about his faith journey and what attracted him to Most Holy Redeemer. People began to free up and express themselves in a conversational rather than a confrontational way. Shore also shared his vocation story.

> So after an hour and a half of just sharing our faith journey, the whole hope was that he would get to see us in a different way, that we weren't militant, that we weren't there to attack him in any particular way, but that we were a faith community.
>
> Jamie Cherrie asked him if he had the videotape history of the gay community made for public television. He gave this video to Levada asking him to watch it so that he might get a broader understanding. . . .
>
> Levada ended with a prayer, and then stayed about twenty minutes for refreshments. Bishop Wester stayed longer to chat. Nobody was rushing out the door. The conclusion was that the dialogue should continue.[16]

The dialogue seems to have stalled somewhat in the past years. Perhaps it has never truly begun. Kathy Carey, formerly on staff at MHR as Pastoral Associate and Director of Religious Education, said that someone in the Chancery asked Levada about the meeting:

> Well, he just kind of shrugged his shoulders and said, "It was a nice evening, but it wasn't anything like I had anticipated." Maybe we were a little too cautious. But I think there is this attempt to do some dialogue.

The ecclesiology is that we are here and we do belong to the church, the general church, and it is saying you know we are not going away. I think he knows that, and so instead of going around making announcements, which he is inclined to do on subjects, I think he is just sort of backing off and staying away. I think that is his way of dealing with it.

And I think that is what the rest of the church does. It's an ecclesiology of, "Well, you know, let them stay in their ghetto." I think it is prejudice.[17]

I sense that Levada's attitude to the parish changed in the time before his appointment to Rome as Prefect of the Congregation for the Faith on May 13, 2005 by Pope Benedict XVI. As time went on he seemed to be more relaxed with the parish. He gave a talk as part of the parish centennial celebration and presided at two Sunday masses in 2002. It may not seem like much, but it represented progress for him to acknowledge the gay community and its contribution in his talk to the parish. Ironic that the angry reaction to his sending sensational news videos to Rome ultimately became a way to break the ice. However, it should be noted that although Levada became more pastoral with time, his views basically did not change. It was Levada who ended the specific ministry for gay and lesbian Catholics in the Diocese leaving this work up to local parishes such as Most Holy Redeemer. Indeed in April 2005 Levada led a march of about 1,000 through the streets of San Francisco to protest gay marriage.

Levada's successor in San Francisco is Archbishop George Niederauer, previously Bishop of Salt Lake City. He was installed as Archbishop of San Francisco on February 15, 2006. Niederauer comes to San Francisco with the reputation of being pastorally sensitive to the gay community. Niederauer, unlike most civic leaders in Salt Lake city, opposed an amendment to outlaw same-sex marriage in Utah saying it was unnecessary. From 1992 to 1994 Niederauer was comfortable living at St. Victor's parish in predominantly gay West Hollywood. In 2007 Niederauer is planning his first visit to Most Holy Redeemer parish.

To my mind, the middle course steered by the parish is both more Christian and more effective than defiance or resentful submission. Fr. James Alison, says it best:

The one sure way to prevent church teaching from being changed except in the direction of more closed-mindedness is to pander to the paranoia, which under girds it by playing its game. While those upholding the teaching and those attacking it are locked in the world of fratricide disguised as sacred paternity, with all its bizarre twists, then no one gets anywhere. Instead we get "innocent children" trying to gang up on wicked "father-figures," or a "victim" hierarchy claiming that it has never hurt anyone, but protesting its need to speak the "divine truth" against those who would sully and "affront" it. This has nothing to do with the revelation of God in Christ—except as a parody of it, on both sides.[18]

I was reminded of Alison's point one day when presiding. After mass, a local TV crew turned up to interview parishioners about something then-Archbishop Quinn had said about domestic partner benefits or some such matter. I was proud of those parishioners who were shown on the news that night. They simply stated both their respect for, and yet their disagreement with the archbishop, as Catholics themselves. They all stated their dissent in conscience from what he had said, and left it at that.

MHR itself has marched as a parish in the San Francisco Gay Freedom/Gay Pride Day parade since 1998. The parish had previously set up information booths at events like the Castro Street Fair and Gay Pride, or sold beer as a fundraiser for the AIDS Support Group, and many, maybe most parishioners had marched in the parade before under the banners of other community groups. The idea of marching as Most Holy Redeemer was an initiative of parishioners. Kathy Carey thinks Father Shore only reluctantly went along with the idea, when it was clear it would go ahead with or without his blessing.[19] He wrote a short letter those marching could hand out to the crowds inviting people to come to church. It was the first time a Roman Catholic parish in San Francisco had marched in a gay pride parade. A gay Internet site reported:

> As if to add paradox to a vast mix of pride-time outpourings, a Roman Catholic group—without begging the Pope's blessing—took part as marchers for the first time in the parade's history. By doing so, San Francisco's Most Holy Redeemer parish thereby positioned itself to be either expurgated or later celebrated by Roman Catholicism's official record keepers.[20]

Actually, it wasn't the first time that a Catholic *group* had marched in the parade. Dignity, the Friends of Peter Claver Community, and Holy Spirit parish in Berkeley had marched on other occasions.[21] But it was a first for a Catholic *parish* in San Francisco. Parishioners who marched were unsure what to expect, some expected the worst, but found themselves moved by the overwhelming positive response from the crowds. Since 1998, taking part in the Pride Parade has become an MHR tradition. Shore's semi-tacit sanctioning of a parish presence in the parade lent the Church's legitimacy to this event of the gay community: "Congregations are places of belonging, but belonging to a religious community has a moral weight not always granted to other memberships."[22] Marching with the parishioners in a Roman collar, I too have been stirred by the response of the spectators. Many are shocked to see us. Some become emotional, weeping openly to see ordinary Catholics assembled as Catholics in such an unexpected context. Our unphotogenic, even drab presence seems to set off a hundred thousand interior fireworks. One amazed woman shouted to me: "But Father—I thought the pope was against this sort of thing!" An elderly woman, conservatively dressed, asked very matter-of-factly, "Father, what times are the masses in your parish?" San Francisco is far removed from Rome, and was certainly no less so in the Jubilee year 2000. In recent years this new parish tradition of taking part in the San Francisco Gay Pride Parade has been encouraged even more explicitly by the present pastor, Fr. Stephen Meriwether.

On the very day Pope John Paul II made a visit to the Roman prison of Regina Caeli to plead for clemency for all prisoners, he also spoke from his window during the recitation of the Angelus. "In the name of the Church of Rome, I cannot but express my bitterness at the insult to the Great Jubilee of 2000, and the offense to the Christian values of a city which is so dear to the hearts of all Catholics in the world." Though the pope did not name the World Pride celebration, the reference was clear. He went on to quote the catechism of the Church, which declares homosexual acts contrary to the laws of nature. "The number of men and women with deeply rooted homosexual tendencies is not negligible. This objectively disordered inclination is for the greater part of them a trial. They must be treated with respect, compassion, and delicacy. Any sign of unjust discrimination against them must be avoided. Such people are called to carry out the Will of God in their lives, and if they are Christian, to unite the difficulties they encounter as a result of their condition to the Lord's sacrifice on the cross."[23] The crowd applauded—just as the San Francisco Pride crowds applauded my fellow parishioners and me as we made our way down Market Street behind a banner that read MOST HOLY REDEEMER CATHOLIC CHURCH.

The images were powerful ones. There was the frail Pope John Paul II asking clemency for prisoners, while brawny prisoners in T-shirts served as altar boys, cried and kissed the pontiff's ring.

Then came the bad news in this year dedicated by the pope to redemption and pardon. John Paul bitterly condemned gays for holding a festival and a parade in Rome the same year as the Roman Catholic Church's jubilee year. The pope said the festival was an 'offense to Christian values' and that homosexual acts are 'contrary to natural law.'

The pope asked clemency for felons who robbed, raped and killed, yet none for gays for holding a parade? There's something very wrong here.

True forgiveness is very hard even for the pope. You might say forgiveness is contrary to natural law. Vengeance, bitterness and jealousy come much more naturally. Why else would Christian teachings spend so much time on the subject to turning the other cheek and forgiving those who trespass against us? As

an admirer of the pope's intellect, courage and kindness toward the poor, I was
moved by his prisoners' mass, and heartened to see his generosity toward them
in a year he has dedicated to redemption and pardon.

Then he proceeded to show how difficult it could be to forgive and love one's
neighbors. I can forgive him. But if I were gay or Catholic, I don't think I
could.[24]

On parade day, June 25, 2000, Father Tom Hayes celebrated the eight a.m.
mass. He asked parishioners to join him in a special blessing for those who
would be marching that morning. Then, with his typical wit, he exhorted
those marching to make sure they gave a special blessing with the sign of the
cross to the television cameras (which show the parade live on local TV):
"You never know who may be watching you!"—a humorous reference to the
tapes the archbishop had sent to the Vatican the previous year.[25]

Then there was the Knight Initiative, Proposition 22, putting to California
voters the question of whether the state should refuse to recognize same-sex
marriages. The initiative did not in fact change existing California law, which
did not sanction same-sex marriage, and was seen by gays as just a fresh ex-
cuse for anti-gay rhetoric and right wing posturing. Nevertheless, the Catholic
bishops of California at their meeting decided to support the Knight Initiative
financially. The Archdiocese of San Francisco contributed $31,724 to the
campaign, claiming it came from a private donor (an odd admission, if strictly
true, some observed, since it could raise legal questions about the donor's
evading campaign-contribution limits). This California bishops' decision was
deeply resented at Most Holy Redeemer. Thomas VanEtten had a strong letter published in *The San Francisco Examiner*,[26] and wrote a more personal
letter to Archbishop Levada, who had published an editorial in the diocesan
newspaper defending the financial contributions:

Your Excellency,
I read your editorial in CATHOLIC SAN FRANCISCO dated March 19,
1999. . . .
Your opinions hurt those of us who are gay and lesbian and Roman Catholic.
I wish you could see our faces and hear our hearts at Most Holy Redeemer when
you say the things you say. . . . Why don't you take the time to come to Most
Holy Redeemer and talk with us and get to know us?
My partner Robert and I have been together for 31 years. . . . I would lay
down my life for Robert. We are very involved Roman Catholics. We love our
parish and we organized last years march in the Gay/Lesbian parade in June. It
was the first year that Most Holy Redeemer marched. We did it because we felt
that we were commanded by our Baptism to spread the good news of God's love
for all. Several people came back to the church as a result of our evangelization
in that parade.

You state in your editorial that "the good order of society itself requires us to draw the line to protect the institution of marriage and family." Robert and I are retired IBM employees. We worked at IBM for 27 years. We were superb performers in our jobs, paid our taxes, contributed money not only to the economy but also to charitable institutions. We volunteer our time. We give good example in our lives of long-term commitment to one another and our love for our faith. How can you possibly say that we are [adversely] affecting the good order of society?

Respectfully yours,
Thomas VanEtten

The California bishops' response to Proposition 22 provoked much soul-searching and anguish at Most Holy Redeemer. It also provoked soul-searching for the pastor, Zachary Shore:

I came home from my retreat and one of the parishioners showed me the headlines of a newspaper that headlined that the Californian catholic bishops were giving money to this Initiative. I didn't know much about it, but after the weekend masses people said to me that they expected me to say something about it. I said to them I honestly don't know enough about it.

That week I went to the Christian brothers camp on my day off at the Russian River and I felt something very negative within myself. I thought I needed to get it out, to express it. So while I was up there I wrote a letter to the Archbishop. I kept it twenty-four hours, then forty-eight hours. and redid a lot of it.

No one on the staff knew I had written that letter. The first time it was read was at mass. I read it at all three Sunday masses that weekend. I simply said I don't ever remember the church giving money for something political like this. At the 5.00 p.m. Saturday Vigil Mass, there was some clapping, maybe standing. At the 8.00 a.m. mass on the Sunday there was some clapping and some silence; that is the make-up of that mass. Then at the 10 a.m. it was overwhelming with standing and clapping, and more besides. I sent it to the Archbishop.[27]

The letter, which brought the parish to tears and to its feet, and thrust the unlikely Shore into the national media limelight:

Dear Archbishop,

A week ago, Friday, October 15, I was appalled to see the headlines of the San Francisco Examiner read: "Catholics' anti-gay funds." As a priest of the Archdiocese of San Francisco and Pastor of Most Holy Redeemer Church, I cannot accept the decision of the Bishops of California to allocate financial assistance to Senator Knight's Protection of Marriage Committee. Is there a right that Bishops have to use money that has been given to a diocese for the purpose of programs for the People of God, to be used for State Politics? I cannot remember whenever this was done before or whether parishioners were aware of it, if it was.

My second concern is, when will the Church start seeing Gay and Lesbian people with true compassion, love and understanding? Statements or publications by civic or religious leaders against the Gay Community are just another form of "Gay-bashing." It is not physical, but it certainly affects the emotions, fears and frustration of the community. Gays and Lesbians do belong to Christian communities and are trying to live out the message of the Gospels. Here at Most Holy Redeemer Church, which is probably the largest concentration of Gays and Lesbians in Northern California, share in the cross of Christ, when they see so many of their friends and parishioners die of AIDS. They take very seriously their role to support these victims by being trained in the Most Holy Redeemer AIDS Support Group as volunteers/caregivers. The parishioners take very seriously their prayer life by joining in the RENEW program, and small Faith communities. Many have been trained to be Eucharistic Ministers, bring Word and Sacrament to the homebound, Lectors and Acolytes. The Liturgy of Most Holy Redeemer Church is probably the best in the Archdiocese and the model for other parishes to strive for. The parish has implemented all that Vatican II asked for, even to a new remodeled Church that lends itself to prayer, excellent liturgies and community.

It is times like this, when the Archdiocese is about to allocate money to State politics that aim at the Gay Community, that the Community here at Most Holy Redeemer becomes very frustrated, hurt and angry. No one from the Archdiocesan Office has bothered to communicate with this parish to see how the parishioners are holding up under all this stress. No one has communicated to find out how the Pastor and his staff are doing under these trying circumstances. At times it feels as if we are an island afloat on our own.

It is very sad, as a Pastor, to hear frustrated parishioners say they are leaving the Church or are no longer going to support the Church or Archdiocesan Ministries. What they thought was a home, a place of acceptance and love and not bigotry, is nothing more than a place of tolerance and lip service.

I would hope, if it were not too late, to not give Archdiocesan money that has come from the people of God for a State issue. I pray that you and the Bishops of California will realize what your actions are doing to Gay and Lesbians in the Church of this State. I pray for the guidance of the Holy Spirit on all your future decisions.

Respectfully yours,

Rev. Zachary Shore, Pastor.[28]

Some time afterward, Shore met with Archbishop Levada and Auxiliary Bishop Wester. Shore forgets how the meeting came about:

It was a 45-minute meeting. I explained to the Archbishop that this was the first time I had ever written to a bishop in such a way. He told me that I had to express my feelings regarding the press coverage. I went through my letter and then he gave me his ideas about the letter. He did not put it down but he said it was the consensus of the Californian bishops, and not just one bishop, to support the Knight Initiative.

So I felt comfortable in that I had met with him, he listened to me. It was a good conversation. And again I tried to emphasize to him to be aware of this particular community, not just Most Holy Redeemer, but the gay community in general, when he was going to speak out, whether it is the church or whatever, there has to be a certain sensitivity. I even brought up the idea of creating a body of priests; maybe gay priests whom he could consult and who know the situation on the ground. He gave a kind of nod, not that I expected him realistically to set up a committee suddenly or anything like that. I wanted to plant an idea.[29]

Shore's letter brought him not only gratitude but great credibility in the gay community. It also helped bring healing with gay Catholics at Dignity, who awarded him a "Pax et Bonum" Award at their annual dinner.[30]

The *Bay Area Reporter* featured an article when Shore left MHR to take up his new appointment as pastor of Our Lady of the Visitacion:

"It's so appropriate. A dinner-dance is such a typical Father Shore event," said Michael Vargas, an administrator at the church, as the lights went down, candles flickered on the tables, and a Madonna song from the new sound system filled the parish hall.

"Do you know what you're getting into?" Shore remembered one of the parishioners asking when he first suggested the dances.

"They have dinner dances. We have dinner dances," Shore recalled he said as the first couple, two guys, both in jeans and button down shirts, ventured out onto the dance floor and executed a disco turn or two.

"We could dance with anyone that we wanted," said Roz Gallo, a chair of the pastoral committee [parish council president]. "We have two or three a year now."

Most Holy Redeemer, on Diamond Street in the Castro, calls itself "an inclusive Catholic community." By that the parishioners mean they invite gays and lesbians into the parish, which is part of a church whose doctrine says that their sex lives are a sin.

"We're a magnet parish for the gay and lesbian community. People come here from all over," said Vargas.[31]

And during Gay Pride week, after Shore's leaving was announced, parishioner Patrick Mulcahey wrote, in a farewell appreciation of his work as pastor:[32]

What Father exemplifies that the [parade] crowds on Market and elsewhere should see is how much further toward fixing the world a sense of fair play will carry you than any ideology, even ideologies we like. Father never thought twice about sticking up for us, whether with the archdiocese or the [*New York*] *Times*, because he never did it out of political correctness or with any agenda at all. His first and only concern was that human beings should treat other human beings with kindness and respect, and it is hands-down the best political tactic going, since nobody dares to oppose it. Do people plague you by asking how on earth you can be gay and Catholic? Tell them it's the only progressive way to be. People like Father Shore make Christianity a far superior plan to Don't ask, Don't Tell.

Sadly, the only car we're loading Father into this weekend is headed in the other direction, to Visitacion Valley and his new parish. Like you I will miss him terribly, his lantern jaw, his goofy smile, his shuffling gait on those big splayed feet, like somebody walking downhill on skis, his awful three-sizes-too-big wardrobe. (His going-away gift from the parish council and finance committee: a gift certificate from the Men's Warehouse.)

And like many of you, when I came back to the Church, Father Shore was the one they had minding the door. The worst bouncer who ever lived.

NOTES

1. Lisa Middleton, interview by author, tape recording: San Francisco, May 4, 2001. In 2000, Middleton was appointed to the MHR parish council. Middleton now lives in San Diego, California.

2. Christine McQuiston, letter to author, San Francisco, May 11, 2001.

3. John Oddo, interview by author, tape recording: San Francisco, April 25, 2001.

4. Rob Lane, interview by author, tape recording: San Francisco, March 14, 2001.

5. Bishop Patrick McGrath, then auxiliary bishop in San Francisco. McGrath, a native from Dublin, Ireland, is presently Bishop of San Jose, California. Shore says that he did not understand that MHR is a parish where there can be cheering and clapping as a matter of course during liturgies. The United States Conference of Catholic Bishops issued the statement: "Ministry to Persons with a Homosexual Inclination," on November 14, 2006. This statement was badly received in the gay catholic community; even so it does at least recognize that the parish was correct to baptize these children: "Baptism of children in the care of same-sex couples presents a serious pastoral concern. Nevertheless, the Church does not refuse the Sacrament of Baptism to these children, but there must be a well founded hope that the children will be brought up in the Catholic religion."

6. Joe Dignan, "Most Holy Redeemer's Pastor Moves On," *Bay Area Reporter,* vol. 32. no. 26, June 27, 2002, A19.

7. In the article "Sunrise Service, Street Party Create an Only-in San Francisco Easter," *San Francisco Chronicle,* April 5, 1999, Peter Fimrite and Steve Rubenstein write about reaction at Most Holy Redeemer to the angry public opposition of Archbishop Levada to the Sisters. The Sisters had applied for, and been granted, a city permit to close the streets around the Castro on Easter Sunday, to commemorate their founding: "Before the festival, at least 700 people, many of them gay, attended mass yesterday at the Castro's Most Holy Redeemer Church. Many of the parishioners supported the sisters, but felt they could have chosen a better day. 'I wouldn't have picked it for this day, but if that's when their anniversary falls, that's when it falls,' said Regis Rosetta, 34, a gay parishioner. 'It's not against nuns. It's theater.' Parishioner Pete Cullinane didn't agree. 'I'm a gay man and I find the sisters offensive,' Cullinane said." Regis Rosetta is also quoted online at http://www.inthelife.com/0_news2.htm,

as saying: "I have no problem with the Sisters having their parade. I think it's a shame that the archbishop is trying to get a red [cardinal's] hat out of Rome by making an issue of this."

8. Burns, *A Journey of Hope*, 46. Ironically, I know several gay and lesbian couples from Most Holy Redeemer who did attend such "recognition ceremonies." The Archdiocese, through Catholic Charities, also became embroiled in disputes with the city. Perhaps the most well known was in 1996 when San Francisco required all businesses who had contracts with the city to provide benefits for domestic partners. Eventually the Archdiocese expanded benefits to one other member of the household, but as it were, under protest, reiterating that it in no way accepted the notion of domestic partners as equal to married partners.

9. Two parishioners, Robert and Thomas Van Etten, a couple, decided to initiate their own dialogue, and asked the archbishop to meet with them. Eventually he agreed and they sat down together for an hour on February 8, 2000. Their email of February 24, 2000 explains that they discussed the Knight Initiative, Levada's perceived negligence in not speaking out immediately after the murder of Matthew Shepard, that the diocese does not have an outreach to the lesbian/gay/transgender community as it does to other minorities, Levada's failure to consult with gay Catholics before making statements, MHR's participation in the Gay Freedom Day Parade, the Sisters of Perpetual Indulgence, the hateful language of the Congregation for the Doctrine of the Faith, Proposition 22, and the Nugent/Gramick censure: "The meeting was amicable and took place without anger. All we can say about the meeting is that we had an opportunity to voice our opinions to the Archbishop in a professional manner representing OUR COMMUNITY with dignity and respect. Will anything change? We don't know. The Hierarchy is a very political body of clergy and the archbishop was very careful in what he said to us. We left feeling that he was grateful for our input and honesty. He listened intently, commented carefully, and we have no idea what the results . . . will be."

10. Michael Vargas, October 5, 2001 interview by author.

11. PlanetOut News Staff, "More Opposition to Rome Pride," May 18, 2000, available at http://www.planetout.com/pno/news/misc/mailarticle/?2000/05/18/1.

12. Ric Meyer and his partner Rob Bodoya left the parish for the East Coast and were blessed together at the end of Mass by Fr. Hayes and the entire congregation on August 27, 2000. Hayes joked that they were moving "to the United States."

13. Ellen Grund, group email, June 14, 2000.

14. Thomas Van Etten, group email, June 14, 2000. The Jordan quotation is from *The Silence of Sodom: Homosexuality in Modern Catholicism* (University of Chicago Press: Chicago, 2000)—and arguably undermines Van Etten's own logic. Van Etten also had a letter published in *Catholic San Francisco,* April 2, 1999: "One of us took the other's last name to make a statement. We worship regularly at Most Holy Redeemer and give of our time, talent, and money. We are two of the many gay and lesbian parishioners who love and support their parish. We cannot speak for anyone other than ourselves, but suffice it to say that if we were able to marry we would. You see, it's about love, nothing else." David Robinson, in "Metaphors of Love, Love as Metaphor: Language, Ritual and Moral Agency in the Theological Politics of Identity,"

Theology and Sexuality no. 12 (2000: 72–73) cites the Van Ettens' relationship as being equivalent to marriage: "The poignant opening quotation comes from a parishioner in a San Francisco parish, where I have become part of a community, as priest and as musician." And: "The language of pastoral concern has surfaced in the Catholic Church [e.g., in *Always our Children*], and in a number of mainline Protestant denominations [to say nothing of Reform Jewish congregations]. At first inspection, this new language may seem a giant leap forward, and it certainly is an improvement over the unbridled vituperation of many earlier documents and public statements. Nonetheless, there is also a potential for psychological and theological deception that could prove invidious over time. I do not mean to defame the legitimate intentions of many religious spokespersons, who honestly seek a compassionate, human base for religious conversation. I do, however, intend to question the efficacy of many contemporary attempts to relocate the debate over gay realities within a set of theoretical or abstract notions regarding human life, love and community. If religious organizations profess to embrace gay and lesbian experience under the umbrella of their institutions and practices, such an embrace can only have meaning if the fundamental elements of human formation and self-expression are included. One cannot be a notional person, an incarnation of a disembodied idea. Love, communal inclusion and moral integrity are grounded in the physicality of human emotion, relationship and concrete, lived decisions."

15. Zobrieta Puckett, letter to Archbishop Levada, June 17, 2000.

16. Zachary Shore, January 22, 2001 interview by author.

17. Kathleen Carey, interview with author, tape recording: San Francisco, January 30, 2001.

18. *Faith beyond Resentment*, 84–85.

19. January 30, 2001 interview by author.

20. John Long, "San Francisco's Mayor Willie Brown: 'A Million Pride Marchers Here!' Colorful, Quick-Stepping Parade Said Most Memorable in 29 Years, Celebration Hosts Anarchist Band, Chumbawamba," *Gay Today,* http://badpuppy.com/gaytoday/garchive/events/0706983v.htm.

21. The Peter Claver community is a Catholic Charities residence for homeless people with AIDS. Archbishop Quinn had forbidden them from marching as the Peter Claver Community. A compromise was reached in allowing the "Friends of Peter Claver Community" to march. Michael Harank remembers marching in the San Francisco gay pride parade with Holy Spirit Parish (the Newman Center), Berkeley in 1996.

22. Ammerman, *Congregation and Community*, 363.

23. Pope John Paul II, address at the Angelus, Sunday July 9, 2000. Associated Press release.

24. Rob Morse, "Forgive Those Whose Parade Rains on Yours," *San Francisco Examiner,* July 11, 2000.

25. Another remarkable outreach to the community, targeting all ages and orientations, and initiated by parishioner Patrick Mulcahey, was to hand out postcard-sized cards at the corner of 18th and Castro Streets. Photos reproduced on the cards were all of people from the parish. One had a picture of a feuding male couple that said: "You know how sometimes you fight, and you know you're not wrong, but all you

want is to go home to him and you know he wants you back?" And on the other side: "One of us had to make the first move"—with the address of the church and the time of the main Sunday mass. Cards showing a lesbian couple were inscribed the same way. Another showed a man and woman in evening dress, the woman looking chagrined, with the words "Got rhythm?" on one side, and on the other, "Nobody said heterosexuality was going to be easy. Most Holy Redeemer, 100 Diamond Street at 18, 10 a.m. Sundays. Your parish Church in the Castro for one Hundred Years. Come Home." One was targeted towards older people, one to the transgender community. On one side transgender parishioner Lisa Middleton was pictured with the prefix: "Trans . . ." (and also, beneath, the words "Executive, Hockey fan, Orchid Grower, Lector, Parish Council Member"); on the other side it continued: ". . . Substantiation, every Sunday at 10 a.m.," etc. The card toward neighborhood seniors (which received some negative feedback: who likes being thought of as old?) said: "We are looking for a Few Gray Hairs." And on the other side: "Yours! Come Home." Another, directed toward families, showed children of the parish: "They say we want your children. They're right."—and on the other side: "And we want them to bring their parents. 10 o'clock mass Sundays. . . ." Another read: "Hot men—Top Tunes—Eternal Life" and showed two handsome men together in dress suits, with the church address and mass information on the reverse. Parishioners seemed reluctant to get involved in this kind of outreach, but it did continue over part of the year.

In a bulletin insert, Mulcahey described the purpose of going onto the streets: "We at Most Holy Redeemer know how lucky we are to have found a place of worship where God's love is not just an abstraction; where we can come together in faith and know that our lives, our struggles, have dignity and meaning, not only in God's eyes but in each other's, in our pastor's and his staff's. How many of us, for how many years, cut ourselves off from the Church because we didn't know such a place existed? This weekend Most Holy Redeemer kicks off an evangelization effort of a very particular sort. We aren't trying to win over Lutherans or Hindus or anyone happy in their religious practice, or people who don't believe in God at all. We're reaching out to people exactly like we were before we first set foot inside MHR; people who'd be here if they knew they'd be welcomed and loved and accepted without reservation. People who'd be our parishioners by virtue of being our neighbors, if they believed anyone would be glad to see them walk through the door."

I helped on two occasions (dressed in lay clothes) and was surprised not to receive a single hostile response. One man told me it really touched his heart. He would love to come, he said. One volunteer did report some negative reactions. To my mind, this outreach shows the enormous potential in San Francisco if the Catholic Church were to make an effort at rapprochement with the gay community. Standing next to, and talking to a young man distributing a very different kind of handout for the gay nightclub MASS while I handed out cards advertising our Mass was an educational experience!

26. Thomas VanEtten, "Are Catholic Church donations to Knight initiative anti-gay?" *San Francisco Examiner,* October 29, 1999.

27. Zachary Shore, interview with author, San Francisco, January 22, 2001, tape recording.

28. Zachary Shore, unpublished letter provided to author.

29. January 22, 2001 interview by author.

30. Although Tom Fry, the founder of Dignity in San Francisco, was always favorably disposed to Most Holy Redeemer, not everyone at Dignity was. In Dignity's June/July 1991 newsletter, the co-chairs write: "Furthermore, this was a community (i.e. Dignity) that watched the Archdiocese sink money into Most Holy Redeemer because we were a growing community presence and it was clear that public ministry to gays and lesbians could not be shut down—or dismissed. In some ways, we posed a threat." I am not aware that the Archdiocese ever did sink money into the parish!

31. Joe Dignan, A19.

32. Patrick Mulcahey, unpublished letter emailed to MHR Wednesday Supper group.

Chapter Five

A Queer Sanctuary

My involvement with Most Holy Redeemer parish began seventeen years ago. I was in San Francisco for the summer of 1990 undertaking several months of pastoral work with homeless people living with HIV at the Peter Claver Community. This work was part of my requirements for the M.Div. degree at the University of Toronto. As a Catholic at the time preparing for ordination, I attended the main Sunday 10 a.m. mass at the parish in shorts and a T-shirt. These days I dress a little bit more formally for mass! At the mass I found myself in tears and profoundly moved. It seemed bizarre to me that I felt so at home when I was in fact thousands of miles away from my geographical home in Ireland. Chris Glaser, now interim pastor at the neighboring congregation at MCC, points out that:

Many lesbian and gay men only know home as an ideal. Some of us suffered physical or emotional abuse growing up. Most of us experienced homophobic abuse. Because we did not feel welcome as we were, the masks came on early: masking our feelings, overcoming our one "bad" trait by overachieving socially, academically, athletically, spiritually, or aesthetically. Or perhaps we covered ourselves another way by becoming as bad or as irresponsible or as unattractive as we believed ourselves to be. That way no one would love us enough to discover our secret. Too many of us hid our difference by choosing death in its literal form or its figurative forms. To choose life meant leaving whatever home we had, often never to return.[1]

The experience of this love is what opens our hearts and allows us to become complete and whole persons, regardless of the double bind that the church can often put us in. James Alison says that the church puts gay people in the situation of the Irish joke. As an Irishman I think I can retell it!

Lost traveler: "How do I get to Dublin?"

Irishman: "If I were you, I wouldn't start from here."

At bottom this is the Church's advice, when it teaches that the homosexual orientation, though not a sin, constitutes a tendency towards behavior that is intrinsically evil, and must be considered objectively disordered.[2] Jesus simply does not always come to us in the way the Church tells us he should! He often seems happy to accompany us, right where we are, without telling us we would be better off starting from somewhere else.

It is when we experience being marginal and vulnerable that we empathize with others who are marginal for a whole host of other reasons. We understand the Gospels better. We come to see that we do not have to earn God's love, but simply to accept it. Until we do this we have not allowed God to be a part of all of our lives.

Charles Bold and the late Michael Fleming, were long term partners and active parishioners for many years. In the words of Bold:

> A guy at Wells (Fargo bank) said to me, why don't you come over here sometime, they have an AIDS support group. I said maybe. I had really been away from the church for a long time.
>
> So one Sunday I went to Mass, and I thought, oh my, this place is so gay. And I felt really at home, and I don't think I have missed many Sundays in the last ten years. I started coming here, and then Michael stopped working on Sundays and started coming with me about eight years ago.
>
> And so I mean this is really a part of our life now. . . . My older sister, she probably belongs to Opus Dei, I brought her here one time, and she wrote a letter saying that all these men who have sex with other men are going to communion. My sister said, "You know, it is social at MHR, and that should not be part of religion. You are there to save your soul. . . ." Her letter said it was her duty to tell me that I was sinning!
>
> This parish is really fulfilling a need for us at this time in our lives. The impression I get about the 10 o'clock mass is that people think it is noisy and everyone is talking, but once the mass starts the whole thing totally changes. At the beginning everyone is relating to each other and then when the mass starts everybody is singing, and most are participating, that is what is really striking. It is a really good feeling. It is the feeling of being at home. It is the feeling of being accepted, it is the feeling of being where you can be who you really are and not have to lie about it. We are taught to lie, the Church makes us lie, and you don't feel that here.
>
> When we both went through the RCIA with Sister Cleta, it was the first time I was ever in a Catholic environment where everything hung out. You could say anything you wanted, and everybody did. Sexuality. Talk about opening windows! It was liberating. With Michael in his late sixties at the time, we had lived this lie for our whole life mostly. If you wanted a job you had to lie, if you

wanted a family you had to lie; you were always made to feel ashamed. And then you come here and there isn't any shame.[3]

Alfredo Amarendez, a friend who died from AIDS complications, was Mexican-American and culturally Catholic. Occasionally Amarendez would attend a mass when I presided at Most Holy Redeemer. For the most part however Alfredo took what he wanted from Catholicism and other traditions as well creating his own special faith, one that drew on many sources. When he was diagnosed with AIDS, Alfredo went shopping and spent all his money, thinking he would die of AIDS anyway. Well, he didn't, and as the gentle, nurturing, stubborn soul he was, he decided to use the rest of his life to help others with HIV, especially those who had recently been infected. He remembered just how traumatic it was for him.

To this end he brought what are called the PLUS seminars from Los Angeles to San Francisco. These weekend seminars are free to attend, because he found public funding for them, and they provide practical, emotional, and spiritual support for people with HIV, their friends, lovers and families. They are open to anyone, but over the years the majority of those attending have been gay men. Volunteers and AIDS experts give their time for free. I attended one of these weekends, and another time I helped provide a spiritual component to the weekend. It dawned on me that many of the gay men present there living with HIV had been brought up Catholic. They did not, however, think of the Catholic Church as a resource for them in living with AIDS. This PLUS seminar did provide an important safe space that allowed people to feel at home; surely, I thought, Church ought to feel the same way. But the participants did not expect to find a welcoming place for them in Church as gay men with HIV. Indeed they were even surprised to find a Catholic priest as part of such a weekend as the PLUS Seminar. For the most part they expected hostility from the Church because they were gay.

It is rather as Fenton Johnson says: "For many years I described myself as having left the Church, but I understand now that I misspoke. These days I say more accurately: The Church left me. Rather than acknowledge the existence of lesbians and gays, it promptly tossed my brothers and sisters and me out on our collective ear."[4] This makes me both sad and angry because it is not as it should be.

I find myself criticized sometimes from within the Church for being too open about such a private matter. I was once described as a "homosexual activist" by Maria Kennedy in *San Francisco Faith.*[5] On the other hand, I am sometimes criticized by gay people for belonging to a homophobic institution so oppressive as the Church. It is ironic, but one reason Kennedy calls me a "homosexual activist" is because I was quoted in a news item on

Gay.Com/PlanetOut network as saying that it was extremely unlikely that seminaries would screen out gay candidates, except perhaps in a few particularly reactionary dioceses.[6] I have to admit that that this article in *Faith* hurt me. But not nearly as much as the document which eventually emerged from the Congregation for Catholic Education:

> That the Church, while profoundly respecting the persons in question, may not admit to the seminary and Holy Orders those who practice homosexuality, show profoundly deep-rooted homosexual tendencies, or support the so-called gay culture. The above persons find themselves, in fact, in a situation that gravely obstructs a right way of relating with men and women. The negative consequences that may derive from the Ordination of persons with profoundly deep-rooted homosexual tendencies are by no means to be ignored.[7]

What does this statement from the Congregation for Catholic Education imply about those who are gay and baptized, many at MHR? What does it say of the ministry of hundreds of thousands of priests who have served, and continue to serve as excellent priests? A surprising number of good vocations to the priesthood are nurtured at MHR. For instance Fr. Joseph Healy who speaks of his struggle to live with integrity as a gay man and a priest in footage from a film Rena Ferrick is making about being both gay and Catholic.[8] In the light of this statement and the attitude of the Church it is not difficult to understand why such a tiny number of gay priests will talk publicly on the issue. This harms not only gay priests but also the whole church. Another priest who faced such a dilemma was Father Mychal Judge, killed in New York in the September 11th attack on the World Trade Center, among the firefighters to whom he was chaplain.[9] This teaching implies that gay men are second-class Christians ineligible for the sacrament of holy orders. This puts in place the kind of structures that placed black people at the back of so many of our churches. Imagine the reaction today if the Vatican proposed barring Latinos or African Americans from ordination. I suppose women have had this experience since nearly the dawn of the Church. Fr. Jim Bretzke speaking of the Vatican document in the *New York Times,* puts it best:

"Unless you get a critical mass of bishops and religious superiors who say, Now we can't admit any gay men, I don't think it's going to have any discernible effect," Father Bretzke said. "There are lots of excellent gay priests and seminarians; and we have a priest shortage. We're not exactly in a buyer's market here. If you're not going to ordain gay men, and not going to ordain married men, and not going to ordain women, well then who's left? It's not exactly a big pool.[10]"

It is fortunate many dioceses and religious orders continue to accept candidates based on the quality of their vocation rather than their sexual orientation. For instance Archbishop George Niederauer of San Francisco, reacting to this document, said that gay men committed to Christ and the Church can effectively minister as priests; and that sexual orientation is a structure of human personality.[11]

The challenge of a parish such as Most Holy Redeemer is to transform the fear that lies behind homophobic church rules like these and pray with St. Francis, patron of the city of San Francisco: "where there is hatred, let me sow love." When the Kingdom that Jesus speaks of finally arrives, it won't be an issue. That is my hope. We will only be asked how we loved, and the acts of love we performed in life that bear us witness will have nothing to do with sexuality.

In a homily at MHR I once said: "I am asked how I can remain in an Institution that is so oppressive. And my answer is usually to say, that yes, there are aspects of the church that are oppressive and dysfunctional, but for myself it is my family and I cannot leave my family. Family is the place where we are at home, and it takes many different shapes, some traditional and some alternative. Jesus does not mind what particular form our family takes and whether Pat Buchanan would recognize it. But Jesus does care about whether in our particular family we put God and God's values at the center. The grace of Christmas, the grace of God can break into our families and transform them. It is into the ordinariness of whatever form our family life takes that God wishes to come."[12]

Patrick Mulcahey, parishioner at MHR, answers the same question:

Why be Catholic is a harder question for me these days, and basically I've stopped trying to answer it. It is the nature of human life that the Mysteries, all we live and die for, are hidden from us, walled off from view.

The Catholic Church is my peephole, my chink in the wall, opened many centuries before I was born and handed down to me by my ancestors. It's as much a part of me as my toenails or my teeth, and sometimes as much of an embarrassment. Personally, I think the clerical hierarchy of the Church is ridiculous, an obscene and alarming vestigial organ from when the Church ruled the known world. For worship, a congregation will always need a temple and a priest—any political structure beyond that I mostly ignore; it belonged to the Middle Ages and is preserved to no point, having nothing real to govern but itself and those gullible enough to be intimidated by it. Intellectually I much prefer the decentralized structure of the Episcopal Church, but intellectualizing can't quite seem to carry me across the threshold into an Episcopal pew. It has something to do with what class distinctions cling to which traditions; and more to do I suppose with the fact that it's just not my chink in the wall.

But these private thoughts don't much affect the business of being Catholic for me. It's a public secret from time immemorial, it's woven into the fabric of life, that we should harbor such reservations about institutions we cherish dearly. The married man thinks it would be a big improvement to have one month off a year from marriage to sleep with whomever he wants—why not? Half of Americans don't understand why we're governed by an idiot we didn't elect, when will we get rid of that Electoral College, and why do we have to have so many people in Congress anyway? My thoughts about Rome are of this same stamp and don't trouble me much. If I were important enough to pay attention to, who knows, I might be excommunicated; but it seems to me one measure of an institution's vitality is the blitheness with which it can tolerate being despised, even by its most ardent adherents.

Thanks to MHR I am able to have the kind of spiritual life I imagine my ancestors had and to find what I trust is very much the same sort of fulfillment in it. I do have frustrations with the parish—principally with people who seem to feel it's so exhausting to declare they are gay and are Catholic, such a feat of mental gymnastics that nothing else should be asked of them. They acknowledge two arms and legs, ten fingers and toes, but that apparently is the end of any commonality they feel with the rest of the human race. If MHR burned down, I have no doubt they'd attend services at a gay synagogue before going to mass at another Catholic church. Hence, to the extent they have any religion, their religion is being gay, or being around other gay people.

Sure, I'm well aware churches around the globe are full of this sort of person, only there because everyone else they know is, only willing to do and say what everyone else seems to do and say. And let's face it, it's especially important to have them in church—if church didn't exist, we'd have to invent it—to keep their dull animal energies from grinding the rest of us down to nubs. But it's not enough to be content with meeting minimum community standards in the gay community, which—unlike, say, Latino or Asian-American communities—has no broad consensus on social standards and no single shared tradition upon which to base them. And herein lies the hazard, to my mind, of Most Holy Redeemer. For the truth is that most people do good because other people expect it of them, not because God does, and no one expects much of us at MHR: other gay people and other Catholics think it's extraordinary enough that we actually go to church. Yes, of course, there are many of us, I could point out thirty to you on any given Sunday, whom the experience of faith leads to ask what it is God wants and expects of us—but I fear they tend to find the answer outside the very little sphere of our parish activity. Maybe that's okay. Because the thing is, they could never have found the question without MHR.[13]

While I know that some parts of my Church are despite all welcoming, I also realize there is substance to the fears of Fenton Johnson and those at the PLUS seminars when I hear their stories of rejection, even hatred. They may be occasioned by people who simply are ignorant or afraid, but it is not what Jesus practiced. Reading the Gospels, I meet a man who learned to become inclusive and compassionate in extraordinary ways.

Take for instance the encounter of Jesus with the Canaanite woman. Here is a woman who cries out for help to Jesus, but he ignores her. When his disciples ask him to send her away, he is rude to her, saying that he only came for the lost house of Israel. Yet she persists and finally Jesus recognizes her faith, even telling her that it is great.[14] In a homily on this text at Most Holy Redeemer I compared the parish at MHR to this unnamed woman. I suggested that she symbolized all voiceless people of all times and places. Jesus was not supposed to talk with her; it would make him unclean and have other serious negative social consequences for him. The purity system then in place made holiness and purity synonymous. As Marcus Borg puts it:

> The effect of the purity system was to create a world with sharp social boundaries: between pure and impure, righteous and sinner, whole and not whole, male and female, rich and poor, Jew and Gentile.[15]

Borg goes on to talk specifically of homosexuality:

> To use a specific example, I am convinced that much of the strongly negative attitude to homosexuality on the part of some Christians has arisen because, in addition to whatever nonreligious homophobic reasons may be involved, homosexuality is seen (often unconsciously) as a purity issue. For these Christians, there's something "dirty" about it, boundaries are being crossed, things are being put together that do not belong together, and so forth. Indeed, homosexuality was a purity issue in ancient Judaism. The prohibition against it is found in the purity laws of the book of Leviticus.[16]

In my homily, I suggested Jesus initially ignored and then rejected this Canaanite woman because of these purity laws. And that what we as a community at MHR are going through today is similar, because of out homosexuality, to what she experienced because of her gender and race. Parishioners at Most Holy Redeemer are sometimes told they are unworthy of sustenance, are ignored, or even insulted by the Institutional Church. Kathleen Carey put it like this:

> It's that people are [at Most Holy Redeemer] because they want to be here. They have made that choice and it has been a hard journey for almost everyone. You know, because. They've had to face, you know, "What the church officially thinks of me," and officially they say you are garbage. But we know we are not garbage here. We know we are esteemed as people. We're raised up, in a sense. That is true community to me. It seems not just, "I need to see people on a Sunday," but "This is where my family is," and that is a whole different thing.[17]

I suggested that the Canaanite woman provided a model of hope for us at the parish, that by persisting in faith, God's inclusive answer would eventually come through, and that this answer would heal that which we love, the Church, which is so sick. The institutional Church is blind, "just doesn't get it," in the same way Jesus was initially blind and didn't get it with regard to this Canaanite woman. A parish such as Most Holy Redeemer calls the rest of the institution to conversion in much the same way that this woman called Jesus to conversion, and so the parish has a prophetic significance beyond an ordinary neighborhood church.

I believe the parish of Most Holy Redeemer can in this way help heal our Church. It is not just individuals who need to "come out," but also churches as institutions, including parishes. MHR is a parish that has come out. Even parishes not in gay neighborhoods need to be safe and affirming places for gay Christians, places where their truth can be shared. As James Alison says: "How do you reconcile the maintenance of the 'closet' with the explicit teaching of the gospel about the fact that everything hidden will be uncovered, and what is said in secret will be preached from the rooftops (Luke 12:3)?"[18] Almost 300 went, on a surprisingly hot spring day to Most Holy Redeemer on February 12, 2006 to hear the question "Is Ethical to be a Catholic?" debated. The conversation, sponsored by the parish along with the Lane Center for Catholic Studies and Social Thought and the LGBTQ Caucus at the University of San Francisco brought together very differing perspectives. Dr. Vincent Pizzuto of the University of San Francisco argued that the ethical response was to leave the Catholic church if you were a gay man such as him. Fr. James Alison had a different position, one surely close to that of many, if not most MHR parishioners. Alison began by saying that he found the question a somewhat surprising one. This question had never crossed his mind; he had never met someone who became a Catholic for ethical reasons. Alison did however agree that there is a place where the ethical bit does come in:

Are we going to allow ourselves to be given new life? What will be the shape of our moving from Creation into New Creation? This means working out what the shape of holiness of life and of heart is for us as gay and lesbian Catholics. It means noting with joy that we are now closer than ever to being able to imagine that a rejoicing gay heart and a rejoicing Catholic heart can be the same heart, and a normal, and healthy and holy thing. We can imagine a seminar reading *Brokeback Mountain* in the light of *Deus Caritas Est* or vice versa,[19] and this would be something that could easily make sense to those, straight or gay, who took part in such a session. And one of the things, which, as the Pope rightly insists, we might find ourselves learning, is how the development of our love should feed into, and be fed by, our development of charitable practices, of practical Catholic outreach to the poor, the sick, the imprisoned and the marginalized. It seems presumptuous of me even to mention it here in this parish Church, in this city of San Francisco, where the ethical response to the HIV-AIDS pandemic by so many Catholic groups and individuals has been such a beacon, but even so, it is worth hammering home this point, the Catholicity of gay love will be seen by the way in which it is part of our empowerment to love the dispossessed. And this is something no one will be able to take away from us.[20]

It is shame that keeps gay Christians from telling their stories. I would agree with Chuck Bold's sister that Most Holy Redeemer is shameless, in that sense.

Stephen Pattison uses the story of Zacchaeus in Luke to illustrate what our church communities need to do in these times. The phrase WWJD is well known: What would Jesus do? But perhaps WIJD is the more Catholic question: What *is* Jesus doing? Jesus is helping gay Catholics leave their shame behind at Most Holy Redeemer just as he helped Zacchaeus in the Gospel. The story of many of us at Most Holy Redeemer, gay or straight, is essentially a reliving of the Zacchaeus story, and of so many other Gospel stories. We see ourselves reflected again and again in the life of Jesus, but rather more rarely in the life of the institutional Church. The paradox remains that it is the institutional Church that introduced us to the liberating person of Jesus. The irony is that it is only when gay Catholics are given the chance to be part of the community that we can truly be the moral agents Jesus so wants us to be.

> This story is apparently a wonderful parable of the respectful overcoming of shame and alienation. Without in any way abusing himself, Jesus looks up into Zacchaeus' face from below, thus being anything but invasive or dominating. He recognizes and honours Zacchaeus' distinct subjectivity and personhood, a fact denoted by the use of the man's name. Jesus then asks for something from Zacchaeus that the latter can easily give in the form of accommodation, thus indicating that he does not despise or reject the man and affirming his efficacy and power. This recognition of personhood and inclusion in the community has the effect of making Zacchaeus want to include himself further. It is at this point, when he has been honoured and had the stain of social shame removed from him, that Zacchaeus is able to become a moral person, taking responsibility for the needs of others and respecting their rights. A lost and outcast, immoral man has been integrated into the community and moral responsibility by the conferral of respect that removes the taint of shame.
>
> It seems to me that it is precisely the kind of shame-removing and morally empowering process figured by the story of Jesus and Zacchaeus that Christian individuals and communities need to explore and emulate today. The Lukan story may provide theological warrant, inspiration and paradigm for doing exactly that.[21]

I interviewed Catherine Cunningham and her partner Roz Gallo, a long time lesbian couple who are active parishioners; Gallo was at the time parish council president.[22] Cunningham makes a similar point, albeit in a stronger and perhaps different way than I would myself:

> I don't believe that the institution and hierarchy and the structure that makes pronouncements about gay and lesbian people is the church Jesus founded. I think it has come a long way from the path that Jesus founded. I think about St. Anthony's and the work they do, and Mercy Housing, those are the people who are doing the work that Jesus asked us to do. If you went to the staff persons of these organizations I am sure they could not care less if I am a lesbian or not. It is just not important; they are doing what is important. To use all this time and energy on this issue is just nonsense. The whole issue of sex—the Catholic Church is so hung up on sex, it is comical.
>
> I think that St. Anthony's and those places that are doing the work Jesus asked of us, and here at Most Holy Redeemer. This may be naïve, but my feeling is we love each other as a community the way Jesus would like us to do. I don't think we do all we could do. But at some level we are part of this picture anyway.[23]

It matters that Most Holy Redeemer is a regular parish, an ordinary part of the institution. Specifically gay catholic organizations such as Dignity are certainly an important means of grace for many; and it is not entirely of their own making that they are unable to bring together being gay and Catholic in quite the same ordinary way as MHR. The BBC recognized this by coming to record a Sunday worship service at MHR. MHR was on top form as Charlie Fermeglia led the fine choir and Fr. James Alison along with Sr. Cleta Herold both shared poignant reflections. Mark O'Brien, the producer, told me they could not have made this program anywhere in the U.K. He added that broadcasting a worship service from a gay perspective was a definite first for the BBC.[24]

I admit I come to this study of Most Holy Redeemer not solely from a scholar's or an historian's perspective. I will not feign academic objectivity: if such a thing really exists. I firmly believe in a new approach and a new vision in this area of ministry. In this I do have "an agenda."[25] I have the responsibility, of course, to be honest with the data I have collected; too, I recognize the importance of charity towards those who disagree with my assessment of this issue. But I also desire to share my passionate faith about what God has done and is doing in this community. What seems critical to me is not what the Church does or does not teach, though that is important, but rather how we treat one another and whether we are able to see God at work in the most unexpected people and places. Can we hear the voice of God in the voice of this parish? MHR has helped me find my own voice and I wish to share the hopes and voices of others in similar situations, such as those who are part of this parish. I want to help unheard voices speak their angry tender cries in prophetic ways to the wider Church—the same Church I feel such a deep ambivalence about, because of our continuing structural and personal sins that exclude and hurt so many; yet it is also the Church I so deeply love.

To me, the story of Most Holy Redeemer has significance for the wider Church; it tells us that integrity and transformation are possible.[26] It is a challenge to the Roman Catholic and other Christian churches to deal with gay people the way Jesus dealt with the socially marginalized in his time. Stories are important. The stories of gay people need to be told and heard. Being in the closet means that a person's ability to give witness is crippled.

Some feminist writers have used the expression "defecting in place" to capture the paradox of their position in relation to the Church. The parishioners of Most Holy Redeemer stand in a similar relation to the institutional Church:

"To defect" usually means to abandon, but the women who are "defecting in place" are not, strictly speaking, "defectors," because they haven't gone anywhere, at least not yet. They are rebels, yes, protesting once again the limits of institutional religion. This time, however, Catholics and Protestants support the same shared values, although they may choose different strategies. Theirs is not a struggle for a new religious expression but a movement *within* the institution in which they pledge allegiance to a whole new paradigm. The movement may be seen by outsiders as rooted in dissent, but proponents believe just the opposite. Their stance is positive, not negative, for their dissent flows from a prior assent to the initiatives of the Spirit. Their "yes" to the Spirit is the basis for their staying within congregations or denominations to work to bring about change. As Toinette Eugene would put it, with a touch of whimsy, there is "no defect here."[27]

There is kinship between "woman-space" and the space created in a parish such as the Castro for gay people. Gays, like women, are finding their voices, connecting with one another, and creating a new culture in the process—a culture that is "alternative" but I believe closer to the values of the Jesus of the Gospel than what passes for "mainstream." The Gospel must be Good News for all, including gay Catholics. The way it is presently presented for gay people, it seems like bad news, or at least very sad news. Father Peter Harris, formerly chairman of Quest, the English organization for gay Catholics, writes:

As long as people are prepared to continue to see themselves as a marginalized group, waiting for the Church to minister to them, they will remain a marginalized group. Once we see the relevance of ministry in our own lives, then true participation in Church begins, and we become truly one of the people of God.[28]

Steven Bevans elaborates:

And so God became flesh (Jn. 1:14)—not generally, but particularly. God became a human being in the person of Jesus, a Jew, son of Mary, a male. God became flesh in a human person of such and such a height, with particular color hair, with particular personality traits, and so forth. Incarnation is a process of becoming particular, and in and through the particular, the divinity could become visible and in some way (not fully, but in some way) become graspable and intelligible.

It follows quite naturally that if that message is to continue to touch people through our agency, we have to continue the incarnation process. Through us, God must become Asian or African, black or brown, poor or sophisticated, a member of twentieth-century secular suburban Lima, Peru, or of the Tondo slum dweller in Manila, or able to speak to the ill-gotten affluence of a Brazilian rancher. Christianity, if it is to be faithful to its deepest roots and most basic insight, must continue God's incarnation in Jesus by becoming contextual.[29]

If God must become Asian or African, then God is also in some sense queer and at work in the gay community.

In a paper presented as part of Gay Pride Week in Derry in 1996, I argued that what we know about Jesus, as the gospels show us, is that he was comfortable with his body, he was able emotionally to be close to both men and women. We do not know his sexual orientation, but this makes no difference theologically and would itself be an anachronistic question. We know he was a sexual person with sexual feelings. However, as churches we have allowed an un-Christian dualism to infect our teachings. We have concentrated on reaching God by our minds and it has brought us to a deep neurosis. It has also led many to reject Christianity when in fact they are only rejecting a caricature of it. As I said speaking to the gay support group Acceptance at St. Canice's church in Sydney: "I don't think we can have a mature relationship to our sexuality until we learn to accept and delight in human bodies, our own and other peoples, the beautiful and the ugly; the sick and the healthy; the young and the old; male and female. For many gay men this will mean confronting stereotypes about women and the elderly. It will also mean dealing with taboo topics such as the sexual, physical, and emotional abuse that goes on in gay relationships just as it does in straight relationships. In a sense the Eucharist we are celebrating shows us the vocation of our human bodies — God became flesh and blood like us. If God has become flesh and blood in this central sacrament of our faith, then surely we can dare to do so as well. Through the transformation of the Eucharist we can become gifts to each other: this is the possibility of communion."[30]

Is it less appropriate for gays to imagine Jesus as gay than for African Christians to picture him as black, Asian Christians as Asian? Through Jesus, God identifies with gay people in the struggle for freedom and liberation. In Jesus, God experiences the stereotypes, the labeling, the hate crimes, and the homophobic violence, physical or emotional. Jesus knew all about stigma, and was not afraid of being called names, nor of being identified with the most marginal and discredited people of his day. Jesus loved them.[31] He also said that the truth will set us free.

Gay Catholics at Most Holy Redeemer know that this God is with them in their journey. There is a need to do a new theology—theology is not the exclusive preserve of theologians. To this end we need safe and sacred places where this is possible, all the time waiting for the day, possibly a long time off, when the whole Church is safe and sacred. And we must proceed in a spirit of genuine love and even forgiveness, without bitterness or hatred, even for those who try to teach people to despise them. It is possible to be strong and truthful and at the same time conciliatory and loving, most powerfully in communities that support rather than seek to silence. Most Holy Redeemer is one such place. The history of this parish reveals a community once so impervious to change that there was blood on its hands, from the killing of a gay man in 1961. One of the three parishioners responsible told police that beating up gay people was all right. Yet as this book shows, the parish changed radically to become a community of inclusion and hope. If such a paradigm shift is possible in one tiny part of the institution such as this parish, then my hope is that other parishes and parts of the wider institutional church will also become open and inclusive one day.

This seems to be happening despite the efforts of some in the church. Most Holy Redeemer is a place where God is active and at work in the gay community and in the relationships between persons gay and straight. Often, it seems, God is more easily experienced when people are marginal, poor or suffering. The Gospel seems to come alive in these situations. As Archbishop Quinn said in his interview with me, [powerful and wealthy persons] sometimes don't have a sense of dependence on God because they can command everything.[32] Hence the coming together of the gay and the gray at Most Holy Redeemer: so often the elderly are also marginalized in California's youth culture. Someone once said that MHR was the "gay 90's"—meaning that everyone in the parish was either gay or in their nineties! Two marginal groups, the "gays and the grays"; gay people devastated by AIDS, and seniors, feeling left behind by the neighborhood, perhaps by life, create a new kind of community. MHR is a kind of parish that is new in the Catholic Church. Even now that other parishes are becoming more welcoming of gay Catholics, it is still unique. It cannot be—it is not even desirable—that many parishes will become similar to Most Holy Redeemer, except for a few in gay neighborhoods. In the vast majority of parishes gay Catholics will continue to be in the minority; but what is most important is that gay people are increasingly welcomed, accepted and an ordinary part of life in these communities. Even here Most Holy Redeemer provides a model of how integration is possible. There are others who come to Most Holy Redeemer to find reconciliation between the parts of them that are gay and Catholic and then find they have the strength to move on to another parish, or to belong in a looser way to the community. These are the people who might only attend Mass irregularly but still have a sense of belonging to the community, and for whom Most Holy Redeemer is an important symbol of possibility.

When I presided to an overflowing congregation at MHR on Sunday September 16, 2001, in the aftermath of the September 11 attack, I welcomed many people who had previously been regular parishioners and no longer attended but who obviously wanted to be present on such a day. Thus MHR becomes a kind of "shrine that symbolizes a culture and an identity similar to other ethnocultural historical and sacred monuments and spaces offering a map of pilgrimages and imageries for experiencing and reinventing one's primary affiliations."[33] In this regard Most Holy Redeemer functions in a similar way to the congregation of Beth Simchat Torah in Greenwich Village, New York. As at MHR, this largely gay Jewish congregation is choosing to confront acute existential problems embedded in the "modern world" within the framework of their ancestors' realm of primordial attachments, religious beliefs, and cultural sentiments. For them it required founding a new congregation. At MHR it meant nothing less than the refounding of a parish. Much of the history of both communities is how people who felt disenfranchised from their faith by their homosexuality have created a safe and supportive environment within the boundaries of their tradition, accomplished in hostile and unwelcoming situations. The question is can a gay person be authentically Jewish or Christian or Catholic? Just as at MHR, some at Beth Simchat move on when the dissonance is resolved or reduced in their identity crisis. I can think of many who now worship elsewhere in more "regular" Catholic parishes or belong now in a much looser sense. In many ways the story of this gay synagogue parallels the story of MHR. One could say of MHR what Moshe Shokeid says of this Jewish congregation:

> The exploration into the politics of identity, suggesting a mainstream social landscape as vehicle for the construction of gay identity and collective action, might disappoint or even antagonize many gay and lesbian activists. Yet I do not claim that gay militancy and fellowship cannot survive unless embedded within another pregay ascriptive category. But "pure" gay political activity cannot provide for the needs of identity and social affiliation of all lesbians and gays. Moreover, the challenge of a stigmatized minority might maintain vis-à-vis mainstream society and the sources of discrimination is far more effective when directed from territories familiar and shared with the dominant society.
>
> Most people are not born into a socially constructed "gay ethnicity," and not many can completely erase and transform the deep layers of social messages, emotional traps, and symbolic conditioning implanted by society since infancy. These remain for better or worse, indispensable components of one's core identity. Inevitably, we are all—heterosexuals, homosexuals, Jews, Gentiles, and the rest of humanity—part of a "text" we can write in only a few lasting novel notes.

The emergence of a new self-assertive social persona and a new type of communitas of gay and lesbian Jews, initiated from the "safe space" of the sanctuaries of gay synagogues, is not a meager achievement in the annals of both contemporary homosexual and Jewish society. I quote Eric Rofes in a gay activist's confession: "I find a great deal of pleasure and happiness in realizing my identities as a gay man and a Jew. I feel satisfaction and comfort in attending services at a gay shul . . . I feel special strength in naming myself publicly as a gay Jew."

Much of the contemporary work on gay men has been limited to their behavior in secluded and covert places where they could mainly express their sexual orientation. The gay synagogue, a place and a "field", offers a far more complex context: it is a gay men's space, but no less a Jewish space, and a lesbian space as well. The development of modern Jewish society entailed the physical, legal, and emotional breakaway from the ghetto walls. Gay liberation was conceived metaphorically as "coming out of the closet." The emergence of gay and lesbian spaces, more visible and familiar to the world outside, where *gay* and *lesbian* encodes more than sex, carries profound consequences for the current living of gay and lesbian communities as well as for the meaning of their identities.[34]

Bishop Randy Calvo, who lived in the parish for many of the years when McGuire was pastor makes a similar point:

[Calvo:] If one was to look at the unhealthy stuff in gay people or any person, one way to offset that, or to move it to mainstream homosexuality is to make it part of life.

[Godfrey:] Isn't that what the church can do in a way that a gay bar cannot?

[Calvo:] Exactly. It is not necessarily something the left wing of the gay community would want. The more the church does to alienate and push in the opposite direction, the more the elements that are harder to reconcile with our own teaching happen. So the more you push to mainstream, the more accountable to virtue is the gay community.

[Godfrey:] The gay community changes by that encounter.

[Calvo:] Sure, well it domesticates, people go home, they are made mainstream. They are like any straight couples.

[Godfrey:] In a way their lives are very ordinary, in many ways they are conservative couples.

[Calvo:] That would be my way.[35]

In this light, I am calling for the most appropriate way to promote the faith in the new world that is gay culture. It is not so different from the different ways that the faith was presented to the New World that was South America in the eighteenth century. Michael Mullins, writing of the film *The Mission*, says:

The Mission was about the rivalry between older-style missionaries who believed the indigenous peoples of South America had to adopt European culture along with the Christianity they were preaching to them, and the Jesuit missionaries who believed in a method that's now termed inculturation. The Jesuit's technique involved studying the culture of the Indians concerned [the Guarani] before presenting the Christian message in a form that harmonized as far as possible with it and so with their experience.

The more traditional missionaries had sought to convert the Guarani not only to Christianity, but also to the European cultural values from which Christianity emerged. They saw that they had to "civilise" the Indians. This would protect them from their own primitive, not to mention evil, culture. The Jesuits, by contrast, gained a foothold among the Guarani through music. They aroused the interest of the Guarani by singing hymns. Then the Jesuits fascinated the Guarani with European musical instruments they produced. Eventually, the Indians were encouraged to use their natural talent for singing complex harmonies as a form of catechesis or teaching. In time the Jesuits gained their trust and respect and the Guarani became Christians without turning their backs completely on their own culture.[36]

I believe, in other words, that the Gospel must always be inculturated into every culture, and this must include gay culture. A parish such as Most Holy Redeemer is an example of how this can happen, with some limitations, in the Roman Catholic Church. Louis Weil explains:

There is, in fact, no way to participate in the Christian tradition except within the framework of some particular cultural, historical, and geographical whole. Christian faith is always incarnate and always reflects the fundamental doctrine of Christianity that in Jesus God has participated in our human reality. By implication it follows that God participates in the whole of our human diversity, not merely in one cultural pattern. Christian faith and practice is more then theoretical; our theory—our theologizing—about that faith and practice is always after the fact. Christian theology reflects on the experience of actual Christians in the living of their faith. This is expressed in corporate worship and in the ordering of their daily lives in accordance with the imperatives emerging from the common life shared by the members of the body of Christ. Christian faith is always grounded in a shared social and cultural context.[37]

My experience over the years working in a number of parishes, retreat houses, and two universities is somehow God breaks into the lives of people when they are in pain. This doesn't make pain, poverty, or suffering, something to be sought in its own right, and of course God is at work in wealthy, happy parishes too. It is just that people who have everything materially don't seem to recognize their need for God as much as those who experience want, of whatever kind. It is easier for the satisfied to be self-sufficient and not really know their need for God. This is certainly true in my personal experience.

My dream is that Church becomes a safe place where we can be open to what God wants for us, where we can be honest and do this kind of soul work. Such openness in church is very rare.

Most Holy Redeemer provides such a place where one can be open about such issues of sexuality and also about the spiritual dimensions of life.[38]

The creation of a safe and consecrated space, which I would call a sanctuary at Most Holy Redeemer is undoubtedly empowering. But as the example of the MHR choir members who came to church bruised after being beaten up in the Castro the night before shows, and as Carter Heyward argues, there are only moments of safe space in the struggle for justice, even at Most Holy Redeemer, no permanent place of safety. Part of the paradox is that: "seeking to find safe space for others as well as for ourselves, we find ourselves in danger. In this sense, our vocation can never be simply to create safety but rather to take the risks involved in standing with those in danger, thereby putting ourselves in danger as well."[39]

Gay people coming to San Francisco often describe themselves as refugees. Even today in many parts of the country it is not possible to live as a gay man or lesbian without persecution and threats—in other parts of the world the situation is worse. Patrick Mulcahey told me:

I came to Most Holy Redeemer at a critical point in my life. Many gay men at a similar juncture in their lives would have looked to a counselor or a therapist, but I think that's just a symptom of how the psychosocial category stunts us and keeps us ignorant of ourselves. We tend to experience unhappiness, even anomie, as somehow owing to our sexuality, I suppose because it is more deeply part of us than anything else we can name. . . .

Lightning did strike me the first time I came to MHR, but not for the reasons you'd think (or maybe you would). It wasn't being in a hall with hundreds of gay men that did it. Lord knows; that wasn't a new experience. It was the Mass itself. It was the homily, given by Fr. Tom Hayes, who seemed to be speaking to me, just to me, to my starved and withered heart and soul. It was what any Catholic would feel after twenty-odd years away; it was the church itself, in all its majesty and mystery and ordinary goodness, in the sturdy beauty of a well-wrought liturgy. With this difference: for the first time since I was old enough to understand myself as a sexual being, it was a church that wasn't pushing me away. That's all. That's it. Any Catholic who'd been on a desert island for twenty years would have felt the same thing upon walking into a church where a wise and decent priest was saying mass. But I couldn't have felt it in any other church. You see?

People don't understand why gay men and lesbians migrate to San Francisco, Los Angeles, Miami, New York, cities all around the world that have flourishing gay ghettos. Usually we don't understand ourselves. To be with "others of our kind," to have wild sex and go to great parties? The truth is, mostly we come here to forget about being gay, to just drop that burden—to just be human. For us, MHR is the church where you can go and just be Catholic.[40]

Mulcahey puts his finger on what we need desperately in every Catholic parish: the creation of sanctuary, so that Catholics who happen to be gay can just be Catholic.[41] Another gay man who found a sanctuary at Most Holy Redeemer is Jeff Ferris:

> First of all, I went and let myself be ministered to. I let my heart soften. It was so ready to be tenderized. I'd go into MHR and I would cry, sitting at the back, and going to the high worship I would lose it. It was all about being made tender. It was not like I was sorry for my sins, or repentant. I guess I was sorry in my heart. It was more the spirit, the sweet spirit of God. He was there. I found him at Most Holy Redeemer. On the right hand side of the back four pews. God is waiting for me there. It started to dawn on me how gay it was only after I started going there—you know the whole social thing, they are looking for boyfriends! [Ferris laughs] The social part dawned on me later. God brought me here, and gave me a home here, and it is only recently that I have socialized over the past couple of months. I want to be part of the community.
>
> There are times I realize this is a really radical thing that we are doing. I find myself back in the Catholic church in a really good way. MHR is the first place I feel I can be gay and serve God. Now the trick is, how do you negotiate your way through the landscape of Catholicism?
>
> Some people tease me for being part of the Catholic Church. I had a date and I mentioned that I went to church and he was an Irish guy from New York. He wanted to know all about it. He said, what do you believe? I started talking about the advent of the human species, I love reading about that sort of stuff. I tried to avoid the topic! He wanted to know more, so I started to tell him some of what I am telling you. Well he cut it to pieces. He ripped the Catholic Church to shreds. He really has a lot of anger towards the Catholic Church. I guess there are a lot of people like that.
>
> That was the end of dating him.[42]

Joseph Stellpflug, a friend of mine and the late Henri Nouwen, the well-known spiritual writer and priest, told me Nouwen would visit Most Holy Redeemer when in the Bay Area. Nouwen apparently found MHR a healing community in his own journey of accepting himself as a gay man. I recalled someone at MHR asking, did I know that Nouwen had attended the mass at which I had just presided? Michael Harank, a friend of mine, describes Nouwen:

> Because of the generation Henri was a part of, because of the Catholic Church which he grew up in, was formed by, and, in my opinion, deformed by, the area of sexuality was repressed by him for many years. What the AIDS epidemic did for him, and for a lot of people like him, was somehow to provide him with a way of connecting with his sexuality and his compassion.
>
> It was very clear to me from the very beginning of our relationship that Henri was a gay man, but was not able to say those words for a very long time. However, he was eventually able to share with a small circle of friends that he was

gay. That he could share this truth gave him an enormous sense of relief. The coming-out process enables you to build a sense of solidarity and community with others who have shared the hellish journey that gay people have to go through in order to come to a new sense of freedom about who we are.

Because of the Western lack of a healthy theology of sexuality, Harank explained, people had not been given the means to understand that sexuality was one of God's most beautiful gifts.

Henri was part of that tragic generation which simply had not tools to work with that gift. Here was Henri in a Church which didn't honor sexuality or give him the tools to deal with the area of sexuality, and which was quite violent in a number of its teachings with regard to homosexuality. How was he going to make that a part of his writings, his life, and his intimate relationships? He couldn't and it was because of his fear.[43]

A gay couple who first came to Most Holy Redeemer in 1994, Les Hribar and Daniel Ray Ollis, describe the contrast between Most Holy Redeemer and their previous experiences of the Church:

[Les Hribar:] I went to confession; it was pretty hard to do. It was in Greendale, not in the big city. It was a Saturday night, seven miles away. My brother was in there; I was so paranoid in that confessional. It seemed like I was in there forever, nobody had ever been to confession for so long! I thought what will my brother think? People knew almost everybody.

I said to the priest, I found places where people like me hung out. I used to dream of a place where there were many kinds of people like me. Anyway, I got all kinds of penance and all kinds of talking to, and the priest said that I must stay away from those kinds of places. "You cannot go to those kinds of places. I said doing that would kill me, and he said, "Would you not be better off dead?" That was heavy, that was hard on me.

How could I answer this? I could not answer this. I wouldn't be surprised if many people committed suicide over something like this. I never went to confession again. I went to church sometimes as if I didn't too many questions were asked, so I faked it. . . .

Then when I came to San Francisco I might go once a year as I was supposed to be Catholic. One Sunday I heard about Most Holy Redeemer in the Castro and it was coming up to Palm Sunday. I said to Dan [his partner of 26 years], let us go to church. I have heard a few things about this church. I looked at him; his health was not the best at the time. It was just like something clicked between us, we had the same feeling at the same time. Dan would go to church with all his pain and walk out without any. He could not walk in; it was like a miracle.

[Dan Ollis:] Church got me through a lot of sickness because of all the members there.

[Les Hribar:] I never felt like I was welcome in church before I came to MHR. Nobody condemned you here. We were welcome. We love the warmth. I could not believe in anything like this. It was like a miracle.

[Dan Ollis:] I decided to get baptized at Most Holy Redeemer. Something told me I should be closer to the Lord. When I was in hospital I was very ill. I was in a convalescent home. Les was to have heart surgery but had to put it off until I got well. I could not walk. We went through RCIA together.[44]

Being part of MHR has totally changed our lives; to be kinder, not talk about our neighbors.

[Les Hribar:] And to be sociable with other people. We used to keep to ourselves. You know, we did not have that love there is today.

[Dan Ollis:] Now we are much more social, we say good day.

[Les Hribar:] It is hard to come up with words, but I feel cleansed, I belong to somebody. Going back to church improved our relationship. We became so much closer. We are just like brothers after all these years. We have never been closer than we are now.

[Dan Ollis:] Now being gay and Catholic is ok.[45]

Ellen Grund, a lesbian parishioner describes something similar:

I felt at the time I had left the church emotionally. I was still going to Mass. I was doing what I needed but my heart and soul were not there. Then all of a sudden at MHR they were. I was bringing my whole person, I was not checking half of my identity at the door here at MHR. And the experience was so overwhelming and so rich. I went to Remembering Church, as well as my partner Kathy. That was great. There were ten or twelve of us. Teresa Caluori and Fr. Tom Hayes were facilitating it. I remember issues being discussed openly, about being gay and so on. Representatives of the church were hearing us, and not only are they not punishing us; but they are entertaining us, and respecting us. . . . We ended up forming a small faith community. We have been together ever since.[46]

As does parishioner Michael Vargas:

I was very active in a Jesuit parish in Tacoma. There was nothing to nourish the gay side of me. I was out to a few good friends on the faculty at the prep school, but there was nothing openly able to nourish me spiritually as a gay man. I went to Seattle to the Dignity Mass at St. Joes. I had two communities.

What I realized existed here, it was one place where all of that could be fed. I didn't have to check my gay identity at the door. Coming to MHR, I could bring it openly. That I could not do at a regular parish. It was very affirming to me as a gay man. It certainly gave me a lot of hope. . . .

I was hoping to meet someone here and I think Marty was too. . . . We were visible from the beginning. We did public displays of affection. Marty in the choir, holding hands after Mass, which was Zachary's first summer here. I applied for a job at the Support Group. The Board went through the list of candidates. Zachary said, do I know him? Someone said, "You know, Michael and Marty." So the pastor knew me as part of a couple before he knew me as an individual! That was remarkable to me. It was a matter of fact attitude that I was in a committed relationship.

We had a commitment ceremony a year earlier. . . . some things I don't expect or demand of the parish community. Things like baptism or the statement of Zachary console me, certainly. Much more hurtful is when either the official magisterium, Levada or the institutional church comes out and says something condemnatory.[47]

James Alison expresses a similar sentiment in his book *faith beyond resentment*. Alison argues in this ground breaking work that the worst lie that gay people have heard and often believe is the one that tells them they are not capable of love, that their love is sick, perverted and can only bring harm and degradation to those to whom gays should reach out. "What you prohibit from incarnation you condemn to the lifestyle of a demon."[48]

Most Holy Redeemer is a community where the whole church can see these lies for what they are. Like any other community, it is flawed, and sinful. But as Alison points out, one of the ironies of Church teaching is that it renders gay people incapable of sin, because only those for whom there is a right way of being can fall short of their created potential. "To be able to get something wrong, and learn from that something of what we can aspire to is, itself, a huge step on the divine road to the humanization of the demoniac."[49] MHR is a community where gay people can get it wrong as well as right.

I often meet former Catholics who are gay here in San Francisco. Quite often they are angry and feel alienated from the church of their upbringing. You may have seen the T-shirt that proclaims "Recovering Catholic." I also meet Catholics at Most Holy Redeemer who tell me that they couldn't be practicing Catholics if it were not for a parish like MHR.

The Catholic Church seems to be pulling us in two different directions in regard to the issue of homosexuality. On one hand, there are statements, such as these from the U.S. Bishops in 1976 that seem to be promoting a kind of inclusion:

> Homosexuals, like everyone else, should not suffer from prejudice against their basic human rights. They have a right to respect, friendship and justice. They should have an active role in the Christian community.[50]

More recently the U.S. Bishops (through their Committee on Marriage and Family) gave a pastoral message to the parents of gay children asking that church ministers and priests:

> Welcome homosexual persons into the faith community. Seek out those on the margins. Avoid stereotyping and condemnations. Strive first to listen. . . . Use

the words "homosexual," "gay," "lesbian," in honest and accurate ways, especially from the pulpit. In various and subtle ways you can give people "permission" to talk about homosexual issues among themselves and let them know that you're willing to talk with them . . .

To our homosexual brothers and sisters we offer a concluding word . . . we need one another if we are to "grow in every way into him who is our head, Christ." Though at times you may feel discouraged, hurt or angry, do not walk away from your families, from the Christian community, from all those who love you. In you God's love is revealed. You are always our children.[51]

On the other hand there are words and teachings that seem to promote exclusion and alienation. For instance, the teaching that says the inclination is ordered towards an "intrinsic evil":

For according to the objective moral order, homosexual relations are acts which lack an essential and indispensable finality. In sacred Scripture they are condemned as a serious depravity and even presented as the sad consequence of rejecting God. The judgment of scripture does not of course permit us to conclude that all who suffer from this anomaly are personally responsible for it, but it does attest to the fact that homosexual acts are intrinsically disordered and can in no case be approved.[52]

This kind of argument finds its way into the most recent document from the U.S. bishops on this issue: "Ministry to Persons with a Homosexual Inclination." In this however the harsh expression "objectively evil" is replaced with "objectively disordered."[53] Once again the bishops distinguish between the immorality of homosexual acts, and having a homosexual inclination which is not sinful to the extent it is not subject to one's free will. In this new statement the bishops stress that saying a person has a particular inclination that is disordered is not the same as saying that the person as a whole is disordered. Nor, they say, does it mean that one has been rejected by God or the Church. This clarification is a welcome improvement, but one has to wonder why the bishops feel they have to keep coming back to this issue.

In 1986 the Vatican had said as much already in a letter that the Sacred Congregation of the Faith sent to the Bishops of the Catholic Church on "The Pastoral Care of Homosexual Persons." This letter was in response to the fact that many in the Church were becoming more open to gay people in relationships with others of the same sex:

That document [the earlier Declaration] stressed the duty of trying to understand the homosexual condition and noted that culpability for homosexual acts should only be judged with prudence. At the same time the Congregation took note of the distinction commonly drawn between the homosexual condition or tendency and individual homosexual actions. These were described as deprived of their essential and indispensable finality, as being "intrinsically disordered," and able in no case to be approved of. (Cf. n., s 4.)

In the discussion which followed the publication of the Declaration, however, an overly benign interpretation was given to the homosexual condition itself, some going so far as to call it neutral, or even good. Although the particular inclination of the homosexual person is not a sin, it is a more or less strong tendency ordered toward an intrinsic moral evil; and thus the inclination itself must be seen as an objective disorder.[54]

Fr. Bernard Lynch in speaking of this letter said it was a cry for help from the institutional church: Help us, we are desperate. The slaves are always the ones who set the masters free. St. Patrick was a slave and he came to Ireland to set us free.

The statements and disciplinary actions of the Vatican seem desperate acts aimed at closing off any real dialogue on this issue. These include the removal of Bishop Giallot and the way that the Vatican has treated Sister Jeannine Gramick and Father Bob Nugent. Their work with the gay community, on the face of it, seems based very much along the lines of the teachings of the U.S. Bishops. Yes, there was some ambiguity in their work, but at no time did either of them ever publicly question the actual teaching of the institutional church. And at no time were they ever allowed due process. Yet both were silenced and later banned from their important work with the gay community, because it seemed to the Vatican that they *privately* dissented from the Church's teaching, or at least were not vigorous enough in presenting it in public.[55] Their silencing caused great pain and many pastoral problems at Most Holy Redeemer. At Most Holy Redeemer I said that they were prophetic, and that prophets and saints were often persecuted by the institutional church. I quoted the words of St. Augustine: "There are many whom the Church has, that God does not have; and many that God has that the Church does not have."[56]

Father Zachary Shore felt obliged to address the July 13 Notification from the Vatican's Congregation for the Doctrine of the Faith dealing with Gramick and Nugent. Shore said he feared that the Vatican's repeated emphasis on "intrinsic evil" would be perceived by many as "not physical but emotional gay-bashing." He also said that, while he could argue with nothing in its content, he wished the Church would "give equal attention" to the "need for respect and dignity" of gays and lesbians. He told the congregation he was "proud to be their pastor" and praised their witness to Jesus Christ. He said, "It is times like these" that can "serve to draw us closer to each other through prayer" and in acknowledging "God's unconditional love for each one of us." The *Catholic San Francisco* reported Shore received a standing ovation for his homily.[57]

For one gay man, Frank Masson, the coverage around this event brought him back to the Catholic Church:

> As a Catholic who grew up in the Church before the changes of Vatican II, and as a gay man, I have always felt like an outsider, someone who is not fully welcome in the Church. I was raised to believe that in order to be a good Catholic—to use a humorous but trite expression, to be a "good Catholic"—a man must pray (at Mass on Sunday), pay, (his offering to the Church), play, (bingo on Thursday nights), and obey (whatever Father said), but not be gay! I tried my best to live as a devout and faithful Catholic, and although I was married for almost thirteen years, and despite my best efforts, deep down I felt that I was not being fully true to myself, or to my family, or to the Church, because I could not be honest about who I am, and be loved and accepted by those from whom I had been taught that I had a right to expect unconditional acceptance and love.
>
> My wife and I eventually divorced in 1989 and I also left the Church for several years after that so I could be gay. Occasionally I would attend Mass, and finally, perhaps four or five years ago, I started to return more regularly. I tried other faith traditions, hoping to find a comfortable place to be, but I was unsuccessful, and now I have fully come to believe that a Catholic cannot really be fully happy anywhere else than in the Church.
>
> About a year and a half ago, and still feeling very definitely as an outsider/observer rather than a full participant, I read in the newspapers about Sister Gramick and Father Nugent, and that they were being silenced because of their ministry to Gay and Lesbian persons. I read everything that I could find about the issue, and in the process learned from the *San Francisco Chronicle* that Fr. Zachary Shore was going to give a homily on the issue at Most Holy Redeemer Church, the "Gay" Catholic parish in the Castro the following Sunday. In the newspaper article, he was quoted as saying that many of his parishioners were openly gay, and that as their pastor he had a duty to talk to them and to support them. I had never heard a supportive statement from someone like that in the church before!
>
> I absolutely had to go to hear what he said.
>
> He gave his homily before the beginning of Mass. Father Tom [Hayes] spoke briefly at the usual place. Two things happened for me. I cried at the homilies. I felt a warm chill in my chest when he spoke. It was obvious to me that others had reacted to his words just as I had done, because the entire congregation who were present burst out into a spontaneous, long, and sustained applause. Many others cried, just as I was unashamedly. I am nearly 60 years old, and I had never seen a homily applauded before in my life, until that day. (I have seen it happen a few times since then, but again at MHR.)
>
> It was the first time in my entire life that I felt completely welcome in church as a whole person. I didn't have to leave part of me outside the door to be able to enter the church to worship my God with others. I could bring all of me as I really am, an American male, Gay, and Catholic.[58]

Despite the ban, Sr. Gramick and Fr. Nugent spoke again at Most Holy Redeemer. Fr. Nugent presided at the main Sunday mass and they participated in a joint service at the Metropolitan Community Church on Eureka Street. Fr. Shore also said a prayer of blessing at this event. In fact, Nugent and Gramick received an increased number of invitations to speak after their ban. Their canon lawyers advised them that canon law should always be interpreted as narrowly as possible and that the ban did not prevent them speaking in public about the decision and about sexuality in general. This interpretation led to a later clarification by the Vatican, which also silenced them from talking about the process or lack of it, or about sexuality. After the second notification from the Vatican, Nugent decided to take a low profile. Sister Jeannine however decided it did not mean she could not talk in public about other issues such as conscience. Furthermore she joined a different congregation of sisters in order to belong to a more supportive community. And Gramick came back to MHR to give a talk at Most Holy Redeemer church on the subject of conscience and the fidelity of doctrine. It was filmed by a German TV crew who were making a documentary about the Congregation of the Doctrine of the Faith.

Sister Jeannine spoke of how conscience is a deep personal conviction about what one has come to believe. Conscience is the place where we hear God and we come to it in an informed way. One listens to the official Church teaching and takes it seriously, and then one asks what does my life experience say to this teaching. One also brings the secular human sciences to bear on the topic, the scriptures, and the experience of the contemporary community. After praying about it, consulting widely, then one goes to that sacred place where you are with God and makes a decision. Gramick explained this is how doctrine develops over time. Whenever our conscience goes against the teaching of the church there is a tension, but it is a healthy tension. We know that the development of doctrine does take place over time. And as we know doctrine has developed over time, for instance with regard to slavery. Once we believed that the earth was the center of the universe. It took our church a long time to recognize that truth. Revelation continues down the centuries. These days we accept and respect our Jewish brothers and sisters but that was not always the case in the church. Vatican II proclaimed the Declaration on Religious Liberty. Even if we are in error we must follow our conscience. This was something new for the church. Gramick struck a chord for many of those listening in the church, for many at MHR remain good Catholics and at the same time dissent in conscience from Church teaching on certain issues, including on homosexuality.

That there are loyal Catholics who dissent in conscience, as at MHR, is what allows theology to grow:

> Are we allowed to differ from the Church's hitherto accepted norms and judgments? Yes, if theology is to grow. Knowledge develops when opposite opinions

are discussed, until an integration is reached. In this process, "theological dissent" forms a creative part. Theological dissent as a means of seeking the truth was defended by the American bishops in their pastoral letter "Human Life in our Day," where they argue that theological dissent is possible and proper, even when it is leveled against statements of the pope and/or bishops of the Church, as long as it is exercised responsibly.[59]

Gramick also spoke of the importance of anger, and urged people at MHR to use it in constructive ways to change things for the better. Gramick cautioned it was important to remember that bishops do their job as they sincerely believe it; that it is important to give others the benefit of the doubt. At this point in the meeting Ramona Michaels called out: "You are too kind, Sister!" Gramick responded, "No, I think that is what the Gospel calls us to. Do we love only those who love us, if we do, we are just like the heathens. We are called to be kind to those who have different views. Cardinal Ratzinger has his branch and I have mine, but we are all part of the one."

Sister Gramick described the role of a community at Most Holy Redeemer:

> I think it can be a model for other parishes. I know every parish has gay and lesbian people in it, but looking at what Most Holy Redeemer does in terms of how it meets the needs of gay and lesbian people can be a model for other parishes . . .
>
> The role of a parish such as Most Holy Redeemer is to make known the experiences of gay and lesbian people, just as with the Knight Initiative, when Fr. Shore spoke out disagreeing with funds being given for this purpose and many others in the parish wrote similar letters. Well, that is what needs to be done. . . .
>
> One of the blessings of what has happened to us, is that it has given the issue higher profile and is causing people to talk about this issue. More Catholics are saying, "Yes, we do have gay and lesbian people in our parish and what are we doing for them?" The action against Father Nugent and me has forced grass roots Catholics to talk about this issue. There is an increase in gay-friendly parishes. That is a blessing, and is a pastoral mystery of dying and rising. Out of something that looks so devastating comes something good.[60]

Gramick is restating what the church actually teaches about conscience, although it is sometimes a well-kept secret. It is important to remind ourselves of it, because many of the Catholics at Most Holy Redeemer live out of just such a space, in the same way that Catholics in other parishes practice artificial contraception while remaining Catholics in good standing. Gay Catholics in relationships are in a similar situation. Catholics can dissent and remain loyal despite what some Catholic fundamentalists would want us believe.[61] Most gay Catholics at MHR do long for that day when the institutional Church will accept and recognize their reality, just as the church now recognizes how wrong we were on slavery. However, most parishioners are realistic and realize that such a change will take a very long time. In the meantime, however, praxis is changing. Gay Catholics are becoming an open and accepted part of parish life in a greater number of parishes. I believe that this movement will grow as gays are more accepted in society. I don't see how it can be stopped. The result is that increasing numbers of gay and queer identified Catholics do feel at home in church. Perhaps a start is being made as the church, in the 2006 document from the U.S. bishops conference drops talk of "intrinsic evil" in relation to homosexuality. This move does not actually change teaching, but at least by doing this the bishops have toned down the rhetoric and thus perhaps are helping the needed conversation. Such language hurts those who are catholic and gay, as Archbishop Quinn agreed, reasoning with Cardinal Ratzinger, now Pope Benedict XVI:

> Given the phenomenon of AIDS, if you put that in there, it will not be understood in the philosophical sense that you want it to be, it will only be regarded as an act of immense cruelty in the face of all this suffering. And that is exactly what happened . . . when the document [the so-called "Halloween Letter" from Cardinal Ratzinger] came out all I could do was sit back and watch what happened. I foretold what happened and it did happen. And to this day it has never been forgotten.[62]

The late Michael Fleming of Most Holy Redeemer speaks of his relationship with the institutional church:

> I don't think the Catholic Church realizes what is going on with the gay community. It is the same thing as is going on in the straight community. My sister-in-law says that our relationships cannot be the same. You know it is no different. I think the church should be blessing any kind of relationship where two people take care of each other, provide for each other, all the things that humans need to have a decent life, to be good to other people, to get involved in AIDS work or social work, or helping other people. Instead the Church just acts like our love counts for nothing, or is evil. That really irritates me . . .
>
> Sometimes I feel like telling the Church, "Well, shove it, I am not going back there." But I think you have to stick with it to be an influence in the Church. . . . To me the church could do a really good service by encouraging these kind of relationships. By saying they are evil they are turning off a lot of people . . .
>
> I think that what you hear officially is not what it is about. We both feel it is the people who are the church. What is important are not the official statements coming out of Rome, but what is going on in your local parish, and how people treat one another there.[63]

Catholics of all kinds, like Fleming, are beginning to create an inclusive and welcoming church for Catholics who happen to be queer, gay, lesbian, bisexual, transgender, inter-sexual, or questioning. They are not waiting for permission. Ordinary Catholics who feel very differently about this subject, whether for or against the present teachings of the church on this issue, can still help create an inclusive space for gay people in the Church. However it is important that the Church is big enough to allow the necessary conversation about both moral teaching and pastoral practice to continue. Efforts to end the pastoral work of Gramick and Nugent destroy the space necessary for a real dialogue to take place. Indeed silencing those who respectfully explore this topic will make the church increasingly irrelevant to a new generation. My impression is that much of the younger generation, whether self-identifying as conservative or liberal, find this a non-issue. The Catholic Church needs to listen to the experience of those who are gay and grapple with the questions that experience raises. Ending the conversation when the questions have hardly even begun to emerge stunts this important process.

Jon Nilson imagines what would have happened if the church had taken the approach encouraged in the Vatican II document *Gaudium et Spes*. This document of the council urged that a conversation on problems of common concern was the most eloquent proof of the Church's solidarity with the human family. Nilson says that a Vatican II approach to the subject would have the pope and his fellow bishops deeply involved in discernment, i.e., consulting biologists, sociologists, and psychologists, reading moral theologians and historians of theology, meeting with individuals and groups of homosexual persons as well as their families and friends:

> The Church's teachers would listen and contribute to the discussions and debates in order to discover the content and appropriate language for the Church's official teaching on homosexuality. If they were pressed for answers before their discernment was complete, they would reply, "We aren't finished with our inquiry yet—and please, don't think that we have all the answers all the time to every question. After all, it's not easy 'to hear, distinguish, and interpret the many voices of our age, and judge them in light of the divine Word.'"[64]

As Nilson points out, the response of the Church to Gramick and Nugent shows this is not the way the Church's practice and teaching has developed on this topic since that council, and that he feels is a great pity:

> The problem is not with the Church's motive, then, but with the ways in which it expresses its concern for human well being when it comes to homosexuality. The content and rhetoric of the official teaching are simply repeated whenever a serious challenge seems put to it. The findings, however tentative, of exegetes, psychologists, sociologists, moral philosophers, and theologians and the experience of gays and lesbians and their families seem to have no impact whatsoever. As a result, the gap between the magisterium on the one side, and the people and

many moral theologians on the other side, grows dangerously wider and wider as their mutual trust breaks down.[65]

The issue will not go away. At some point, however distant, the Catholic Church will have to face it in realistic ways at a larger, institution-wide level. A parish such as MHR is the kind of place that will facilitate that eventual necessary conversation. For it is a sacred place where the conversation within the Church and also between the Church and the world on this issue has been taking place for a considerable time. Thus we are preparing for the future. Lisa Middleton describes the situation at Most Holy Redeemer:

> MHR is on the front line of a huge debate that has been going on in the Church and is going to continue to go on for decades to come. And the church, depending on your point of view, has dealt with the issues of sex and gender either poorly or as well as it could. Largely the thinking of the hierarchy is patriarchal. It is steeped and rooted in a world that [has been left behind]. I think the debate will not go away. It will continue, and it is going to be hard, so many of the issues as they relate to gays and lesbians get very close to home. And they are taken personally. You cannot help but take them personally.
>
> I find that the parish leadership here, especially the Parish Council, the elders of the church if you will, is trying to keep a balance between the need to be responsive and express dissent with where the hierarchy is at, and also with some of the more inflammatory things that are said. There are examples in different places of parishes that have become highly charged and in which open confrontation with leadership has taken place, and frequently what you find when that happens is that a parish ends up dividing. Then the sense of spirituality becomes secondary to the political issues of the day, and maybe there is some progress on some of the social issues, maybe not; but it is a very tough place to be. I think MHR is trying to avoid that kind of divisive politics and stay true to our individual souls that tell us that ours is a Church that needs to change. It is a balancing act. It would be wrong to give ourselves too much credit and say we have the balance right. It would be right to say that this is a very tough task. Doing it right is hard work.[66]

It is hard to get the balance right. For some such as Rev. Jim Mitulski, a former Catholic who was a friend of the parish and pastor at MCC for many years, the parish does not go far enough:

> MHR has something to say to the wider Catholic community. The first thing I would say to them is: Say it! Don't be afraid to say it. You do have something to say. What I've observed when I've been there is a caring community, intergenerational, to some extent mixed gay and straight, much more gay than straight—but still it's a cooperative, it's an exercise, it's a social experiment, and they know how to take care of one another. They know the same things we know

at MCC, the wholesomeness and beauty and God-given character of gay identity and gay relationships. Whereas on the margins we have the freedom to say
it, they too have the freedom to say it, and I would say to them, your freedom
will come when you say it. And live with the consequences. It's a risk. . . .

I think MHR epitomizes what the Catholic Church could and should be. And
it's a base community walking a very thin line. I mean, ironically, in the seminary in the Eighties we were studying liberation theology, we would look at the
gap between the base communities in Latin America and the evil cardinals and
archbishops who were opposed to them. And to some extent that culture has
been replicated now in the United States where you have pockets of liberal
Catholicism that are very much at odds with the hierarchy. So a parish like MHR
has nothing to lose by being more public and by saying what they know to be
true. And I understand how painful that can be and how difficult that can be, but
even from a spiritual perspective we know about how you have to lose in order
to gain. You have to die in order to live. . . .

I think, because I grew up in the Catholic Church, I understand the contradic-
tions that the people of MHR live with. There is a built-in schizophrenia to Catholicism that you hate to leave it, you never really do leave it on one level, you're willing to put up with a lot, because what you get is a lot too. I think that people who
are not Catholic are going to be a lot harsher in their assessment of what is happening at MHR. Certainly people say about MHR that it's people worshipping their
own oppression and participating in it. And I've heard the same critique of MCC,
because it's Christianity, so I'm not pointing fingers and saying, "They are like this,
and we're not like this," because I think the same critique can be applied. But at
MCC I felt we had the freedom to engage that critique and really reinvent Christianity if we had to. And I'm not sure they have the same freedom at MHR. . . .

Now I am going to contradict what I just said! Those who are really comfortable with their identity, and unwilling to invest their energies elsewhere are
probably on Eureka Street [MCC], and people who feel some commitment to
trying to change the institution from within, and who are also proud of their
identity, are probably on Diamond Street [MHR]. And then you have everything
in between. And people go on both ends, but I do think that there comes a point
in the spiritual lives of many gay and lesbian people where it's just not an option to set foot in a Catholic Church. You know, they feel too good about themselves, and they recognize how the Church functions in society. It's not just a
spiritual or interior organization. It has a social dimension that influences public policy, and they want to hold it accountable.

But so it does have power in society, and there are many women who come
to MCC whose primary conflict with the Church isn't even simply lesbianism.
They would say, and they do say, it's about being a woman. Just that weekly insult of going into a building and never seeing a woman at the altar. Once they've
experienced that, it makes them nuts. You know what is that about? So, there are
many challenges that the Church faces, but to underestimate its political power
is naïve. It does have tremendous social and political influence, less and less in
a place like San Francisco, but still very strong in other areas.[67]

Mitulski and Middleton give some good reasons why the parish is a wonderful resource for the whole church, albeit one as yet largely unrecognized.

> Yet the magisterium has apparently terminated the effort toward rapprochement questions related to the family. Today its response to these complex moral issues, including homosexuality, is not that conversation urged by Vatican II as the "most eloquent proof of the Church's solidarity with the human family." Instead, contemporary experiences and perspectives on sexuality are taken as *prima facie* erroneous. In place of a conversation between Church and world there is the clear, consistent, and unchanging moral teaching.
>
> Despite some short-term gains, the costs of this strategy are very high; theological incoherence, the appearance of arrogance in seeming to dismiss the tentative findings of the social sciences, and dismissal of the testimony of its own homosexual members and even marginalizing them (as well as their families and friends) by the claim that their sexual orientation, unlike that of their heterosexual sisters and brothers, is "objectively disordered," and the resulting loss of credibility by the Church's teaching authority.[68]

The Catholic Church is not a credible moral voice within the gay community. If you ever read the gay press at times you might think that war had been declared between the two. I hear many gay people say that they did not leave the church but rather that the church left them when they accepted themselves as gay. Rather than be a search for scapegoats, the present crisis might better point us to the deeper malaise, our seeming inability as an institution to deal in healthy ways with issues of power and sexuality.

Andrew Sullivan is both Catholic and gay. He says the church is like the family that cannot talk about the subject even though its own daughter or son is queer. Sullivan says that queer Catholics need to make themselves known so that the rest of the church can listen and learn:

> Why not a teaching about the nature of homosexuality and what its good is? How can we be good? Teach us. How does one inform the moral lives of homosexuals? The church has an obligation to *all* its faithful to teach us how to live and how to be good—which is not the mere dismissal, silence, embarrassment or a "unique" doctrine on one's inherent disorder. Explain it. How does God make this? Why does God make this?
>
> I grew up with nothing. No one taught me anything except that this couldn't be mentioned. And as a result of the total lack of teaching, gay Catholics and gay people in general are in crisis. No wonder people's lives–many gay lives–are unhappy or distraught or in dysfunction, because there is no guidance at all. Here is a population within the church, and outside the church, desperately seeking health and values. And the church refuses to come to our aid, refuses to listen to this call.[69]

This process of creating safe space is a challenge both for gay Catholics and for the rest of the church. Most Holy Redeemer is a model. As Archbishop Quinn said:

> I think Most Holy Redeemer does an important service, an important role for the church in the city of San Francisco. I think if there weren't a Most Holy Redeemer we should create one. It has proved repeatedly to be a very effective witness of the church, and a very effective service on the part of the church. I think many other places could learn from it, in Europe and the United States. . . . I will say it was one of the most reverent and beautiful parish liturgies of any parish I ever visited; it was spirited and reverent, and beautiful, uplifting. I thought it was beautiful. There was an evident spirituality in that community.[70]

Gay Catholics are learning to be more assertive, to come out, and ask for change. However this requires the willingness of others to listen, people such as Archbishop Quinn, who are willing to take action to make our churches safe and inclusive spaces.

Silence on this topic is, as Sullivan argues, simply an inadequate response. Silence forces people to split themselves into two, to live a hidden life that is a lie, to live in fear; and it also deprives the wider community of so much. Silence alone, or mere toleration, does not make a parish a welcoming community. Most Holy Redeemer is a community where this conspiracy of silence has been broken. Energies that have been used up in keeping something a secret are released for the sake of the whole community. A parish such as Most Holy Redeemer puts a human face on what is for many in the church an abstract issue. Bishop Holloway presents this point compellingly:

> We struggle intellectually or psychologically with an abstract issue: can women be ordained? Should gay and lesbian people be allowed the blessing of the Church in their relationships? At this stage it is a theoretical issue in our own hearts and heads, but soon it becomes a person knocking at the door like Cornelius,[71] and we are called out of the refuge of abstraction to confront real human beings who are being victimized by those same abstractions. That has certainly been my experience. What begins as abstract theorizing, almost as an intellectual game, soon becomes flesh and blood that makes its challenge directly and will not let me escape into theory. Your theory, this abstraction you struggle with, is actually about *me,* and it is causing me to suffer. Your theology *hurts* me, gets me beaten up, sometimes even killed: think about it![72]

The role of straight Catholics, and there are a significant and growing number at Most Holy Redeemer is to act as allies in making such change possible. Ramona Michaels became the parish secretary as a grandmother and not only found her life changed, but found that her children had some adjusting to do:

I told my children I was going to work for a community that was largely gay and there was no reaction. And then I as I worked here, I was full of stories. And so I would talk about it, and I was met with silence from all four of my daughters and their husbands. No response. Or, "That is nice, come to eat," or changing the subject, all very uneasy.

Gradually some of my children came to visit the church, but the men never came. The first time one of my daughters came to mass here it was midnight mass in 1993 or 92. She came and sat there and was breathing nervously, deeply. Afterwards she said to me, "Do you mind if we don't go to coffee?" Now when she visits she will chat away with everyone. Now my son-in-law said, "I am never going to that church." I said, "Well you are not coming to my funeral then." Also this happened among life long friends.

Well being the person that I am, I am going to talk about it for ever! I want people to know that it is not all bars, what I see in church is a healthy thriving community. A bunch of people who worship the Lord in the same manner I do, very familial and very comforting. Little by little, I am talking about this, my grandchildren were younger and they were listening very carefully. Among the first responses I got from my grandchildren was, "I am glad you really like your job, Nana," "Okay, Nana," and "How long have they lived together?" and "They go to church?" Yes, they say the family that prays together stays together.

My grandchildren were very accepting. They come to visit two or three at a time. I don't feel any tension with them. One of them when in high school wrote an essay about her grandma who worked with the gays. She won some sort of class prize for it. I probably have a copy of it. The forty-somethings forget it, and my friends in their sixties were just silent.

One day we sat around, these friends from my kindergarten days and we were talking about our funerals. Well, my funeral, they all said, we are not going to your funeral, you are just going to have a big old show. I said you are going to miss something because you will all be in tears. That broke the ice and now I can talk about gay people to my old time friends. They admittedly say they never knew a gay person. Well my goodness, my girlfriend, I went to the kindergarten with her. She has got a gay son. We have never spoken about Sal, he has been here to church, and then she had another son who killed himself and Sal said he put a bullet through his head as he could not accept himself as gay. We have never talked about that.

I think I want to say to the wider church just love us as we love God and you. Don't be so harsh on us, we are much like you Bishop, Father.

When I went to Rome and I saw all those priests running around, some kind of fear and coldness gripped my heart. I thought so many people who won't admit who they are, and that is their business. I will not judge that, but the politics and the rest of the stuff that goes on here, it put a fear in my heart, people were just too righteous.

My faith here has deepened over the years. My conversion has been slow. When I saw faith filled people reaching out and practicing their faith, more than I saw in heterosexual parishes if you will, where if you reached your hand out for the sign of peace they barely offer you a finger, and do not look at you and did not want to touch you. Some people are terribly affronted by our sign of peace. All the demonstration and hugging and kissing, same-sex hugging and kissing. I could go for an hour and do the whole church and most of us could. We try to contain ourselves, I have heard people say it is too much, but I am getting older and I have an open mind. What is wrong with it? The older people enjoy it. When Nick [Andrade] goes around and hugs some of the old ladies, they are waiting with a sparkle in their eyes. Who else hugs these old people?[73] And in other churches they want to do their duty and that is it.

Ten o'clock mass here is not a duty. People come here out of love. It is not just the love of the coffee hour, which we all like. I have heard it called the cruising hour. I say, Come and visit us we have a wonderful coffee hour, you might meet a nice guy. But there is a hook, once you take part in the service you are hooked by other things. It is a way to God. Another way to find God.

Sometimes I go to Call to Action. Quite a few of us here belong to CTA. Kathy Jenkins, Sr. Cleta, Mary Quinlin. It was started by bishops and others. It is all about openness. My eyes were opened. We could have this kind of church, people of all sexualities, all kinds of people. It was marvelous. To see that we could be this kind of church, the one you dream about. But this is not happening. It seems like we are tightening up again.

I don't want the Church of my childhood. I really don't. It was so strict, yet of course it brought me to where I am today! I did not like the fact that you had to go, I was forced to go. However I do remember the churches were packed in ways they are not now. For the future I want an open and better Church. I know you live in Kansas, but honest to goodness, Dorothy, you need to accept those who are different from you in your family. You cannot refer to them as the little brown ones or the homosexuals, or be ashamed of them. Jesus accepted everybody no matter what they did, and that is the way we need to be.[74]

I do not believe that there is an "us" or a "them" in the light of the gospel. There is only a "we." John and the late Evelyn Squeri are a good example of straight parishioners at Most Holy Redeemer who have become allies and friends to their fellow gay parishioners. Born in the 1930s they lived in the neighborhood and been active parishioners their whole lives:

We were raising a young family and there were these make-out scenes on the corner. I had led a very sheltered life. . . . When the gay people first came into the area—you know, people just never talked about things like that, and the outlandish stuff really kind of scared people off. . . .

Then we got to know them as people in the church and we saw that people are people. My daughters worked at the store and they got to see the people. They called us in the parish the Gays and the Grays. Some people left the parish. We were never tempted to leave however. Then a dying church started to fill up again. People like Marie Krystofiac would get the young men under her wing.

She would phone up and say: "We need a couple dozen cookies, you have them here, right?" You could not say no! Men with AIDS responded to her. She would have dozens and dozens of cookies. The parish became their family too.

We were parents; it made us feel terrible. In some way these guys found their mothers in these old ladies. It created a bond of dignity and acceptance after that time around sexual orientation. . . . With Fr. Tony it was always God loves you, no matter what; it was an eye opener for us at our age. . .

I think the church has grown up. You can say whatever you want now. Today I think the church should applaud gay commitments, not just casual relationships. I think it's too hard to live a life alone. I think people need each other. Yes, the people we have seen in long time relationships, it is so sweet, one almost forty-five years long. A relationship is a relationship.

My mother's hair would curl if she heard me! She was also here in the parish too in the 1920s. People say to us, "Oh—you go to *that* parish!" They really feel sorry for you. I just think they see the gay freedom parade and think that is what church looks like. Not like normal people coming to Sunday worship. I've gotten all kinds of comments. It's very hurtful to hear them. It's like that Joan Collins song, my friends are acting strange, and they shake their heads and say I've changed. Once they hear what we are doing in the parish they say, Hey that is good. And we do get positive comments too. What a great parish, doing good things, we get positive comments too. Sometimes I make a comment back about the parish. It depends who the person is and what the situation is, not however in St. Mary's hospital where I am Eucharist minister. I don't want to cause a heart attack!

I think people really need to speak for themselves at MHR. I think when people come once or twice and see the spirit working; they will be convinced people are people.[75]

Gay people at MHR no longer see themselves as the recipients of ministry but as rather the very ones, along with straight allies, who will bring about the change by doing the ministry themselves, by being prophetic and challenging the silence and fear that surrounds this issue. In this regard parishioners and former parishioners at Most Holy Redeemer have taken a lead. Jamie Cherrie and Jim Gunther are a committed gay couple in a long-term relationship that, like a considerable number of other gay couples actually met at Most Holy Redeemer. This is a letter they wrote to the Archbishop after Levada had written an article defending the status quo for marriage in California:

Dear Archbishop Levada,

As members of Most Holy Redeemer Catholic Church in San Francisco, we are writing to let you know of our disappointment in you as our Archbishop. As you continue to write and speak to and about the gay and lesbian community of San Francisco you are slowly rendering apart the very fragile fabric of faith that we have worked hard to create here in this city. Not once in your most recent article on DOMA did you mention the Catholic Church's teaching on compassion toward the homosexual. Not once did you mention the on-going development of the Catholic Church's understanding of homosexuality in the light of modern psychology, medicine, and psychiatry. Your desire to undermine the Catholic gay and lesbian community's efforts to live stable, committed lives is very apparent today. To say the least, we are deeply grieved by your words and actions.

When you visited us most recently for the re-dedication of our church, you saw for yourself the handiwork that Catholic gays and lesbians have helped to create. You even spoke eloquently regarding the necessary and wonderful outreach the community was providing to the city at large. You were able to affirm the great faith and dedication of gays and lesbians and their contributions to the church in ministry. You saw firsthand what the faith of gays and lesbians can do, gays and lesbians who have found faith, nourishment, and support in committed relationships and have brought these wonderful gifts to Most Holy Redeemer to be shared. Even after all of this you still preach a message of disdain for what we are trying to achieve, accusing us of being subversive, and fostering a spirit of fear among the people in the Catholic Church that the very essence of the sanctity of marriage is at risk. It is that very sanctity that we have emulated, and now want protection for, and will continue to work for in the church and society as a whole.

Archbishop, we don't need you in order to continue living out the very basis of our faith: "Where two or more are gathered, there I am in their midst." We have experienced the power of Christ flowing through our relationship. We shall continue to participate and share that truth with all people, especially with the parishioners of Most Holy Redeemer. You see, Archbishop, we're not going to leave. You can't drive us out. This isn't your church. It is ours. We know and live out our responsibility as participants in the priesthood of the laity. We shall continue to preach the Good News of Jesus Christ here in this community, the Good News that God loves gays and lesbians, and most especially that God loves and supports the committed, stable, and loving relationships that we have created despite your protests. We shall preach it loudly and clearly, Archbishop, and let the people know in word and example that the message of Christ is a message of love and compassion. Jesus was not afraid to stand up to the erroneous teachings of the religious leaders of his day. Neither shall we run from our responsibility to speak out against the demeaning and violent rhetoric that is couched in theological terminology, and to help members of our community to do the same.

Two men were recently murdered as a result of prejudice against gays and lesbians: Matthew Shepard and Billy Jack Gaither. There have been countless others. Your inflammatory rhetoric is what perpetuates the belief that gays and lesbians are deserving of such attacks. Why haven't you spoken up against the darkness of evil that plagues our community? Where are your words of hope for us who live in fear for our lives because we are gay? Have you forgotten that you are supposed to be a shepherd of our souls too? Or are we outcasts that you shun? Your silence, Archbishop is not only deafening, but demonstrates your participation in this genocide that is occurring in this country.

Archbishop, there is a story of a village that was hiding a Jew from the Nazis. One individual in the village turned the man over to the Nazis. Once done, the village people confronted him. "Why did you do it? He was a holy man!" "How would I know he was a holy man?" the individual replied. "If only you had looked in his eyes," was their reply. "If only you had looked in his eyes." We wish you could look into the eyes of every committed couple in our parish, Archbishop. We wish you could learn more about our stories, our struggles, and our dreams. Then, and only then, would you come to know us as holy men and women, disciples of Jesus Christ, and realize that we pose no threat to society or to the Catholic Church? Our prayers are with you, Archbishop, that you may come to know the fullness of Truth as revealed in the Spirit of God, as present in the lives of gays and lesbians in committed and loving relationships at Most Holy Redeemer.[76]

Roman Catholic Bishop Gumbleton has a closer relationship with the gay community than Archbishop Levada. Gumbleton often speaks of the need for gays to come out in order to break down stereotypes and prejudices. Gumbleton tells the story of how his family was changed when his brother came out.[77] Catholics, like anyone else, usually change and become more open to the issues when they know a friend or family member who is openly gay, that is part of the point that Cherrie and Gunther make in their letter to the Archbishop. In theology class I was always told that the church is not just a teaching church but also a listening church. Right now on this issue we need a lot more attentive listening so that the voices of gay Catholics are finally heard. Then the Catholic Church may begin to represent for gay people a place of hope rather than the memory of rejection.

It is sad for me to admit that these are new ideas for the largest part of the Roman Catholic Church. The good news is that they are no longer new ideas everywhere in the Catholic Church. Things are changing. And yet, in another way, aren't they very old ideas indeed? Those of us who call ourselves Christians do after all profess to follow Jesus of Nazareth, a man who especially befriended the marginalized in society. I remember once hearing Bono of U2 saying that Jesus would have felt at home hanging out in a gay bar; I would add maybe more so than in some of our churches. For something is seriously wrong when, with exceptions such as at Most Holy Redeemer, Dignity, the Newman Center, and a small but thankfully growing number of parishes, gay people such as Patrick Mulcahey, Jim Gunther, Jamie Cherrie and Thomas O'Connor do not feel comfortable, welcome, or at home in most of our churches. I am convinced that unless we are willing to go into a real and equal dialogue with those who are struggling with their sexuality in terms of their faith, we are not responding as Jesus would.

The choice, as Richard Smith suggests as the thesis of his book: *AIDS, Gays and the American Catholic Church*,[78] is not between an inherited tradition and the latest politically correct fashion. Rather it is between a tradition that has become rigid and strangling to many people, and one that is flexible enough to grow. A living tradition, one that springs from our faith in Jesus, from the scriptures, and for Catholics from church teaching and the tradition, needs a willingness to interact with other cultures, and this must include gay culture. The call of the Second Vatican Council was that we read the "Signs of the Times." In other words we need to ask what is it that God is trying to say to us through the experience and voice of gay Catholics, voices being heard for the first time in history. Can we try to discern together what gifts God is bringing to the wider church through gay Catholics? This is a very different approach from seeing gay people as a threat and as somehow undermining what we are about.

In the context of the dialogue between gay people and the wider church, as Smith argues, we need a mutual and respectfully critical assessment of each side's symbols and values, a recognition of the legitimate and positive elements within, and where appropriate, an assimilation of those positive elements of the other culture into one's own. This is not the same as an uncritical acceptance of everything as found either in the church or in the gay community. And this kind of dialogue is precisely what has been going on for some decades now at Most Holy Redeemer parish. Most Holy Redeemer is an example of a run of the mill parish becoming a mission outpost. It is an example of the fact that unless the church can become open and inclusive to the gay community it will have nothing to say to a whole generation of gay people, simply becoming irrelevant.

As Vincent Genovesi say there is neither justice nor merit in the mentality that claims to tolerate gays and lesbians as long as they know their place and keep to it. For far too long, such a mentality made racial minorities and women into victims.[79] The challenge today is to see homosexuality as a blessing rather than as a curse, and then the church's pastoral role is to help gay people embrace who they are, created in the image of God. Can people be helped to see their sexual orientation as part of their Christian calling and vocation? As I suggested in a homily at MHR we need new models of holiness and Most Holy Redeemer shows the wider community models of people who are holy and gay at the same time:

> The Saints help us to see how the Gospel can be lived in many different ways and under many different social and historical circumstances. The list of canonized saints still tends to be white, European, middle and upper class. Seventy percent of the saints in the calendar are men and of the saints canonized up to 1978 79% were clergy. It strikes me that we need new models of holiness in our age. More lay people, more women. I certainly hope that the day comes when

an openly gay person is canonized. For the church needs role models of openly gay and lesbian persons.

The basic mystery of our faith is, after all, not that God has created a world different from God and in which God must be served and glorified, but rather that grace, which is identical with God, has permeated the world with God's own presence, and this includes the world of gay, lesbian, bisexual and transgender people. To have sexually alive saints of all sexual orientations is the challenge for our own time. Presently a gay person's route to holiness is suspect in our churches, but as Christians we believe in a God who turns the world's ways of order upside down.

I recognize that no road to holiness is easy. I am not suggesting a soft option. However holiness does not have to mean aloofness, grim-faced duty, a denial of the core of ones sexual identity, but should rather include celebration, delight and pleasure. Our sexuality can serve to make us holy with the call to be in touch with the transforming center, the God within and beyond.[80]

I would like to see dioceses around the world implement plans based on such strategies. As Arthur Berliner says:

> A form of affirmative action is required of the churches. It is not enough to preach tolerance. The churches can, and should, in concert with other groups, work actively to eradicate discriminatory laws. They should not merely admit homosexuals to membership in their congregations, but actively seek such members. The gay church may then disappear, as an anachronism belonging to a time when a segregated church was acceptable.[81]

Important organizations such as the Association of Catholic Diocesan Lesbian and Gay Ministries, Dignity, and New Ways already raise many of these questions in the context of North America. The statement of the U.S. Catholic Bishops: *Ministry to Persons with a Homosexual Inclination*[82] seems redundant. Everything in this document has been said somewhere else before. The Catholics of Most Holy Redeemer already know what the Church says on this issue. What a shame that no MHR parishioners or any other gay Catholics were consulted in drawing up this statement. Asking parishioners at Most Holy Redeemer, as the bishops' statement does, not to come out except to a few select people is clearly a case of trying to close the door after the horse has bolted! It seems very odd that no gay Catholics were consulted, especially when you read the statements' call for just such a respectful dialogue. The bishop's definition of dialogue is impressive, it is a pity that the bishops didn't follow it in writing their statement:

> Authentic dialogue, therefore, is aimed above all at the rebirth of individuals through interior conversion and repentance, but always with profound respect for consciences and with patience and at the step-by-step pace indispensable for

modern conditions. Such dialogue facilitates an ongoing, interior conversion for all parties truly engaged in the exchange.[83]

What is there not to like about this definition of dialogue? Certainly I long to hear my church acknowledge the sin of homophobia, ask for forgiveness from gay people, and to take action to create an inclusive church. However I am not sure that is what the bishops had in mind! It is probably true to say that the Church needs the gay community more than the gay community needs the Church, but the reality is we need each other. For after all, it is part of the body of Christ that is gay. For too long we have seemed to make this issue an exception to the rule of Christian love. Certainly I see signs of hope that this is changing. I am confident that the words that Archbishop Tutu once said of the Christian churches will one day no longer be true. Tutu said that the churches make gay and lesbian people doubt if they are children of God, and that, he said, must be almost the ultimate blasphemy.

I know that gay people differ greatly on this issue as on all, but I sense a growing wish to no longer be the object of pity or mere tolerance let alone hostility. Increasingly Catholic gay people want to be seen as equals, capable of collaborating with straight Catholics in the Christian task of helping to build the world that Jesus is on about in the Gospels, the world that he so deeply desires for our world today, a world that is just and humane for all. The creation of safe space for gay Catholics is still very much resisted. Such space must be created if we are to be true to our mission as followers of Jesus Christ.

Let me conclude with something I said at Most Holy Redeemer:

> I believe that Jesus invites us here at Most Holy Redeemer to be a community that confesses our brokenness, one that reaches out and ministers a healing reconciliation between the races, between the young and the old, liberal and conservative, gay and straight, gay, lesbian and bisexual, male and female, the rich and the poor. A truly prophetic community must embrace all people regardless of their differences.
>
> The trouble begins when one group claims exclusive right to the title of Church and shuts out all who will not conform to its model. As you know I am Irish. Well, in the early Irish Church, which long resisted the effort to force its practice into the Roman model, the Holy Spirit was represented not by a white dove, but by a wild goose. As you know geese are not controllable, they make a lot of noise, and even bite people who try to contain them. Incidentally they also make great guard dogs! Christians of all denominations who are marginalized within their churches know that God's spirit comes not only as a tame dove, but also as a wild goose. And it is one that makes its home in unlikely places. The spirit sometimes comes as a goose demanding to be heard. And its sound may not be too sweet to many because the spirit urges us to become noisy, passionate, and courageous guardians of the gospel of Jesus. As Dr. Elizabeth Stuart has

written I too hope it will not be take too long before the whole flock is daring to speak, sing, and dance love's name.[84]

NOTES

1. Chris Glaser, *Come Home! Reclaiming Spirituality and Community as Gay Men and Lesbians* (Harper & Row: San Francisco, 1990), xi–xiii. Glaser is currently the interim pastor of MCC San Francisco.

2. James Alison, "Unbinding the Gay Conscience," talk for Quest Conference, London, Colney, July 26–28, 2002.

3. Charles Bold and Michael Fleming, interview with author, tape recording: San Francisco, March 27, 2001.

4. Fenton Johnson, *Geography of the Heart* (Scribner: New York, 1996).

5. Maria Kennedy, "They Face No Censure: California Jesuits Promote Gay Rights" in *San Francisco Faith*, October 4, 2002.

6. Tom Musbach, "Gay Priests will be on Vatican Agenda," *Gay.com/PlanetOut .com, Network,* April 22, 2002: "I think it is very unlikely that any such screening could or will take place as a general principle," Donal Godfrey, a Jesuit priest in San Francisco, said, via e-mail. "It may happen in some specifically reactionary dioceses." . . . The current scandal raises several other concerns for him. "It makes me grieve for the suffering innocents," he said. The Congregation for Catholic Education did eventually issue: *Instruction concerning the criteria of vocational discernment regarding persons with homosexual tendencies, considering their admission to seminary and to Holy Orders,* Rome, 2005. On an ordinary reading I was proved wrong. However because of the ways this document has been, or rather has not been, implemented; I don't see much change of previous practice. See the article: "The Vatican blames gays for priest scandal: analysis by Matthew Bajko," *Bay Area Reporter,* March 28, 2002, A 10: "The question is: do the present structures serve us well? For the structures are meant to serve us and not the other way around. Jesus didn't set up any specific structures for the Church, and so we must renew and change them in our time to enable us to be what we are meant to be," said Donal Godfrey during a St. Patrick's Day Mass at Most Holy Redeemer in the Castro. Could such a change be in the church's future? Possibly. But for years the church has denied its priests to be sexual beings, and has chastised homosexuals for acting on their sexual desires. Maybe the best that can be hoped for is a more frank discussion of sexuality. And a renewed push for the church to be fully accepting of its gay parishioners."

7. Congregation for Catholic Education, *Instruction concerning the criteria of vocational discernment regarding persons with homosexual tendencies, considering their admission to seminary and to Holy Orders.* Rome, 2005.

8. Rena Ferrick is the daughter of MHR parishioner Roz Gallo. At the time of writing Rena had interviewed many MHR parishioners in the making of this film.

9. For an interesting examination of Judge, see the book by Michael Ford, *Father Mychal Judge: An Authentic American Hero* (Paulist Press: New York, 2002).

Judge had a special ministry not only to the fire department but also to those living with HIV and the gay community. His fire helmet was presented to Pope John Paul II. Maybe Judge can help people see that one can integrate being gay and Catholic at the same time, as Jack Wintz points out in his review of the book. ("Life of Sept. 11 Hero was Driven by Love," *National Catholic Reporter,* October 4, 2002, 38.)

10. Laurie Goodstein, "Priests Citing New Problem in Gay Policy," *The New York Times,* November 24, 2005.

11. Archbishop George Niederauer, quoted by Wyatt Buchanan, "A New Archbishop for San Francisco: views tolerant attitudes toward gays. Homosexuals can minister as priests Niederauer says." *San Francisco Chronicle,* December 16, 2005.

12. Homily by author, Most Holy Redeemer, December 28, 1992.

13. Patrick Mulcahey, written at request of author, October 24, 2001.

14. Matthew 15: 21–28.

15. Marcus J. Borg, *Meeting Jesus Again for the First Time: The Historical Jesus and the Heart of Contemporary Faith* (Harper: San Francisco, 1994), 52.

16. Borg, 59.

17. January 30, 2001 interview by author.

18. *Faith beyond resentment*, 52.

19. *Brokeback Mountain* is a film of 2005 that explores the hidden love of two gay cowboys. *Deus Caritus Est,* the first encyclical of Pope Benedict XVI, promulgated in January 2006, is a well-received reflection on the nature of love.

20. James Alison, "Is it ethical to be Catholic?" "The Communities in Conversation" 2006 Project, held at Most Holy Redeemer parish, February 12, 2006. Co-sponsored by MHR parish and the Lane Center for Catholic Studies and Social Thought along with the LGBTQ Caucus at the University of San Francisco.

21. Stephen Pattison, *Shame: Theory, Therapy, Theology* (Cambridge: Cambridge University Press, 2000), 308.

22. Cunningham and Gallo were featured in Annie Nakao, "Three Diverse Bay Area Families Share Universal Joys of the Holiday," *San Francisco Examiner,* December 26, 1993: "This Christmas snuck up with a vengeance, but Roz Gallo and Catherine Cunningham caught up with the help of their multitude of a family. Crowding their warm Mission District flat on Christmas Day were a son and daughter, grandparents, ex-in-laws and even an ex-husband—all milling around a Christmas tree trimmed with candy canes, tiny bears and white doves.

"At the center of this: Gallo and Cunningham, who have been together as a couple for 6 1/2 years. 'We're just two moms,' said Gallo, whose 20-year-old daughter is the same age as Cunningham's son. Both children were in their early teens when their mothers divorced and got together. It was a time of turmoil for young Rena Ferrick. . . . Sitting next to her, Jeremiah Crowell, Cunningham's son, a student at Columbia University, said he looks at his two mothers as an example of a 'nice married couple. It's what I aspire to in a relationship. Sometimes, though, it's a little overwhelming— they're both so very motherly.'

"Both women have busy lives. They are informal hospice workers to friends dying of AIDS. They are also active at Most Holy Redeemer Catholic Church in the Castro, where Cunningham is an acolyte and the two attend Midnight Mass every Christmas Eve." In January 2007 Nick Andrade was the parish council president.

23. Catherine Cunningham and Rosalyn Gallo, interview by author, tape recording: San Francisco, March 10, 2001.

24. This BBC Radio 4 program was recorded on October 22, 2006 and was broadcast on April 29, 2007. The text of the broadcast is available at http://www.bbc.co.uk/religion/programmes/sunday_worship.

Pictures of this and other significant parish events may be found on the MHR parish website at www.mhr.org.

25. See the interesting discussion by Fr. Peter Liuzzi on "Issues versus Agendas" in *With Listening Hearts: Understanding the Voices of Lesbian and Gay Catholics* (Paulist Press: New Jersey, 2001), 8.

26. Bernard Schlager, program director for the Center for Lesbian and Gay Studies in Religion and Ministry at the Pacific School of Religion, agrees: "Like Sparks, Godfrey says gay men and women should not be defined by a small part of who they are. 'At a place like Most Holy Redeemer, gays and lesbians can pray as whole human beings,' Godfrey says, 'he or she can pray without shame.' For Schlager, a parish like Most Holy Redeemer is symbolic of his hope for change." Jenny Diamond, "Catholic Priest Speaks About Church Stance on Sexuality," *Daily Californian,* May 14, 2002.

27. Miriam Therese Winter, Adair Lummis, & Allison Stokes, *Defecting in Place: Women Claiming Responsibility for Their Own Spiritual Lives* (Crossroad: New York, 1994), 197.

28. Peter Harris, "Speaking the Truth in Love," in *The Vatican and Homosexuality: Reactions to the "Letter to the Bishops of the Catholic Church on Pastoral Care of Homosexual Persons,"* eds. Jeannine Gramick and Pat Furey (Crossroad: New York, 1988), 114.

29. Stephen B. Bevans, *Models of Contextual Theology* (New York: Orbis Books, 1992), 8.

30. Unpublished, August 1999.

31. See also "A Place at the Table: Towards a Positive Gay Theology," paper given by author, Gay Pride Week, Derry, Ireland, 1996. This event was organized by James Grant.

32. February 13, 2001 interview by author.

33. Mosche Shokeid, *A Gay Synagogue in New York* (Columbia University Press: New York, 1995), 240. This study of a congregation that was specifically founded for gay Jews can be contrasted with the unpublished study of how a mostly straight New York Jewish congregation became open and affirming of the gay community. Rabbi Linda Henry Goodman's thesis was submitted in partial fulfillment of the requirements for the Doctor of Ministry degree, "Gay and Lesbian Inclusion at Union Temple of Brooklyn" at Hebrew Union College–Jewish Institute of Religion Graduate Studies Program, New York, March 1999.

34. Shokeid, 242–43.

35. March 28, 2001 interview by author.

36. Michael Mullins, from the manuscript of "The Next Generation," chapter 6 in *A Long Way From Rome: Why the Australian Catholic Church Is in Crisis,* eds. Chris McGillon, and Geraldine Duogue (Allen and Unwin: Sydney, 2003).

37. Louis Weil, *The New Church's Teaching Series: A Theology of Worship,* vol. 12 (Cowley Publications: Cambridge, 2002), 55.

38. For example, see Evelyen Nieves, "At a Largely Gay Church, a Test of Faith: Some San Francisco Catholics Have Harsh Words for Hierarchy," *New York Times,* April 29, 2002, A20. "For Roy King, 40, an accountant, the hierarchy remains a part of the religion he holds in little regard. He tries to ignore what it says, he said, even though he believes it has handled the scandals poorly. "There is far too much emphasis on celibacy and homosexuality in regard to the scandal," said Mr. King, who left the church as an adult and then returned to Catholicism in the early 1990's because Most Holy Redeemer welcomes gay men and lesbians." Roz Gallo is also quoted: "The crisis calls for a whole new understanding of sexuality. They are not even talking about celibacy. They are missing the boat and holding onto very old, narrow views." But like so many members of Most Holy Redeemer, she said her faith was intact. "The foundation of my religion is not in the institution," she said. "It's with my parish."

39. Carter Heyward, *Staying Power: Reflections on Gender, Justice, and Compassion* (Pilgrim Press: Cleveland, 1995), 43.

40. October 24, 2001.

41. It was a parishioner, Peter Millington who first suggested to me the idea that Most Holy Redeemer ought to be declared a shrine rather than a parish. In some respects it already functions as one for many in the gay community. As described in *A Gay Synagogue in New York*, a shrine symbolizes a culture and an identity similar to other ethnocultural historical and sacred monuments and spaces, offering a map of pilgrimages and imageries for experiencing one's primary affiliations.

42. Jeff Ferris, interview by author, tape recording, San Francisco, May 4, 2001.

43. Michael Harank, quoted by Michael Ford, *Wounded Prophet: A Portrait of Henri Nouwen* (Darton, Longman, and Todd: New York, 1999), 66.

44. The Rite of Christian Initiation for Adults, or the Catechumenate, was restored in the Roman Catholic Church after Vatican II by Pope Paul VI.

45. Lester Hribar and Daniel Ray Ollis, interview by author, tape recording, San Francisco, March 11, 2001.

46. Ellen Grund and Kathy McAdams, interview by author, tape recording, San Francisco, April 21, 2001.

Kathy McAdams, the partner of Ellen Grund is an ordained priest in the Episcopal Church. In this interview McAdams spoke of an elderly MHR parishioner: "Ann Farrelly had just given me an alb before she died. I wore it at my ordination. She would have been so excited about my ordination. An older proper Catholic woman who really took us in, our sexuality and all. I would not have expected it at all." Rev. McAdams and her partner Ellen Grund have moved to Boston.

47. October 22, 2001 interview by author.

48. *Faith beyond resentment*, 137–38.

49. *Faith beyond resentment,* 139.

50. National Conference of Catholic Bishops, *To Live in Christ Jesus: A Pastoral Reflection on the Moral Life,* 1976, p.19.

51. A Statement of the Bishops Committee on Marriage and Family, National Conference of Catholic Bishops, *Always Our Children: A Pastoral Message to Parents of Homosexual Children and Suggestions for Pastoral Ministers*, 1997.

52. CDF (Congregation for the Doctrine of the Faith), *Declaration on Certain Questions Regarding Sexual Ethics*, 1975.

53. United States Conference of Catholic Bishops, *Ministry to Persons with a Homosexual Inclination. Guidelines for Pastoral Care.* November 14, 2006.

54. CDF (Congregation for the Doctrine of the Faith), "Letter to the Bishops of the Catholic Church on the Pastoral Care of Homosexual Persons," published in *The Vatican and Homosexuality: Reactions to the "Letter to the Bishops of the Catholic Church on the Pastoral Care of Homosexual Persons,"* ed. Jeannine Gramick and Pat Furey (Crossroad: New York, 1988), 2.

55. Dan Morris-Young, "Gay and Lesbian Ministry: Controversial Pair Issue Challenge, Outline 'Concerns,' *San Francisco Catholic,* February 4, 2000, 19: "Speaking at Most Holy Redeemer . . . Sister Gramick later echoed the charge in comments about ongoing 'developments of doctrine' on homosexuality which, she said, 'is at the heart of the nervousness on the part of the Vatican.' Stating that polls indicate that about half of all Catholics and 'most Catholic moral theologians disagree with the Church' that homosexual activity is intrinsically evil, she said she feels 'that what the Vatican is really trying to head off' is the notion same-sex couples should not be denied a loving (sexual) relationship."

56. Homily by author, Most Holy Redeemer, January 28, 2001.

57. Dan Morris-Young, "Reaction Varies Widely to Vatican Ministry Ban on Priest, Nun," *San Francisco Catholic.*

58. Frank Masson, letter to author, September 16, 2001. Used with permission.

59. A Pastoral Minister, "What Are We Doing to Our Gay People?" in *The Furrow*, January 29, 1990.

60. Jeannine Gramick, interview by author, tape recording: San Francisco, February 6, 2001.

61. Christian Armstrong wrote to Archbishop Levada about the silencing of Nugent and Gramick on October 2, 1999: "My partner encouraged me to go to Mass after my arrival even though she knew that I had been away from the Church for many years. She told me that this parish was 'different' from any other that I had tried. . . . The first Sunday I attended Mass at Most Holy Redeemer, I had the experience of being surrounded by a loving community who had truly come together to give praise to God. Here were men and women, gay and straight, embracing one another in complete acceptance and love. I had waited for this experience for a very long time. It didn't stop there, I came to know that these were men and women who were very serious about finding their way to God through the action of the Holy Spirit.

"Their love extends far beyond mass on Sunday mornings. It extends to the homeless, the sick, the old, the dying, the faint of heart, the rejected, etc, etc and the wonderful part is they REALLY do mean what their actions show. I felt that I was accepted into a very good and holy community of men and women and I felt blessed that they wanted me to participate in this love. I am not unique in this acceptance—it is extended to all who come to our church. You have felt it too, haven't you?

"To say that the statement silencing Fr. Nugent and Sr. Gramick came as a blow to the gay/lesbian community is an understatement. We search for answers and we find none. We have asked that you visit with us and discuss this matter in open forum but you have not agreed to do so. When you visited our parish, and especially at the rededication of our church, you gave a homily that seemed genuinely caring about us. You seemed to recognize that our parish is a place that has seen much suffering and death and that the presence of God is most evident here.

"We are not asking so much for answers as we are asking for dialogue. We are asking that you meet with us and listen to us with your heart and respond as the Holy Spirit directs you."

62. February 13, 2001 interview by author.

63. March 27, 2001 interview by author. Michael Fleming is now deceased.

64. Jon Nilson, "The Church and Homosexuality: A Lonerganian Approach," in *Sexual Diversity and Catholicism, Toward the Development of Moral Theology,* ed. Patricia Beattie Jung with Joseph Andrew Coray (The Liturgical Press: Collegeville, 2001), 61.

65. Nilson, 68.

66. May 4, 2001 interview by author.

67. February 1, 2001 interview by author.

68. Nilson, 71–72.

69. Thomas H. Stahel, S.J., "I'm Here: Interview with Andrew Sullivan," *America,* May 1993, vol. 168 no. 16, 11.

70. February 13, 2001 interview by author.

71. Acts of the Apostles: 10: 1–16.

72. Richard Holloway, *Doubts and Love, What Is Left of Christianity* (Edinburgh: Conongate, 2001, 43.

73. In an article in the September 2002 issue of the right-wing local Catholic newspaper, *San Francisco Faith,* "Roamin' Catholic: Liturgical Life in the Bay Area: Most Holy Redeemer, San Francisco, The Men's Church," there is a profile of the parish by Stephen Frankini which spoke of the sign of peace: "For many, it seemed as if the kiss of peace was the high point of the Mass. Many went well out of their way (and for what seemed an eternity) to show very warm signs of affection to their friends. One man sitting to my left stretched past me to kiss the man to my right on the lips." Frankini adds: "I was a bit apprehensive about attending Mass at Most Holy Redeemer Church in the Castro. En route to the Church, I encountered local establishments with names like Hot n'Hunky Donuts, Moby Dick Bar n'Grill and The Men's Room, that confirmed my fears. Many of these establishments tried to lure customers with lewd photos of men. What would Mass be like in a church set in this neighborhood?" Frankini also comments on the preponderance of men in the church and that the singing was striking as it was reminiscent of a monastery.

74. Ramona Michaels, interview by author, tape recording: San Francisco, February 28, 2001.

75. Evelyn Squeri, interview by author with her husband John Squeri, tape recording; San Francisco, January 22, 2001.

76. Jamie Cherrie and Jim Gunther, undated letter provided to author, December 2001.

77. Chuck Colbert, "For Gay Catholics, Conscience is the Key," *National Catholic Reporter,* January 16, 1998, 17.

78. Richard Smith, *AIDS, Gays and the American Catholic Church* (Pilgrim Press: Cleveland, 1994).

79. Vincent Genovesi, "Human and Civil Rights for Gays and Lesbians," *America,* April 22, 1995, 20.

80. Homily by author at mass for Acceptance group, at St. Canice's Church, Sydney, 1998.

81. Arthur Berliner, "Sex, Sin, and the Church: The Dilemma of Homosexuality," *Journal of Religion and Health,* vol. 26, no. 2, Summer 1987, 142.

82. *Ministry to Persons with a Homosexual Inclination. Guidelines for Pastoral Care.* The United States Conference of Catholic Bishops, November 14, 2006. www.usccbpublishing.org "New Titles." This statement was developed by the Committee on Doctrine of the United States Conference of Catholic Bishops and approved for publication by the full body of bishops at their general meeting in November 2006.

83. *Ministry to Persons with a Homosexual Inclination,* p. 24.

84. "Homily given at Most Holy Redeemer Church, San Francisco. Sunday, July 3, 1994. By Father Donal Godfrey, S.J." *Gay Community News,* November 1994. (It did rather surprise me that the only Irish gay newspaper decided to publish this homily in full. They also showed a picture of me in rainbow vestments with other parishioners Ramona Michaels and Stephen Rossi. This chasuble and stole were made for me as a gift by Sr. Adele Appleby, BVM.)

See Dr. Elizabeth Stuart's book: *Daring to Speak Love's Name: A Gay and Lesbian Prayer Book* (London: Hamish Hamilton, 1992). Stuart speaks of the Holy Spirit as a Goose on page 15.

Appendix

Succession of pastors and administrators at Most Holy Redeemer Parish:

Fr. Joseph P. McQuade, 1900–1905;

Fr. Patrick McGuire, 1905–17;

Fr. Charles E. O'Neille, 1917–32;

Rt. Rev. Msgr. William P. Sullivan, 1932–48;

Rt. Rev. Msgr. Henry J. Lyne, 1948–68;

Fr. John G. O'Connell, administrator, 1966–68, pastor, 1968–76;

Fr. John M. Sweeney, administrator, 1973–76;

Fr. Donald E. Pyne, 1976–79;

Fr. Cuchalain K. Moriarty, 1979–82;

Fr. Anthony McGuire, 1982–90;

Fr. Zachary Shore, co–pastor, 1989, pastor, 1990–2002;

Fr. Edward Phelan, administrator, 2002–4;

Fr. Stephen Meriwether, 2004–

Bibliography

Abelove, Henry, Michele Aina Barale, David Halperin, eds. *The Lesbian and Gay Studies Reader*. New York: Routledge, 1993.

Adam, Barry. *The Rise of a Gay and Lesbian Movement* (Revised edition). New York: Twayne Publishers, 1995.

Alexander, Neil J. *This Far by Grace: A Bishop's Journey Through Questions of Homosexuality*. Boston: Cowley, 2003.

Alexander, Scott, W. *The Welcoming Congregation. Resources for Affirming Gay, Lesbian and Bisexual Persons*. Boston: Unitarian Universalist Association, 1990.

Alison, James. *Faith Beyond Resentment: Fragments Catholic and Gay*. London: Darton, Longman & Todd, 2001.

————. *On Being Liked*. London: Darton, Longman & Todd, 2004.

————. *Undergoing God: Despatches from the Scene of a Break-in*. London: Darton, Longman & Todd, 2006.

Altman, Dennis. *Homosexual Oppression and Liberation*. New York: Dutton/Outerbridge and Dienstfrey, 1971.

Ammerman, Nancy Tatom. *Congregation and Community*. New Brunswick: Rutgers University Press, 1997.

Ammerman, Nancy, editor, with Jackson W. Carroll, Carl S. Dudley, and William McKinney. *Studying Congregations: A New Handbook*. Nashville: Abingdon Press, 1998.

Ammerman, Nancy Tatom and Carl S. Dudley. *Congregations in Transition: A Guide for Analyzing, Assessing, and Adapting in Changing Communities*. San Francisco: Jossey-Bass, 2002.

Arpin, Robert L. *Wonderfully, Fearfully Made: Letters on Living with Hope, Teaching Understanding, and Ministering with Love, from a Gay Catholic Priest with AIDS*. San Francisco: HarperSanFrancisco, 1993.

Batchelor, Edward, ed. *Homosexuality and Ethics*. New York: The Pilgrim Press, 1980.

Barzan, Robert. Ed. *Sex and Spirit: Exploring Gay Men's Spirituality*. San Francisco: A Publication of White Crane Newsletter, 1995.

Bawer, Bruce. *A Place at the Table: The Gay Individual in American Society*. New York: Simon and Schuster, 1994.

——. *Stealing Jesus: How Fundamentalism Betrays Christianity*. New York: Three Rivers Press, 1997.

Beaudoin, Tom. *Virtual Faith: The Irreverent Spiritual Quest of Generation X*. San Francisco: Jossey-Bass, 1998.

Becker, Penny Edgell and Nancy L. Eiesland, eds. *Contemporary American Religion. An Ethnographic Reader*. Walnut Creek: AltaMira Press, 1997.

Becker, Penny Edgell. *Congregations in Conflict: Cultural Models of Local Religious Life*. Cambridge: Cambridge University Press, 1999.

Berrigan, Daniel, *Sorrow Built a Bridge, Friendship and AIDS*. Maryland: Fortkamp Publishing, co., 1989.

Bevans, Stephen B. *Models of Contextual Theology*. New York: Orbis Books, 1999.

Birkett, Stephen. *Ulster Alien*. London: Gay Men's Press, 2000.

Blasius, Mark and Shane Phelan. *We Are Everywhere. A Historical Sourcebook of Gay and Lesbian Politics*. New York: Routledge, 1997.

Block, Gil. *Confessions of a Jewish Nun. The true life adventures of Sister Sadie, Sadie, the Rabbi Lady . . . as told through Gil Block*. San Francisco: A Fog City Production, 1999, revised 2000.

Boff, Leonardo, and Clodovis Boff. *Introducing Liberation Theology*. New York: Orbis Books, 1987.

Bogdan, Robert, and Stephen Taylor. *Introduction to Qualitative Research Methods: A Guidebook and Resource,* New York: John Wiley & Sons, Inc., 1998.

Boisvert, Donald L. *Out on Holy Ground. Meditations on Gay Men's Spirituality*. Cleveland: The Pilgrim Press, 2000.

——. *Men, Homosexuality, and the Gods: An Exploration into the Religious Significance of Male Homosexuality in World Perspective*. Binghamton, NY: Harrington Park, 2004.

Borg, Marcus. *Jesus A New Vision: Spirit, Culture, and The Life of Discipleship*. San Francisco: HarperSanFrancisco, 1987.

——. *Meeting Jesus Again for the First Time: The Historical Jesus and The Heart of Contemporary Faith*. San Francisco: HarperSanFrancisco, 1994.

Borsch, Frederick H. *Sexuality and Christian Discipleship*. Cincinnati: Forward Movement, 1993.

Boswell, John. *Christianity, Social Tolerance, and Homosexuality*. Chicago: University of Chicago Press, 1980.

——. *Same-Sex Unions in Premodern Europe*. New York: Villard Books, 1994.

Bouldrey, Brian, ed. *Wrestling with the Angel: Faith and Religion in the Lives of Gay Men*. New York: Riverhead Books, 1995.

Bouthillette, Anne-Marie & Retter, Yolanda, eds. *Queers in Space: Communities/Public Spaces/Sites of Resistance*. Seattle: Bay Press, 1997.

Boyd, Malcolm. *Gay Priest: An Inner Journey*. New York: St Martin's Press, 1987.

Boyd, Malcolm, and Nancy L. Wilson, eds. *Amazing Grace: Stories of Lesbian and Gay Faith*. Freedom, California: Crossings Press, 1991.

Boyd, Malcolm, and J. Jon Bruno. *In Times Like These: How we Pray*. New York: Seabury, 2005.

Boyd, Nan Alamilla. *Wide Open Town. A History of Queer San Francisco*. Berkeley: University of California Press, 2003.

Boyle, Eugene, and Paddy Monaghan, eds. *Adventures in Reconciliation: Twenty-Nine Catholic Testimonies*. Guildford: Eagle Publishing, 1998.

Burns, Jeffrey. *San Francisco: A History of the Archdiocese of San Francisco*. Vols. 1–3. (Strausbourg: Editions du Signe.)

Bradshaw, Timothy, ed. *The Way Forward? Christian Voices on Homosexuality and the Church*. London: Hodder & Stoughton, 1997.

Brennan, Patrick. *Re-Imagining the Parish*. New York: Crossroad, 1990.

Cahill, Lisa. *Between the Sexes: Foundations for a Christian Ethics of Sexuality*. New York: Paulist Press, 1985.

Catholic Bishops of Washington State, *The Prejudice against Homosexuals and the Ministry of the Church* (1983).

Cherry, Kittredge, and Zalmon Sherwood, eds. *Equal Rites: Lesbian and Gay Worship, Ceremonies, and Celebrations*. Louisville: Westminster John Knox, 1995.

Clark, J. Michael, and Michael L. Stemmeler. *Homophobia and the Christian Tradition*. Dallas: Monument Press, 1990.

Clark, J. Michael. *Defying the Darkness: Gay Theology in the Shadows*. Cleveland: The Pilgrim Press, 1997.

Cleaver, Richard. *Know My Name: A Gay Liberation Theology*. Louisville: Westminster John Knox, 1995.

Clendinen, Dudley, and Adam Nagourney. *Out for Good. The Struggle to Build a Gay Rights Movement in America*. New York: Simon and Schuster, 1999.

Coleman, Gerald D. *Homosexuality: Catholic Teaching and Pastoral Practice*. Mahwah, NJ: Paulist Press, 1996.

Comstock, Gary David. *Gay Theology Without Apology*. Cleveland: The Pilgrim Press, 1993.

——. *Unrepentant, Self-Affirming, Practicing. Lesbian/Bisexual/Gay People within Organized Religion*. New York: Continuum, 1996.

——. Ed. *A Whosoever Church: Welcoming Lesbians and Gay Men into African American Congregations*. Louisville: Westminster John Knox Press, 2001.

Comstock, Gary David, and Susan E. Henking, eds. *Que(e)rying Religion: A Critical Anthology*. New York: Continuum, 1997.

Congregation for Catholic Education. *Instruction concerning the criteria of vocational discernment regarding persons with homosexual tendencies, considering their admission to seminary and to Holy Orders* (Rome, 2005).

Congregation for the Doctrine of the Faith. "Letter to the Bishops of the Catholic Church on the Pastoral Care of Homosexual Persons," October 31, 1986. In *The Vatican and Homosexuality*, ed. Jeannine Gramick and Pat Furey, 1–10. New York: Crossroad, 1988.

———. *Letter to the U.S. Bishops: Some Considerations Concerning the Response to Legislative Proposals on the Non-discrimination of Homosexual Persons* (Rome, 1992).

Conner, Randy P., David Hatfield Sparks, and Mariya Sparks. *Cassells Encyclopedia of Queer Myth, Symbol, and Spirit*. London: Cassell, 1997.

Coriden, James, A. *The Parish in the Catholic Tradition: History, Theology and Canon Law*. Paulist Press: New Jersey, 1997.

Countryman, William L. *Dirt, Greed and Sex: Sexual Ethics in the New Testament and Their Implications for Today*. Philadelphia: Fortress Press, 1988.

———. *Living on the Border of the Holy: Renewing the Priesthood of All*. Harrisburg: Morehouse Publishing, 1999

———. *Love, Human and Divine: Reflections on Love, Sexuality, and Friendship*. Harrisburg: Morehouse, 2005.

Countryman, William L. and MR Ritley. *Gifted by Otherness, Gay and Lesbian Christians in the Church*. Harrisburg: Morehouse Publishing, 2001.

Cozzens, Donald B. *The Changing Face of the Priesthood: A Reflection on the Priest's Crisis of Soul*. Collegeville, Minn.: Liturgical Press, 2000.

Cromey, Robert Warren. *In God's Image: Christian Witness to the Need for a Gay/Lesbian Equality in the Eyes of the Church*. San Francisco: Alamo Square Distributers, 1991.

De Jim, Strange. *San Francisco's Castro*. San Francisco: Arcadia Publishing, 2003.

De La Huerta, Christian. *Coming Out Spiritually: The Next Step*. New York: Putnam, 1999.

D'Emilio, John, and Estelle B. Freedman. *Intimate Matters: A History of Sexuality in America*. New York: Harper and Row, 1988.

D'Emilio, John. *Sexual Politics, Sexual Communities: The Making of a Homosexual Minority in the United States, 1940–1970*. Chicago: University of Chicago Press, 1983.

Dilley, James, W. and Michael Helquist. *Face to Face. A Guide to AIDS Counselling*. Berkely: Celestial Arts, 1989.

Dolan, Jay P., ed. *The American Catholic Parish: A History From 1850 to the Present*. 2 Vols. New York: Paulist Press, 1987.

Dorsey, Gary. *Congregation: The Journey Back to Church*. Cleveland: The Pilgrim Press, 1998.

Duberman, Martin. *About Time. Exploring the Gay Past* (Revised edition). New York: Meridian, 1991.

Duberman, Martin Bauml, Martha Vicinus, and George Chauncey. Jr., eds., *Hidden From History. Reclaiming the Gay and Lesbian Past*. New York: New American Library, 1989.

Duncan, Geoffrey, compiler. *Courage to Love. Liturgies for the Lesbian, Gay, Bisexual, and Transgender Community*. Cleveland: The Pilgrim Press, 2002.

Empereur, James L. *Spiritual Direction and the Gay Person*. New York: Continuum, 1998.

Faderman, Lillian, and Stuart Timmons. *Gay L.A.: A History of Sexual Outlaws, Power Politics, and Lipstick Lesbians*. New York: Basic Press, 2006.

FitzGerald, Frances. *Cities on a Hill: A Journey through Contemporary American Cultures*. New York: Simon & Schuster, 1986.

Freedman, Samuel G. *Upon This Rock: The Miracles of a Black Church*. San Francisco: HarperCollins, 1993.

Ford, Michael. *Wounded Prophet: A Portrait of Henri J. M. Nouwen*. New York: Doubleday, 2002.

———. *Father Mychal Judge: An Authentic American Hero*. New Jersey: Paulist Press, 2002.

———. *Disclosures. Conversations Gay and Spiritual*. London: Darton, Longman & Todd, 2004.

Fone, Byrne. *Homophobia. A History*. New York: Metropolitan Books, 2000.

Fortunato, John E. *Embracing the Exile: Healing Journeys of Gay Christians*. Minneapolis: Winston-Seabury Press, 1983.

———. *AIDS: The Spiritual Dilemma,* San Francisco: Harper & Row, 1987.

Foucault, Michel. *The History of Sexuality*. Translated by Robert Hurley. Vol. 1. An Introduction. New York: Random House, Vintage, 1980.

Foster, Charles, R. *Embracing Diversity: Leadership in Multicultural Congregations*. An Alban Institute Publication, 1997.

Gaede, Beth Ann, ed. *Dialogue on a Difficult Issue: Congregations Talking about Homosexuality*. An Alban Institute Publication, 1998.

Gaillot, Jacques. *Voice From The Desert: A Bishop's Cry for a New Church*. New York: Crossroad, 1996.

Gates, Gary J. and Jason Ost. *The Gay and Lesbian Atlas*. Washington, D.C.: The Urban Institute Press, 2004.

Gearhart, Sally and William R. Johnson. *Loving Women/Loving Men. Gay Liberation and the Church*. San Francisco: Glide Publications, 1974.

Genovesi, Vincent. *In Pursuit of Love, Catholic Morality and Human Sexuality*. Washington: Michael Glazier, 1987.

Godfrey, Donal. *An Examination of the Roman Catholic Church and HIV Disease with Particular Reference to Method, Moral Teaching, and Pastoral Practice*. An S.T.L. thesis: Jesuit School of Theology at Berkeley, 1993.

Gomes, Peter J. *The Good Book*. New York: Avon Books, 1996.

Goss, Robert. *Jesus Acted Up: A Gay and Lesbian Manifesto*. San Francisco: Harper & Row, 1993.

———. *Queering Christ, Beyond Jesus Acted Up*. Cleveland: The Pilgrim Press, 2002.

Glaser, Chris. *Come Home! Reclaiming Spirituality and Community as Gay Men and Lesbians*. New York: Harper & Row, 1990.

———. *Coming Out to God: Prayers for Lesbians and Gay Men, Their Families and Friends*. Louisville, Westminster John Knox, 1991.

———. *Coming Out as Sacrament*. Louisville: Westminster/John Knox, 1998.

Graham, Larry Kent. *Discovering Images of God: Narratives of Care among Lesbians and Gays*. Louisville: Westminster John Knox Press, 1997.

Grahn, Judy. *Another Mother Tongue: Gay Words, Gay Worlds*. Boston: Beacon Press, 1984.

Gramson, Joshua. *The Fabulous Sylvester: The Legend, the Music, the Seventies in San Francisco*. London: Picador, 2006.

Gramick, Jeannine, ed. *Homosexuality and the Catholic Church*. Chicago: The Thomas More Press, 1983.

Gramick, Jeannine, and Robert Nugent, eds. *Building Bridges: Gay and Lesbian Reality and the Catholic Church*. Connecticut: Twenty-third Publications, 1992.

Gramick, Jeannine, and Pat Furey, eds. *The Vatican and Homosexuality: Reactions to the 'Letter to the Bishops of the Catholic Church on the Pastoral Care of Homosexual Persons.'* New York: Crossroad, 1988.

Gramick, Jeannine, and Robert Nugent, eds., *Voices of Hope: A Collection of Positive Catholic Writings on Gay and Lesbian Issues*. New York: Center for Homophobia Education, 1995.

Greeley, Andrew. *The Catholic Imagination*. Berkeley: University of California Press, 2000.

Guindon, Andre. *The Sexual Language: An Essay in Moral Theology*. Ottawa: The University of Ottawa Press, 1976.

———. *The Sexual Creators. An Ethical Proposal for Concerned Christians*. Lanham, MD/London: University Press of America, 1986.

Hanigan, James P. *Homosexuality: The Test Case for Christian Ethics*. New York: Paulist, 1988.

Hanvey, John Michael. *God in Dark Places*. Dublin: Columba Press, 2006.

Hartman, Keith. *Congregations in Conflict. The Battle over Homosexuality*. New Jersey: Rutgers University Press, 1996.

Hardy, Richard. *Knowing the God of Compassion: Spirituality and Persons Living with AIDS*. Ottawa: Novalis, 1993.

———. *Loving Men: Gay Partners, Spirituality and AIDS*. New York: The Continuum Publishing Company, 1998.

Harrison, Beverly Wildung. *Making the Connections*. Boston: Beacon Press, 1985.

Harvey, Andrew, ed. *The Essential Gay Mystics*. San Francisco: HarperSanFrancisco, 1997.

Harvey, John F. *The Truth about Homosexuality: The Cry of the Faithful*. San Francisco: Ignatius Press, 1996.

Hasbany, Richard. *Homosexuality and Religion*. New York: Harrington Park Press, 1989.

Haughton, Rosemary. *The Catholic Thing*. Springfield, Ill.: Templegate, 1979.

Hay, Harry and Will Roscoe. *Radically Gay: Gay Liberation in the Words of Its Founder*. Boston: Beacon Press, 1996.

Hazel, Dann. *Witness. Gay and Lesbian Clergy Report From the Front*. Louisville: Westminster John Knox, 2000.

Helminiak, Daniel A. *What the Bible Really says about Homosexuality*. San Francisco: Alamo Square, 1994.

———. *Sex and the Sacred: Gay Identity and Spiritual Growth*. New York: Harrington Park Press, 2006.

Herdt, Gilbert, editor. *Gay Culture in America. Essays from the Field*. Boston: Beacon Press, 1992.

Heyward, Carter. *Saving Jesus From Those Who are Right: Rethinking What It Means to be Christian*. Minneapolis: Fortress Press, 1999.

——. *Touching our Strength. The Erotic as Power and the Love of God*. San Francisco: Harper and Row, Publishers, 1989.

——. *Our Passion for Justice. Images of Power, Sexuality, and Liberation*. New York: The Pilgrim Press, 1988.

——. *Staying Power: Reflections on Gender, Justice, and Compassion*. Cleveland: The Pilgrim Press, 1995.

Higgs, David, ed. *Queer Sites: Gay Urban Histories since 1600*. London: Rutledge, 1999.

Holben, L.R. *What Christians Think About Homosexuality: Six Representative Viewpoints*. North Redlands Hills, TX: Bibal Press, 1999.

Holtz, Raymon C., ed. *Listen to the Stories: Gay and Lesbian Catholics Talk About Their Lives and the Church*. New York: Publishing, Inc. 1991.

Hopcke, Robert H. *Jung, Jungians and Homosexuality*. New York: Shambhala, 1991.

——. *Same-Sex Love and the Path to Wholeness*. Boston: Shambhala, 1993.

——. *There are No Accidents: Synchronicity and the Stories of Our Lives*. New York: Riverhead Books, 1998.

——. *Living the Mysteries: The Spiritual Power of the Rosary in the Lives of Contemporary People*. New York: Crossroad, 2003.

Hopewell, James. *Congregations: Stories and Structures*. Philadelphia: Fortress Press, 1987.

Hunt, Mary. *Fierce Tenderness: A Feminist Theology of Friendship*. New York: Crossroad, 1991.

Hume, Cardinal Basil, *A Note on the Teaching of the Catholic Church Concerning Homosexual People*, February 1995 (revised April 1997).

Iles, Robert H, Ed. *The Gospel Imperative in the Midst of AIDS*. Wilton: Morehouse Publishing.

Jagose, Annamarie. *Queer Theory. An Introduction*. New York: New York University Press, 1996.

Jennings, Theodore W., Jr. *Men Jesus Loved: Homoerotic Narratives from the New Testament*. Boston: The Pilgrim Press, 2003.

Johnson, Fenton. *Geography of the Heart: A Memoir*. New York: Scribner, 1996.

——. *Keeping Faith: A Skeptic's Journey*. Boston: Houghton Mifflin, 2003.

Johnston, Toby. *Gay Perspective: Things Our Homosexuality Tells us About the Nature of God and the Universe*. Los Angeles: Alyson Books, 2003.

——. *Gay Spirituality*. Maple Shade, NJ: Lethe Press, 2004.

Jones, Alan. *Sacrifice and Delight. Spirituality for Ministry*. San Francisco: Harper-SanFrancisco, 1992.

Jones, William Clossen, ed. *AIDS in Religious Perspective*. Papers by Paul Johnson, William P. Zion, and Bruce L. Mills. Kingston, Ontario: Queen's Theological College, 1987.

Jordan, Mark D. *The Invention of Sodomy in Christian Theology*. Chicago: The University of Chicago Press, 1997.

────. *The Silence of Sodom: Homosexuality in Modern Catholicism*. Chicago: The University of Chicago Press, 2000.

────. *Telling Truths in Church. Scandal, Flesh, and Christian Speech*. Boston: Beacon Press, 2003.

Jung, Patricia Beattie, and Ralph F. Smith. *Heterosexism: An Ethical Challenge*. Albany: SUNY, 1993.

Jung, Patricia Beattie, with Joseph Andrew Coray, eds. *Sexual Diversity and Catholicism. Towards the Development of Moral Theology*. Collegeville, Minn: Liturgical Press, 2001.

Jung, Patricia Beattie, with Jeffrey Siker, Elliot Dorff, Frederick Borsch, Rebecca Alpert, and Donal Godfrey. "New Jewish and Christian Approaches to Homosexuality." An offprint of the 2002 Swig Lecture, April 21, 2002. The Swig Judaic Studies Program at the University of San Francisco.

Kaiser, Charles. The Gay Metropolis. The Landmark History of Gay Life in America Since World War II. New York: A Harvest Book, 1998.

Kaufman, Gershen, and Lev Raphael. *Coming Out of Shame. Transforming Gay and Lesbian Lives*. New York: Doubleday, 1996.

Katz, Jonathan. *Gay American History. Lesbians and Gay Men in the U.S.A*. New York: Thomas Y. Crowell Company, 1976.

Keane, Philip. *Sexual Morality. A Catholic Perspective*. New York: Paulist Press, 1977.

Keeler, Robert F. *Parish! The Pulitzer Prize-Winning Story of A Vibrant Catholic Community*. New York: Crossroad Publishing Company, 1997.

Keenan, James, ed., with Jon Fuller, Lisa Sowle Cahill, and Kevin Kelly. *Catholic Ethicists on HIV/AIDS Prevention*. New York: Continuum, 2000.

Kelly, Kevin, *New Directions in Sexual Ethics: Moral Theology and the Challenge of AIDS*. London: Geoffrey Chapman, 1998.

Kelsey, Morton. *Prophetic Ministry: The Psychology and Spirituality of Pastoral Care*. New York: Crossroad Publishing Co., 1984.

Kennedy, Eugene. *The Unhealed Wound: The Church and Human Sexuality*. New York: St. Martin's Griffin, 2001.

Killen, Patricia O'Connell, and John De Beer. *The Art of Theological Reflection*. New York: Crossroad Publishing Co., 1994.

Kendall, R.T. *Is God for the Homosexual?* Basingstoke: Marshall Pickering, 1988.

Kennedy, Eugene. *The Unhealed Wound: The Church and Human Sexuality*. New York: St. Martin's Griffin, 2001.

Kirkpatrick, Bill. *AIDS: Sharing the Pain: Pastoral Guidelines*. London: Darton, Longman, and Todd, 1988.

Kosnik, Anthony, et al. *Human Sexuality: New Directions in American Catholic Thought*. Paulist Press, 1977.

Krauss, Krandall, *Bardo,* Los Angeles: Alyson Books, 1999.

Krauss, Krandall, and Paul Borja, *It's Never About What It's About: What We Learned About Living While Waiting to Die*. Los Angeles: Alyson Books, 2000.

Kramer, Larry. *Faggots*. New York: Random House, 1978.

────. *The Normal Heart*. New York: Penguin, 1985.

Krondorfer, Bjorn, ed. *Men's Bodies, Men's Gods: Male Identity in a (Post-) Christian Culture.* New York: New York University Press, 1996.

Kushner. Tony. *Angels in America. Part 1: Millennium Approaches.* New York: Theatre Communications Group, 1993.

———. *Angels in America. Part 11: Perestroika.* New York: Theatre Communications Group, 1993.

Laquer, Thomas. *Making Sex: Body and Gender from the Greeks to Freud.* Cambridge: Harvard University Press, 1990.

Law, Robert H.L. *Inclusion, Making Room For Grace.* St. Louis: Chalice Press, 2000.

Lea, Jeffrey. *Daily Advent and Christmas Meditations for Gay & Lesbian Christians.* Cleveland: The Pilgrim Press, 2005.

Leas, Speed, and George Parsons. *Understanding Your Congregation as a System: The Manual.* Herndon, VA: The Alban Institute, 1993.

Lee, Jung Young. *Marginality: The Key to Multicultural Theology.* Minneapolis: Fortress Press, 1995.

Leyland, Winston, ed. *Out in the Castro: Desire, Promise, Activism.* San Francisco: Leyland Publications, 2002.

Lipskey, William. *Gay and Lesbian San Francisco.* San Francisco: Arcadia Publishing, 2006.

Loftus, John Allen. *Clergy and Religious Exposed to AIDS, An Invitation to Care.* Emmanuel Convalescent Foundation, Ontario, 1989.

Liuzzi, Peter J. *With Listening Hearts: Understanding the Voices of Lesbian and Gay Catholics.* New York: Paulist Press, 2001.

Lynch, Bernard. *A Priest on Trial.* London: Bloomsbury, 1993.

Lee, Jung Young. *Marginality: The key to Multicultural Theology.* Minneapolis: Augsburg Fortress Publishers, 1995.

Leib, Frank B. *Friendly Competitors, Fierce Companions: Men's Ways of Relating.* Cleveland: The Pilgrim Press, 1997.

Lopata, Mary Ellen. *Fortunate Families: Catholic Families with Lesbian Daughters and Gay Sons.* Oxford: Trafford Publishing Co., 2006.

Loughery, John. *The Other Side of Silence: Men's Lives and Gay Identities: A Twentieth Century History.* New York; Henry Holt and Company, 1998.

Lowenthal, Michael, ed. *Gay Men at the Millennium: Sex, Spirit, Community.* New York: Jeremy P. Tarcher/Putnam, 1997.

Lussier, Jean-Guy. "The Roman Catholic Archdiocese of San Francisco and Its Response to the AIDS epidemic." MA Thesis. Graduate Theological Union, Berkeley, 1989.

Maher, Michael. *Being Gay and Lesbian in a Catholic High School: Beyond the Uniform.* New York: Harrington Park Press, an imprint of the Haworth Press, 2001.

Marcus, Eric. *Making History. The Struggle for Gay and Lesbian Rights. 1945–1990.* New York: HarperCollins, 1992.

Marsden, George. *Religion and American Culture.* San Diego: Harcourt/Brace/Jovanovich, 1990.

Massa, Mark S. *Catholics and American Culture: Fulton Sheen, Dorothy Day, and the Notre Dame Football Team.* New York: Crossroad, 1999.

Martin, Del, and Phyllis Lyon. *Lesbian/woman*. San Francisco: Calif.: Volcano, 1991.

Maupin, Armistead. *Tales of the City*. New York: Harper Perennial, 1989.

McBrien, Richard, ed. *The HarperColliins Encyclopedia of Catholicism*. San Francisco: HarperSanFrancisco, 1995.

McCormick, Richard. *The Critical Calling: Reflections on Moral Dilemmas Since Vatican II*. Washington, D.C.: Georgetown University Press, 1989.

McDonald, Helen B. and Audrey Steinborn. *Understanding Homosexuality: A Guide for Those Who Know, Love, or Counsel Gay and Lesbian Individuals*. New York: Crossroad, 1993.

McGinley, Dugan. *Acts of Faith, Acts of Love. Gay Catholic Autobiographies as Sacred Texts*. New York: Continuum, 2004.

McNaught, Brian. *On Being Gay: Thoughts on Family, Faith and Love*. New York: St. Martin's Press, 1988.

McNeill, John. *The Church and the Homosexual*. Kansas City: Sheed, Andrews and McMeel, 1976.

——. *Freedom Glorious Freedom: The Spiritual Journey to the Fullness of Life for Gays, Lesbians, and Everyone Else*. Boston: Beacon, 1995.

——. *Both Feet Firmly Planted in Midair: My Spiritual Journey*. Louisville: Westminster John Knox Press, 1998.

Miller, Neil. *Out of the Past: Gay and Lesbian History from 1969 to the Present*. New York: Vintage, 1995.

Monette, Paul. *Borrowed Time: An AIDS Memoir*. San Diego: Harcourt/Brace/Jovanovich, 1988.

——. *Becoming a Man: Half a Life Story*. San Francisco: HarperSanFrancisco, 1992.

Moon, Dawne. *God, Sex and Politics: Homosexuality and Everyday Theologies*. Chicago: University of Chicago, 2004.

Moore, Gareth. *A Question of Truth: Christianity and Homosexuality*. London: Continuum, 2003.

Morris, Charles. *American Catholic. The Saints and Sinners Who Built America's Most Powerful Church*. New York: Random House, Inc., 1997.

Morrison, David. *Homosexuality: Christ Above All: The Church's Teaching on Same Sex Attraction*. London: Catholic Truth Society, 2004.

Myers, Bryant L. *Walking With The Poor: Principles and Practices of Transformational Development*. New York: Orbis Books, 2002.

Myers, William R. *Research in Ministry: A Primer for the doctor of ministry program*. Chicago: Exploration Press, 1997.

Naughton, Jim. *Catholics in Crisis: The Rift between American Catholics and Their Church*. New York: Penguin, 1997.

Nelson, James B. *The Intimate Connection: Male Sexuality, Masculine Spirituality*. Philadelphia: The Westminster Press, 1988.

Nelson, James B., and Sandra P. Longfellow, eds. *Sexuality and the Sacred: Sources for Theological Reflection*. Louisville, Westminster John Knox Press, 1994.

Nimmons, David. *The Soul Beneath the Skin: the unseen hearts and habits of gay men*. New York: St. Martin's Press, 2002.

Nissinen, Martti. *Homoeroticism in the Biblical World*. Minneapolis: Fortress Press, 1998.

Nouwen, Henri J.M. *The Wounded Healer: Ministry in Contemporary Society*. New York: Doubleday, 1972.

Nord, David. *Multiple AIDS-Related Loss: A Handbook for Understanding and Surviving a Perpetual Fall*. Washington: Taylor and Francis, 1997.

Nugent, Robert, ed. *A Challenge to Love: Gay and Lesbian Catholics in the Church*. New York: Crossroad, 1983.

O'Brien, Glen. *Praying from the Margins: Gospel Reflections of a Gay Man*. Dublin: The Columba Press, 2001.

O'Connell, Timothy. *Principles for A Catholic Morality*. New York: The Seabury Press, 1976.

Olivero, Karen, Kelly Turney and Traci West. *Talking about Homosexuality: A Congregational Resource*. Cleveland: The Pilgrim Press, 2005.

Olyan, Saul, & Martha C. Nussbaum, eds. *Sexual Orientation and Human Rights in American Religious Discourse*. New York: Oxford University Press, 1998.

O'Meara, Thomas Franklin. *Theology of Ministry*. New York: Paulist Press, 1983.

O'Neill, Craig, and Kathleen Ritter. *Coming Out Within: Stages of Spiritual Awakening for Lesbians and Gay Men*. San Francisco: Harper & Row, 1992.

Pattison, Stephen. *Shame, Theory, Therapy, Theology*. Cambridge: Cambridge University Press, 2000.

Peddicord, Richard. *Gay and Lesbian Rights: A Question of Ethics or Social Justice?* Kansas: Sheed and Ward, 1996.

Pepper, Michal Ann. *Reconciling Journey. A Devotional Workbook for Lesbian and Gay Christians*. Cleveland: The Pilgrim Press, 2003.

Perry, Rev. Troy D., with Thomas L.P. Swicegood. *Don't be Afraid Anymore: The Story of Reverend Troy Perry and the Metropolitan Community Churches*. New York: St. Martin's, 1990.

Presbyterian Church (U.S.A.) *Presbyterians and Human Sexuality*. Louisville, Kentucky: Presbyterian Church (U.S.A.), 1991.

Polledri, Paolo, ed. *Visionary San Francisco*. Munich: Prestel and San Francisco Museum of Modern Art, 1990.

Quinn, John R. *Pastoral Letter on Homosexuality*. San Francisco: The Chancery Office, 1980.

Reid, John. *The Best Little Boy in the World*. New York: Ballantine Books, 1977.

Reuther, Rosemary Radford. *Sexism and God-Talk: Towards a Feminist Theology*. Boston: Beacon, 1983.

Richards, David. *Identity and the Case for Gay Rights: Race, Gender, Religion as Analogies*. Chicago: The University of Chicago Press, 1999.

Richards, Rand. *Historic Walks in San Francisco. 18 Trails Through the City's Past*. San Francisco: Heritage House Publishers, 2002.

Richo, David. *The Five Things We Cannot Change . . . and the Happiness We Find by Embracing Them*. Boston: Shambhala, 2005.

Ritley, M.R. *God's Tribe. Laying the Foundations of Communal Memory*. New Haven, Beloved Disciples Press, 1994.

Rodriguez, Richard. *Days of Obligation: An Argument with My Mexican Father*. New York: Penguin USA, 1993.

———. *Brown: The Last Discovery of America,* New York: Viking, 2002.

Rogers, Eugene, Jr. *Sexuality and the Christian Body: Their Way into the Triune God*. Oxford: Blackwell Publishers, 1999.

Rogers, Jack. *Jesus, the Bible, and Homosexuality: Explode the Myths, Heal the Church*. Louisville: Westminster Knox, 2005.

Roscoe, Will. *Queer Spirits. A Gay Men's Myth Book*. Boston: Beacon Press, 1995.

Rudy, Kathy. *Sex and the Church: Gender, Homosexuality, and the Transformation of Christian Ethics*. Boston: Beacon Press, 1997.

Schmidt, Thomas E. *Straight and Narrow? Compassion and Clarity in the Homosexuality Debate*. Downers Grove: Intervarsity Press, 1995.

Schreiter, Robert J. *Constructing Local Theologies*. New York: Orbis Books, 1985.

Scroggs, Robin. *The New Testament and Homosexuality*. New York: Harcourt Brace & Co., 1983.

Senate of Priests, San Francisco. *Ministry and Homosexuality in the Archdiocese of San Francisco*. 1983.

Seow, Choon-Leong, ed. *Homosexuality and Christian Community*. Louisville: Westminster John Knox Press, 1996.

Shallenberger, David. *Reclaiming the Spirit: Gay Men and Lesbians Come to Terms with Religion*. New Brunswick, N.J.: Rutgers University Press, 1998.

Signorile, Michelangelo. *Queer in America: Sex, the Media, and the Closets of Power*. New York: Random House, 1993.

Siker, Jeffrey, ed. *Homosexuality in the Church: Both Sides of the Debate*. Louisville: Westminster John Knox Press, 1994.

Shilts, Randy. *And the Band Played On. Politics, People, and the AIDS Epidemic*. New York: St. Martin's Press, 1987.

———. *The Mayor of Castro Street. The Life and Times of Harvey Milk*. New York: St. Martin's Press, 1982.

Shinnick, Maurice. *This Remarkable Gift: Being Gay and Catholic*. St Leonards, NSW: Allen and Unwin, 1997.

Shokeid, Moshe. *A Gay Synagogue in New York*. New York: Columbia University Press, 1995.

Siegel, Stanley and Ed Lowe, Jr. *Unchartered Lives. Understanding the Life Passages of Gay Men*. New York: Penguin USA, 1994.

Signorile, Michelangelo. *Queer in America: Sex, the Media, and the Closets of Power*. New York: Random House, 1993.

Siler, Mahan. *Exile or Embrace? Congregations Discerning Their Response to Lesbian and Gay Christians*. Cleveland: The Pilgrim Press, 2005.

Simmons, David. *Most Holy Redeemer Church Restoration Project: Project Commemorative Book*. San Francisco: Most Holy Redeemer Church, 1998.

Smith, Walter. *AIDS: Living and Dying with Hope: Issues in Pastoral Care*. Ramsey, N.J.: Paulist Press, 1988.

Smith, Richard. *AIDS, Gays, and the American Catholic Church*. Cleveland: The Pilgrim Press, 1994.

Sontag, Susan. *AIDS and Its Metaphors*. New York: Farrar, Straus, and Giroux, 1989.

Sparks, Richard. *Contemporary Christian Morality: Real Questions, Candid Answers*. Edinburgh: The Crossroad Publishing Co., 1996.

Stevenson, Thomas. *Sons of the Church. The Witnessing of Gay Catholic Men*. New York: Harrington Park Press, 2006.

Steinfels, Peter. *A People Adrift: The Crisis of the Roman Catholic Church in America*. New York: Simon & Schuster, 2003.

Stryker, Susan and Jim Van Buskirk. *Gay by the Bay. A History of Queer Culture in the San Francisco Bay Area*. San Francisco: Chronicle Books, 1996.

Stuart, Elizabeth. *Daring to Speak Love's Name: A Gay and Lesbian Prayer Book*. London: Hamish Hamilton, 1992.

———. *Chosen: Gay Catholic Priests Tell Their Stories*. New York: Geoffrey Chapman, 1993.

———. *Just Good Friends: Towards a Lesbian and Gay Theology of Relationships*. London: Mowbray, 1995.

———. *Religion Is a Queer Thing. A Guide to the Christian Faith for Lesbian, Gay, Bisexual and Transgendered People*. Stuart, Elizabeth, with Andy Braunston, Malcolm Edwards, John McMahon, Nancy Wilson, and Tim Morrison. London: Cassell, 1997.

Sullivan, Andrew. *Virtually Normal: An Argument about Homosexuality*. London: Picador, 1995.

———. *Love Undetectable: Reflections on Friendship, Sex and Survival*. London: Random House, 1998.

———. (Editor) *Same-Sex Marriage: Pro and Con. A Reader*. New York: Vintage Books, 1997.

Sweasey, Peter. *From Queer to Eternity: Spirituality in the Lives of Lesbian, Gay, and Bisexual People*. London: Cassell, 1997.

Switzer, David. *Pastoral Care of Gays, Lesbians, and Their Families*. Minneapolis: Fortress Press, 1999.

Task Force on Gay/Lesbian Issues (Roman Catholic Diocese of San Francisco). "Homosexuality and Social Justice" San Francisco: Consultation on Homosexuality, Social Justice, and Roman Catholic Theology, 1982.

Tedesco, Mark. *That Undeniable Longing: My Road to and from the Priesthood*. Chicago: Academy Chicago Publishers, 2006.

Tigert, Leanne McCall. *Coming Out While Staying in*. Cleveland: Pilgrim, 1997.

Tigert, Leanne McCall. *Coming Out While Staying in: Struggles and Celebrations of Lesbians, Gays, and Bisexuals in the Church*. Cleveland: United Church Press, 1996.

Thompson. Mark. *Gay Spirit: Myth and Meaning*. New York: St. Martin's Press, 1987.

———. *Gay Soul: Finding the Heart of Gay Spirit and Nature with Sixteen Writers, Healers, Teachers, and Visionaries*. San Francisco: HarperSanFrancisco, 1994.

Thompson, Mark, ed. *Long Road to Freedom: The Advocate History of the Gay and Lesbian Movement*. New York: St. Martin's, 1994.

Troy, Perry. *The Lord Is My Shepherd and He knows I'm Gay*. New York: Bantam Books, 1973.

——. *Don't Be Afraid Anymore: The Story of Rev. Troy Perry and the Metropolitan Community Church,* with Thomas L. Swicegood. New York: St. Martin's Press, 1990.

United States Conference of Catholic Bishops. "Always Our Children: A Pastoral Message to Parents of Homosexual Children and Suggestions for Pastoral Ministries." Washington, D.C.: United States Catholic Conference, Inc., 1997.

——. "Ministry to Persons with a Homosexual Inclination: Guidelines for Pastoral Care." Washington, D.C.: United States Catholic Conference, Inc., 2006.

Weakland, Rembrant. *Who Is My Neighbor?* Milwaukee: The Chancery Office, 1980.

Webber, Francis. *Catholic Footprints in California.* Newhall: The Hogarth Press, 1970.

Weil, Louis. *The New Church's Teaching Series: A Theology of Worship.* Vol 12. Cambridge: Cowley Publications, 2002.

White, Edmund. *States of Desire: Travels in Gay America.* New York: Penguin, 1991.

White, Mel. *Stranger at the Gate: To Be Gay and Christian in America.* New York: Simon & Schuster, 1994.

Whitehead, James D. and Evelyn Whitehead. *Community of Faith: Models and Strategies for Developing Christian Communities.* Minneapolis: Seabury Press, 1982.

——. *A Sense of Sexuality: Christian Love and Intimacy.* New York: Crossroad, 1990.

——. *The Promise of Ministry: A Model for Collaborative Ministry.* San Francisco: HarperSanFrancisco, 1991.

——. *Method in Ministry: Theological Reflection and Christian Ministry.* Kansas City: Sheed and Ward, 1995.

Whitehead, Sally Lowe. *The Truth Shall Set You Free: A Memoir, a Family's passage from fundamentalism to a new understanding of faith, love, and sexual identity.* San Francisco: HarperSanFrancisco, 1997.

Wilkes, Paul. *Excellent Catholic Parishes: The Guide to Best Places and Practices.* New York: Paulist Press, 2001.

Wills, Garry. *Papal Sin: Structures of Deceit.* New York: Doubleday, 2000.

——. *Why I Am a Catholic.* New York: Houghton Mifflin Company, 2002.

Wilson, Nancy. *Our Tribe. Queer Folks, God, Jesus, and the Bible.* San Francisco: HarperSanFrancisco, 1995.

Wind, James P. and James W. Lewis. *American Congregations: Vol 1: Portraits of Twelve Religious Communities.* Chicago: University of Chicago Press, 1994.

American Congregations: Vol 2: New Perspectives in the Study of Congregations. Chicago: University of Chicago Press, 1994.

Wink, Walter, ed. *Homosexuality and Christian Faith: Questions of Conscience for the Churches.* Minneapolis: Fortress Press, 1999.

Winter, Miriam Therese, Adair Lummis, and Allison Stokes. *Defecting in Place: Women Claiming Responsibility for Their Own Spiritual Lives.* New York: Crossroad Publishing Company, 1994.

Wolf, James, ed. *Gay Priests.* San Francisco: Harper & Row, 1989.

Woods, Richard. *Another Kind of Love. Homosexuality and Spirituality* (3rd edition) Fort Wayne: Knoll Publishing Co., Inc., 1988.

Woodward, James, ed. *Embracing the Chaos, Theological Responses to AIDS.* London: SPCK, 1990.

World Council of Churches: *The Church and AIDS.* Church and Society Documents, March 1987. No 1.

Wuthrow, Robert. *The Restructuring of American Religion.* Princeton: Princeton University Press, 1988.

Vaid, Urvashi. *Virtual Equality.* New York: Anchor Books/Doubleday, 1995.

Vasey, Michael. *Strangers and Friends: A New Exploration of Homosexuality and the Bible.* London: Hodder and Staunton, 1995.

Zanotti, Barbara, ed. *A Faith of One's Own: Explorations by Catholic Lesbians.* Trumansburg, New York: Crossing Press, 1986.

Index

About the Author

Donal Godfrey was born in Liverpool, England in 1959. Educated at Stony-hurst College and University College, Cork, he was then called to the Irish Bar. He is a Catholic priest and a member of the Irish province of the Society of Jesus. He also has degrees in philosophy from the Milltown Institute of Dublin, theology from Regis College at the University of Toronto, a licentiate in sacred theology from the Jesuit School of Theology at Berkeley, and a Doctorate in Ministry from the Church Divinity School of the Pacific in Berkeley. Fr. Godfrey has worked at Clongowes Wood College, Ireland; the Jesuit Centre of Spirituality in Belfast; Loyola University, Chicago; and is presently Executive Director of University Ministry at the University of San Francisco.